The Legacy of HarlemLIVE

Empowering Youth Through Journalism and Experiential Learning

RICH CALTON &
THE HARLEMLIVE ALUMNI

Cover Design: Shem Rajoon
Interior Design: Laura Boyle
Cover Photograph: Jim Belfon
Back Cover Photograph: John Crum

Feedback and comments: editor@harlemlive.org
Printed in the United States.

Trade Paperback Edition
ISBN: 978-1-7334713-8-1

Registered under the copyright laws of the United States of America with the copyright registration number: TXu 2-346-987

CONTENTS

A TRIBUTE TO TRAILBLAZERS

To the remarkable young people of HarlemLIVE: Your strength, resilience, and creativity have not only shaped this narrative but continue to inspire many. This book stands as a testament to your profound impact. It is my hope that this work serves as a gesture of gratitude and a commitment to supporting the vibrant legacy of HarlemLIVE.

Nyiesha Showers and Melvin Johnson

Prologue

THE VOICES OF TRANSFORMATION: HARLEMLIVE'S LEGACY

HarlemLIVE, a world-renowned and award-winning initiative that operated from 1996 to 2011, was rooted in the vibrant heart of New York City. This groundbreaking program was a trailblazer in the digital age, championing youth journalism through an entirely youth-led and produced web magazine at a time when the internet was just beginning to reshape our world.

As a dynamic digital platform, HarlemLIVE empowered young people to cultivate resilience, hone their self-expression, and amplify their unique perspectives through reporting and storytelling. Though no longer in direct operation, its pioneering model continues to inspire initiatives worldwide.

This book unveils the powerful narratives that underscore HarlemLIVE's transformative influence. This introduction features stories from four individuals—alumni and early contributors—whose experiences serve as a prelude to the wider story of HarlemLIVE. The main body of the book incorporates over two dozen firsthand accounts from other HarlemLIVE alumni and participants.

Writing Her Own Destiny

In the summer of 2006, Nyiesha Showers plunged headlong into redefining her own path through the thriving HarlemLIVE program.

"It's ten p.m. Do you know where your children are?" I'm sure you're familiar with that daunting voiceover that loomed on ABC News *for the last twenty years. Or what about this saying: "The most dangerous time for children is between the hours of three p.m. and seven p.m." This rings true especially for inner-city kids because their parents are normally at work or traveling from work during these times, and if children aren't occupied and doing something enriching that piques their interest, they are liable to do anything and be led astray.*

HarlemLIVE, an online teen publication, was created to cultivate a tribe of young reporters through curriculum, professional mentorship, and hands-on experience. Clearly, the objective of HarlemLIVE was to foster writing professionals, but for an inner-city girl like me who was born in prison and had sex at the young age of twelve, HarlemLIVE was a lifesaver.

Reading and writing were always my passions and allowed me, an only child, to escape. When I joined HarlemLIVE at twelve, I fell in love with reporting, interviewing, and shooting video. It was super cool to run around the city doing something productive, attending events, interviewing artists, politicians, and laypeople, and having published articles online.

Most of all, the relationships I cultivated and the diverse cultures and experiences I was exposed to at HarlemLIVE were truly life-changing and made me well-rounded.

I was thirteen years old when I attended the inauguration at the Newseum in Washington, DC, for the private viewing as President Barack Obama was sworn in. I met Mary J. Blige twice at HarlemLIVE, and I was even featured on an episode of Extreme Makeover: Home Edition *with her.*

I have countless stories about HarlemLIVE, but the most important thing you should know is that HarlemLIVE was a staple in my journey from little lost black girl to the Howard University graduate and the published author that I am today.

Programs like HarlemLIVE help to cultivate the youth—personally, professionally, mentally, and even emotionally. I learned about conflict resolution at HarlemLIVE. I learned about healthy eating at HarlemLIVE. I learned about the range of professions in communications at HarlemLIVE. I visited Thompson Reuters, NBC, CBS, and the New York Times, and rode on the spiral escalator at Bloomberg News via HarlemLIVE.

HarlemLIVE helped me raise the bar for myself, and since then I have yet to look back. All girls and boys need a HarlemLIVE.

Melvin's Legacy: Molding Future Voices

Moving on from Nyiesha's journey, we come to another integral figure in HarlemLIVE: Melvin Johnson. It's important to note that a substantial part of Nyiesha's guidance and mentorship stemmed from Melvin himself. His older sister, Wanda, offers a moving account of how Melvin transitioned from a participant to one of the organization's most influential figures. Melvin's story and HarlemLIVE's trajectory were deeply intertwined. Although his life was tragically cut short, his legacy continues to echo, particularly in the lives of those he mentored, like Nyiesha, and many others he influenced.

HarlemLIVE helped Melvin become the man he was. He grew up in the South Bronx during a time that it was very easy for a young black man to get caught in the negative life of the street. It was all around us: drug abuse, selling drugs, robbing, stealing. HarlemLIVE was a haven for Melvin.

It exposed him to things that he would not typically see in the inner city. He was there all day, every day. He reported, he wrote stories, he edited, he interviewed, he was an interviewee, he represented the program at various functions... He learned computer languages independently—JavaScript, HTML... We would buy a textbook; he would read it and learn the languages. All he needed was guidance, and that guidance came from HarlemLIVE. Rich and the mentors opened their hearts and space to Melvin as well as to many others, and I'm happy that Melvin took it and ran with it. The way HarlemLIVE blessed him, Melvin paid it forward and blessed others.

Melvin had a lot of charisma, and he could speak to anyone. You could work at a Fortune 500 company or be a bum lying on the street in a cardboard box, and he would speak to you with the same authenticity. The exposure he received opened his eyes to a world that I don't think he ever imagined was there or was accessible to people like us. He went to Italy to attend an award ceremony for HarlemLIVE's Clickable Map of Harlem, and he participated in workshops and spoke to an international audience. He didn't have to pay a cent for this trip; HarlemLIVE raised the funds.

After that, the world was his oyster.

Igniting Change

From the indomitable spirit of Melvin, we shift to Kelvin Christie's compelling narrative. Joining HarlemLIVE during its temporary residency at Bloomberg's Midtown headquarters, Kelvin's life evolved from a turbulent past to an inspiring story of redemption and resilience. The following essay he penned during his early days with HarlemLIVE unveils the depth of his struggles and the power of self-expression.

I remember my first hospitalization for my temper like it was yesterday. I was just 11, terrified that the medication they were forcing on me would ruin me for life, as my mother warned. Four adults were needed to restrain me for the injection.

Contrary to my fears, the mental hospital was almost normal, save for the gang-related activities among the residents. I was taken there after losing control at my Brooklyn middle school, after which they brought me to King's County Hospital rather than home. Trapped, I felt suffocated, fearing a loss of normalcy.

When my mother arrived, pride held me back from running into her open arms. I shed a single tear, trying to hide my vulnerability. My toughness came from resisting my mother's comfort.

At the J building, I was overwhelmed with paranoia. In a desperate attempt to escape the looming admission, I tried to bolt from the doctor's office but was caught and restrained. I screamed under the weight of the needle until the medication silenced me.

Awakening in the hospital, disoriented, being institutionalized gradually became a part of my daily routine, less terrifying with each repetition.

As I grew within the hospital, I began to rebel against both my confinement and the medication. Rebellion made me tired but also incited a determination to resist more. The more I rebelled, the higher they raised my dosage.

My resistance and defiance resulted in numerous arrests, often driven by a desire to hurt those forcing the medication upon me. I had become someone to be feared, even by my psychiatrist. After attacking him, I woke up handcuffed and facing jail time, which led to my court cases.

While in jail, I began questioning my involvement in the gang lifestyle. On meeting a fellow gang member, we shared a cigarette and stories. Over time, I revealed my desire to leave the gang. He was taken aback but understood my decision.

In court, paranoia consumed me. My heart raced as my lawyer tried to keep me calm. However, when the judge declared me not guilty and not crazy, I felt a surge of triumph. Finally, the validation I had longed for: "Not guilty." "Not crazy."

Kelvin embraced the freedom of expression that HarlemLIVE offered, flourishing as a writer of poetry, essays, and stories. Each word he penned echoed his experiences and growth. Now working toward his doctorate after achieving four master's degrees, Kelvin's narrative is evidence of the revolutionary power of the HarlemLIVE model—proof that no past is too difficult to overcome.

Underestimated to Undaunted

After Kelvin's experiences with hands-on journalism at HarlemLIVE, the narrative evolves further back in time. Before HarlemLIVE was even a concept, there was the school newsletter. Miriam was at the heart of it. Through her lens, we not only witness the nascent stages of what would become HarlemLIVE but also the passion and dedication of early participants.

Like many parents, mine were skeptical of this white male teacher who looked like a surfer boy they saw on television. He wasn't like the teachers we, or they, had had in the past. Who was this guy? A common practice of charter schools today (still greeted with skepticism from many Title I families who have been systemically mistreated), Mr. Calton might actually come to your home and speak with your family.

A common practice of elite private schools, Mr. Calton would plan trips outside of school hours that were focused on controversial topics in the "adult" world. Mr. Calton took us to see a Basquiat exhibit, which made us view Black art as not only legitimate but also fascinating. He took a group of 6th graders to see Malcolm X *when it came out in theaters (could you imagine the grasping of the pearls today?!), lighting a lifelong fire in me for the ongoing fight for equity.*

While my family said "no" often out of concern for my safety and well-being, they said "yes" enough to allow me to very actively participate in the launch of Kids Newsday *as an editor and reporter. They said "yes" enough to allow me to go into local businesses and sell advertising space in our paper, which taught me to use my voice, to persuade others, and to feel comfortable working in fundraising—skills that came in handy during my years in the nonprofit sector. They said "yes" to special assemblies and classroom speakers who taught us to feel pride in our African American and Afro-Latinx backgrounds.*

I once read that a child growing up in difficult circumstances really only needs one adult who believes in them and is genuinely there for them to "make it." Rich Calton came into my life at a critical time in my development, right before my exceptionally difficult teenage years, and showed me that I had agency. Resilience. A voice. Choices. He treated me, and all of his students, as if we were capable of making adult decisions and self-advocating for our wants, needs, and futures. It was never just a newspaper, or just a play we were producing and performing, or just a guest speaker. It was always a way to give us the tools needed to mine the depths of our own strength and power, and prepare us to continue in a world that viewed us as less than because of what we looked like and where we came from.

The lessons I learned served me through high school, college, and successful careers in finance, the nonprofit world, and education. I look back at that sweet little people-pleasing mouse of a girl and am so pleased that chance and timing gave her what she needed most in that classroom at P.S. 206.

* * *

These stories are the heart and soul of HarlemLIVE. They serve as a testament to the enduring power of learning while doing and journalism as an innovative educational tool. HarlemLIVE's model showcases a unique approach to nurturing youth potential and equipping them with the skills needed to navigate the future successfully.

* * *

Enhance your reading experience and delve deeper into our story by visiting our online resources at https://www.harlemlive.net/publications. Discover a collection of images, video, and content that align directly with the text, enriching your understanding and immersing you further in our book.

Photo by John Crum

ABOUT THIS BOOK

In the summer of 2006, a chipped plaster in the stairwell of our HarlemLIVE newsroom became an unexpected battleground. Exposing an old brick wall, the city declared it a safety hazard and threatened to shut us down. To our young participants, this was a call to action. They prepared to confront a challenge that would test HarlemLIVE's very essence.

But this was just one riveting chapter in the incredible fifteen-year journey of HarlemLIVE. Dive into this chronicle for an intimate look at how the youth, with grit and determination, rode the waves of the digital revolution, carved out a space for their stories, and reshaped both their destinies and that of their community.

As a public school educator and founder of HarlemLIVE, I discovered that teaching journalism to teens awakened their inherent curiosity. Equipped with a press badge and a digital platform for self-expression that they managed and developed, these students unearthed confidence and grew into various roles, including journalists, photographers, public speakers, graphic artists, administrators, and more.

* * *

Part 1, The HarlemLIVE Narrative: An Educator's Odyssey and a Trailblazing Platform, comprises two sections.
Section A, The Accidental Educator, details my journey into education and the philosophy that became the foundation of HarlemLIVE. This philosophy

emphasizes giving kids a broad range of experiences and the agency to make decisions and manage projects. Within this narrative, educators will find practical methods. These include letter writing, after-school trips, theatrical plays from African Folktales, guest speakers, and a student-led newspaper. Each technique offers effective ways to engage students.

Section B, The Story of HarlemLIVE, unfolds the narrative of HarlemLIVE, tracing its beginnings and evolution. These chapters serve as a blueprint for creating your own youth program by highlighting the practical steps taken to establish a strong foundation and achieve impactful change. As the story unfolds, you'll witness the challenges faced and conquered by our participants, offering insights for those aiming to establish a successful program. This journey explores HarlemLIVE's evolution from its inception to navigating myriad complexities over time.

Part 1 is predominantly told in my voice, with many contributions from outside voices to enhance the storytelling.

* * *

Part 2, Building on Legacy: Strategies, Success Stories, and Resources, contains three sections offering valuable insights, success stories, and practical guidance on implementing youth-oriented programs. While it adopts a more informational and resourceful tone, it draws on real-life experiences and examples from HarlemLIVE alumni.

Section C, Tenets of a Successful Youth Program, presents a detailed exploration of the key elements that underpinned HarlemLIVE's success. This section showcases how experiential learning, trust building, community involvement, mentorship, and fostering a sense of ownership, among other tenets, significantly impacted youth development. While it doesn't serve as a step-by-step guide, it provides a thorough examination of principles that can inform and inspire other youth enrichment initiatives.

An additional chapter within this section, **Creating Youth Journalists**, offers practical insights on establishing youth-oriented journalism programs and nurturing the skills of young journalists.

Section D, From HarlemLIVE to the World: Alumni Updates, underscores the profound and lasting impact that HarlemLIVE had on its participants, many of whom have since embarked on diverse and interesting projects, both nationally and internationally. In the book, you'll directly hear from these alumni through over two dozen detailed interviews woven into the narrative.

Finally, **Section E, Resources**, offers extensive links to organizations and articles supporting issues, practices, and philosophies explored in this book.

* * *

HarlemLIVE's legacy has never been more relevant than it is today. As we navigate an increasingly digital world where young people's engagement is crucial, the need for spaces that foster creativity, critical thinking, and self-expression is paramount. This book provides not only a historical account of such a space but also explores the universal components that made it a success—lessons that can be replicated and adapted to today's context. For educators, policymakers, parents, and anyone interested in empowering the next generation, HarlemLIVE's story offers invaluable insights and inspiration.

The pandemic highlighted the need to reevaluate how we educate and engage our youth. The story of HarlemLIVE offers hope, showcasing methods that empower young people to take control of their future and ameliorate negative social behaviors brought on by lockdowns and isolation.

PART 1

The HarlemLIVE Narrative: An Educator's Odyssey and a Trailblazing Platform

Section A

THE ACCIDENTAL EDUCATOR

Chapter 1

UNCONVENTIONAL PATHS: FROM CALIFORNIA TO NYC

I was just shy of my seventeenth birthday when my dad's old buddy convinced him to let me loose in the city that never sleeps. I'd be staying with him and his coworkers in a cramped storefront apartment on Saint Mark's Place, in the gritty, vibrant East Village. Their sound engineering company was putting in a new system for CBGB, the legendary punk rock venue.

The friend had told my father he was tired of hearing me brag about how nothing could beat California. Little did I know that New York City would change everything.

During that first visit, I saw Lily Tomlin on Broadway, feasted on delicious Chinese food in Chinatown, hung out in Washington Square Park, and got hopelessly lost on Delancey Street. Something about the chaos and energy of the city piqued my interest, so I returned three months later.

It was 1977, and the infamous Son of Sam was on the prowl. The city had just suffered a massive blackout in July, followed by fires and looting. Later, a sanitation strike left mountains of garbage piled high in a city on the brink of financial collapse. But to me, it was all part of the thrill. New York was a hot mess: vibrant, gritty, dangerous, and SO much fun.

That August, I stayed in that same East Village apartment, and this time I mostly had it to myself. I made new friends while hanging out in the parks and bars and on the streets. The drinking age was eighteen back then, and I could pass. I dropped acid for the first time and went to Max's Kansas City and Studio 54.

One night, I went to a house party and met Ellis Amburn, the editor in chief of Delacorte Press. I mentioned my passion for drama and how I'd had bit parts in productions back in Pleasanton, California.

"Quit drama," Ellis commanded. "Join the school newspaper and become a journalist."

* * *

When I returned to California in the fall of '77 for my senior year, I followed Ellis's advice. I had more success in a few months on the school paper than I'd ever had as a thespian. I became the coordinating editor, and my passion for journalism only grew from there.

I returned to NYC for a third time over Christmas break. The city was alive with disco mania. *Saturday Night Fever* had just come out, and wild, showy dance clubs were popping up everywhere. I knew then that New York was where I wanted to be.

A week after my high school graduation in June 1978, I made my way across the country on a Greyhound bus with nothing but some clothes and my trusty bicycle. I left my things with friends and went backpacking through Europe for a couple of months before returning to New York and getting hired at the original Barnes and Noble Bookstore on 5th Avenue. I moved into a small East Village apartment with several others. The rent was a mere $140 a month.

Instead of following the expected path of going straight to college, I chose a different route. When my father offered me a car, something that is typically seen as a rite of passage for young adults in California, I refused. I didn't want to be like everyone else.

"When you see people going this way," my father instructed during a break in our boxing lesson, drawing clockwise circles on my open palm, "go the other way," he continued, drawing counterclockwise circles. "Do things differently. Go against the grain. Think outside the box."

I was only five years old at the time, but his words stayed with me. They became a guiding principle in my life. I refused to conform in every way I could. I even protested going back to kindergarten class after recess. I chose Apple over Windows PCs in the '90s, when most thought Apple was a lost cause; I ignored a "No Trespassing" sign on an island off Istanbul to get a better view of the city. Anything that went against convention, I was willing to try.

* * *

For three years, I worked at some fascinating jobs, including as an editorial assistant on a few *New York Times* bestsellers. I even brought tuna fish sandwiches and black and white malts to actress Shelley Winters in her Upper West Side apartment, where her memoir pages were strewn about the place like confetti. Her large muumuu was the same pattern as the couch, so you couldn't tell where Shelley ended and the couch began.

During the years 1978 to 1981, I came to better understand that many careers required a college degree, something I wasn't going to do just because "that's what's done." After a three-year break from school, I enrolled at New York University, majoring in journalism and, on the advice of a forward-looking professor, minoring in computer science.

It was a combination that would prove to be invaluable. These skills led me down an unexpected path to HarlemLIVE, a groundbreaking online magazine that would go on to receive worldwide acclaim.

5th grade in Brooklyn: My first teaching job with visiting aerobics instructor.

Chapter 2

IN THE TRENCHES: A FIGHT FOR EDUCATION

The year was 1985, and amid the celebrations of the Brooklyn Bridge's centennial and the blockbusters of the year—*Back to the Future*, *Beverly Hills Cop*, *Cocoon*, and *Pee Wee Herman's Big Adventure*—New York City was facing a growing crack cocaine epidemic. The crime and murder rates were skyrocketing, and the city was also battling a severe outbreak of AIDS.

On top of that, the board of education was dealing with a critical teacher shortage.[1] Recruiters were sent overseas to hire teachers from Spain, Puerto Rico, and Germany. They even sent letters to retired teachers, begging them to come back. It was a desperate situation, and the board was willing to do just about anything to fill the vacancies.

They lowered the standards and started giving out temporary teaching certifications to anyone with a bachelor's degree. It was a running joke, really. They called it the "mirror test."

"You put the mirror under the nostrils; if it fogs, you're a candidate," said former New York City schools' chancellor Anthony Alvarado.[2]

As a recent graduate, I was a prime candidate for the board of education's "mirror test." I had a bachelor's degree, and that was all that mattered. Never

---

1. Larry Rohter, "New York Schools Facing a Shortage of Over 4,200 Teachers," *The New York Times*, August 11, 1985, Page 1.

2. Joyce Purnick, "City's Poor Districts Are Hit Hard by a Shortage of Teachers," *The New York Times*, February 29, 1984, pp. A1 & B5.

mind the fact that I'd never considered teaching as a career or that I'd never taken an education class in my life.

* * *

During my senior year at NYU, after an internship at CNN, I was hit with a wave of self-doubt. I loved journalism. I enjoyed working on the school newspaper, and I had a blast doing person-on-the-street interviews with veteran CNN reporter Jeanne Moss. But something just wasn't clicking for me.

That's when a friend of mine, a former public school teacher, saw the educator in me—the potential I had to make a difference in the lives of young people. He encouraged me to apply.

I was skeptical at first. I had no experience in this field aside from playing school with my youngest sister, Joelle, six years my junior, when we were kids. From before kindergarten until she reached fourth grade, I turned her bedroom into a makeshift classroom and taught her reading, writing, and arithmetic. The head start I gave her kept Joelle consistently ahead of her class.

Maybe teaching was my calling. Maybe it was the path I was meant to take all along.

* * *

I went through all the motions of applying: filling out paperwork, taking tests, getting fingerprinted. But it was an intense in-person interview with a panel of three veteran educators that really got me sweating. They peppered me with questions, and I was certain I had failed. After all, why would the city consider hiring someone with no background in education?

To my surprise, just nine weeks after starting the process and signing an agreement to complete required coursework, I was deemed ready to teach. However, I still felt I was in way over my head.

So I called up my former high school French teacher in California, looking for some words of encouragement. What she told me wasn't exactly reassuring.

"Oh, boy," Madame Miller warned me. "You have a triple whammy. It's your first time teaching, you have no training, and you're starting in the middle of the school year. Your job is to survive without losing your faith in humanity."

Indeed.

* * *

In late October 1985, I sat in a classroom at Public School 262, located in the Bedford-Stuyvesant section of Brooklyn, surrounded by three fifth-grade female teachers. Their classes had been overflowing with about forty students each for the first two months of the school year, and now they were giving me 5" x 8" index cards with the names of their most challenging students.

"Here are Kenmore, Jermaine, Tammy, Kenneth, and Sherode," said the most experienced teacher.

"Maybe you'll do well with Thelma, Earl, Martin, Bakari, Princess, Gary, and Kisha," said the next.

"See how Darnell, Cassandra, Sheena, Clifton, and Eldrika work out," said the third.

Before I knew it, I had a class of twenty-nine, and I had no idea what I was in for. I was given just half a piece of chalk and an old sponge for an eraser and instructed to give it a go.

* * *

On my first day, I entered the smoky teachers' lounge wearing slacks, a freshly pressed shirt, and a tie. I may have worn dress shoes, but I quickly learned that comfortable sneakers were a teacher's best friend. As I sat down, one of the older male teachers scoffed.

"That won't last long," he said, referring to my shirt and tie.

"You remind me of us when we first started," said another, who wore jeans and a patterned shirt with several buttons undone, revealing a hairy chest and a gold chain necklace.

However, I didn't allow their negative attitude to affect me. Instead, I befriended other teachers, counselors, and support staff who showed a sincere interest in the children's welfare. As for those older white men who had become teachers to avoid the Vietnam War draft and who despised both their jobs and the children they taught, I couldn't comprehend how individuals like them were permitted to teach in schools.

Pots and Pans

In 1985, P.S. (Public School) 262 was a floundering school with a reputation that was circling the drain.

The state had caught wind of the shoddy performance, launched an investigation, and sent in state monitors. In an effort to fix things, the district's superintendent brought in a seasoned administrator to act as vice principal.

Gloria Simmons was a formidable figure, tall and stern, with a no-nonsense attitude that could cut through steel. Her thick-rimmed glasses only added to her intimidating presence. But beneath her tough exterior lay a heart of gold, and she would become my biggest ally.

My first few weeks of teaching were a disaster. I yelled until I was hoarse, banged on pots and pans to get the students' attention, and wrote affirmations in my journal in a desperate attempt to turn things around. But nothing seemed to work.

I found myself struggling to connect with the students and earn their respect. My self-confidence waned, and I couldn't help but wonder if I was even cut out for this profession. One day, I had my grade book stolen, and another day I confiscated comic books in a fit of rage, only to have a student confront me and call me out on my incompetence.

"How do you walk in here, almost a teenager, and think you can teach?"

I was lost and alone. What was I doing there? How could I possibly make a difference when I had no idea what I was doing? All over the city, teachers were quitting within weeks of being assigned to schools where they didn't want to be.[1]

I sought out advice from anyone who would give it. One old friend told me to show them who was boss, and another suggested I give the unruly students a firm grip on their shoulders to show my strength. It all felt so... outdated.

---

1. Joyce Purnick, "City's Poor Districts Are Hit Hard by a Shortage of Teachers," *The New York Times*, Feb 29, 1984, pp. A1 & B5.

But things took a darker turn when I sought help from the teachers' union leader, a chain-smoking man who exuded a sense of world-weary cynicism. I poured out my heart to him, admitting my shortcomings and the negative effect I might be having on the children.

He took a long drag on his cigarette and let out a cloud of smoke.

"Don't worry about them," he said, with a dismissive wave of his hand. "They're just n******."

I was stunned, sickened, and angry all at once. In that moment, I knew I could never trust him. It took time for me to find my voice and speak out against his toxic attitude, but I eventually did. Unfortunately, he would be behind efforts that eventually led to my dismissal. The memory of that encounter still haunts me, a reminder of the deeply ingrained racism and indifference that can infect even the most trusted institutions.

* * *

After the December holiday break, I almost lost my job.

I was bumped on a return flight from Costa Rica. Forced into a several days' layover, I returned to my East Village apartment to find my roommate strung out on heroin. Many of my belongings were missing.

Traumatized and afraid to leave, I called in sick for one, two, three days. Finally, one of my colleagues phoned.

"People are starting to talk," she explained. Perhaps they thought I was not returning. "You better come in."

Threatened with possible termination, I knew I had to act. I stored my important belongings with friends and went in with renewed vigor. But it wasn't easy.

As I grappled with the challenges of teaching, I found solace in my students. Despite their defiance, I grew fond of them. I learned not to take their actions personally.

I discovered the importance of keeping notes of any incidents that occurred in the classroom. I silently jotted down any misbehavior, catching the attention of the students and reminding them that their actions were being documented. These notes became a crucial tool in my defense when confronted by administrators or parents. They helped me become a more effective and respected teacher.

To keep my students engaged, I decorated the classroom with large, colorful book posters that I got from my friend Margot, who managed the popular Shakespeare Books on Manhattan's Upper West Side. I had assistance from Ms. Simmons and the teachers I befriended. They were there to offer guidance, and I took many of the scheduled workshops around the city to become a better educator.

I spent hours in the library at NYU, poring over books by Herbert Kohl, a prolific writer on progressive education methods, and studying the works of Chicago educator Marva Collins, who instilled confidence in her students.

Building confidence was one of my crucial goals as an educator, and it was something I had struggled with myself.

As a child, my father meant well, but his actions often left me feeling uncertain about my own capabilities. In fifth grade, I had to create a model of an early American town for school. Despite my efforts, my father scoffed at my work and took over the project.

Dad built an incredible piece of art on painted plywood, complete with cardboard buildings and fruit trees. My classmates and teacher marveled at his creation, with my name on it. But I knew I was an imposter. His feeling that only he could do it right in so many instances had a lasting impact on my self-confidence, making me feel as though my efforts were never adequate.

I never wanted my students to feel that way. I wanted to be the teacher who inspired confidence and fostered creativity.

Bringing the World to the Classroom

To improve the classroom experience, I borrowed a practice from one of my favorite high school classes: frequent guest speakers. First up was Ellis Marsalis, a photographer and younger brother of the famous Wynton Marsalis. Having worked together on NYU's student publication, I knew that his passion for capturing the world through his lens would inspire my students. A friend and NYU film school graduate, Paul Duffy, came to speak about the magic of filmmaking, and we viewed his final movie project. Margot, my bookstore manager friend, brought art supplies and taught a lesson in drawing and also read a short story. My aerobics teacher even taught a class in the gym later that year.

I wanted my students to be exposed to professionals in different fields, to glimpse a world beyond their own and perhaps discover something that would ignite their passions. This type of exposure became a cornerstone of HarlemLIVE's philosophy: to open doors and broaden horizons, to help the students see a world of opportunity.

Over time, my students began to warm up to me as they sensed my sincerity in wanting to help them succeed, but it was an uphill battle. The school was dysfunctional, and the strife among the staff was palpable. Supplies and books were scarce or nonexistent. I was given a set of tattered social studies books, relics of a bygone era, that announced in one chapter, "Someday, we will land on the moon." Their yellowed pages were a testament to the neglect that had plagued the school for far too long.

* * *

To address this problem, in early February I had the students write letters to Mayor Edward Koch describing the deplorable condition of the school and the lack of current textbooks or sufficient supplies. I gave the letters to the school secretary, Mrs. White, who put them in a large manila envelope and mailed them to City Hall.

I had no idea those letters would have such profound consequences.

* * *

In March, I took the class to the Brooklyn Museum. It was our first field trip, and it went surprisingly well. I figured out that students make the best line monitors. Sheena Evans, who was taller than most everyone in the class, fulfilled that duty well.

Later that month, the eagerly awaited letter came—the New York City schools' response to our pleas for help. I tore open the letter and read it aloud to the class. I couldn't help but feel disappointed by its content. The chancellor thanked the students for their letters and assured them that the principal knew the proper procedures for obtaining resources. But to me, the letter sounded empty, and even dismissive.

Without a second thought, I announced to the class, "This is BS" and ripped the letter in half.

Meanwhile, tensions were brewing among the staff. The union leader, a man who had shockingly used a racial epithet in our conversation earlier, and some of the other white teachers were trying to get rid of Ms. Simmons. I signed a counter-petition, along with the rest of the teachers who believed in providing a quality education to our students.

* * *

In mid-April, the principal sent for me.

I was summoned to the nurse's office, which seemed odd. The principal was waiting for me in a tiny, windowless room I'd never laid eyes on before. It was filled with stacks of miniature chairs meant for kindergarteners, but he beckoned me to sit down as he placed two of the tiny chairs in the center of the small room, our knees practically touching.

"I didn't know your class sent letters to the mayor," the principal said.

"I gave them to Mrs. White, your secretary. She mailed them on our behalf," I replied, trying to sound calm.

"Well, that was a very naive thing to do," he said, before launching into a rambling, self-important speech about his experience in the education system.

Then he leaned in close and wagged a finger in my face. "Mayor Koch is coming to this school next week, but it's not because of those letters," he said.

Perhaps the mayor's visit was precisely due to the letters, and the principal was clearly upset about it. I realized that, as a per diem teacher with no job protections, my days might be numbered.

* * *

Tensions reached a boiling point at an after-school staff meeting in early May, as accusations were hurled regarding the union leader's alignment with the principal and those attempting to oust Ms. Simmons, the vice principal. In a sudden interruption, members of the PTA burst into the meeting, demanding chairs to sit on.

The focus shifted to the school improvement committee, where the union leader strongly opposed teachers collaborating with state monitors. I was among the teachers selected by the state to serve on the committee tasked with addressing school issues. The union leader argued that if there were any problems, we should raise them through the union.

"It shouldn't be teachers against teachers. It should be teachers against the administration," he said.

"No!" I yelled, standing up as my chair slid behind me. "It's not us against them! We should be working together to educate the children."

The room fell silent, save for a smattering of applause. The union leader seethed with rage, his face contorted.

* * *

When I clocked in the next morning, a staff member informed me that the principal wanted to see me immediately.

I went into his shoebox-shaped office, the air heavy with smoke and foreboding. The gym teacher was at the principal's desk, mysteriously counting cash, while the union leader paced around the room with a cigarette in hand, his eyes narrowed behind wire-rimmed glasses.

The principal leaned uneasily on the back of a blue vinyl cushioned chair, his shoulders slumped. He looked down at the floor. The gym teacher quickly bundled the cash and left, leaving me alone with the principal and the union leader.

"There have been complaints, so we are sending you to the district office for reassignment," said the principal.

"What? I don't want to be reassigned."

"We think it's best."

"Why? I don't want to go! I'll fight this."

"You don't have any say in the matter," snapped the union leader between puffs on his cigarette. "You're just a per diem teacher. Go up to your classroom and retrieve any personal items. You will report to the district office. They'll reassign you."

"Do I get to say goodbye to my kids?"

The principal shook his head. "It's better this way. A clean break."

I was in shock. Reeling, but with no recourse, I gathered what I could carry and walked the quarter mile down to the district office. The rest of my things would be put in storage until I could pick them up at another time.

* * *

Late that morning, sitting in an empty conference room at the district, I was notified that I had a phone call. It was Vice Principal Simmons.

"The principal had to go to a meeting and will be out of the building for a few hours. Get over here now and say goodbye to your children."

Ms. Simmons met me at a fire exit away from the building entrance. She took me up a side staircase to my former third-floor classroom.

"Take a break," she ordered my replacement, who was standing at the head of the class.

"I already took my break, Ms. Simmons. I'm right in the middle of…"

"Take another."

In a heartfelt and tearful farewell, I went to each student's desk and spoke to them individually, expressing what I appreciated about each of them. I felt like Dorothy bidding goodbye to her friends in the Land of Oz.

Shortly after, Ms. Simmons arrived and instructed the children to inform their parents that they no longer had a teacher. I quietly exited through the rear entrance and made my way back to the district office.

* * *

District 16 assigned me to finish the remaining weeks at a better-run school. I provided break, or "prep" periods, to first- through third-grade teachers.

I missed my fifth graders at P.S. 262. Over time, I had built a strong bond with my class. Since my new school got out earlier, most days I walked to P.S. 262 to see my former colleagues, to say hi to my students as they were dismissed, to attend some of the end-of-year school ceremonies, or to pick up my check, which was still delivered there.

An effort was mounted to try to get me back in the school; parents protested at the district, and staff held meetings, but the principal and his cronies were not having it. They were steadfast in their opposition, even objecting to my presence at performances in the auditorium.

Then one day in mid-June, I arrived at P.S. 262 just as an ambulance was pulling away. The principal had finally cracked under the weight of it all. The turmoil surrounding the school—the state monitors, the warring teachers, the visit from the mayor—had all become too much. He would never set foot in the school again.

I knew my return to that mess wasn't in the cards, not with the union rep and his allies on the school board. So I researched other school districts, eventually landing an offer from the superintendent of nearby District 19. He said people like me often made good principals, but I knew better. I couldn't handle that kind of stress. Principals get hit from all sides—kids, parents, teachers, administration, bureaucracy, and the whole community.

Visionary Seeds

It started with a seed of an idea, one that took root in the last weeks of the school year in 1986. I wanted to spend more time with my former fifth graders, to show them a side of life beyond the classroom. So I passed out a flyer with a parent permission slip attached, inviting them to join me on an excursion into the heart of the city.

I planned the trip for a Saturday and enlisted my friend Margot to help make sandwiches in advance and to join us. Our first stop was the observation deck of the original World Trade Center, a breathtaking view that left us all feeling a bit awestruck. But that was just the beginning—we walked down Broadway to the southern tip of Manhattan to have a picnic in Battery Park.

There was a lot going on in the park. A protest by Native Americans next to where tourists lined up for the boat to the Statue of Liberty. Acrobats performing for tips from a gathered crowd. Elders learning folk dances in another section. It was sensory overload, but one that allowed me to observe what sparked each child's interest.

There was none of the performative behavior one would normally see in the classroom. We were just a group of humans, connecting on a level that transcended the typical teacher-student dynamic. They were alive with curiosity and excitement, and I felt a sense of purpose that filled me with hope.

This practice of taking smaller groups of kids on after-school excursions would become the secret sauce of my success as a public school teacher and the reason I left the public school system a decade later to create an after-school program called HarlemLIVE.

Chapter 3

TEACHING BEYOND THE WALLS

My tumultuous year in Brooklyn, combined with my tenuous living arrangements, kept me from taking the education courses I needed to maintain a per diem teaching certification. That meant I could only work as a substitute teacher while I took classes at City College.

By subbing all over the city the following year, I happened upon P.S. 206, a third- through sixth-grade elementary school on 120th Street in East Harlem, right by the East River. It was part of District 4, one of over thirty-two geographical divisions of the NYC school system at the time. Meanwhile, my living conditions improved when I moved in with my friends Margot and Scott in their nearby East Village apartment.

District 4 was the precursor to the charter school movement that would become popular nationally. Starting with the work of Deborah Meier in the early 1970s at Central Park East Secondary School (C.P.E.S.S.) and continued throughout the district by Superintendent Anthony Alvarado, several small schools existed within larger school buildings, each of them organized around a specific instructional model and specialized curriculum. The district allowed families to choose the school they thought would be the most effective place for their kids to learn. In ten years, District 4 went from being the worst school district in New York City (32nd out of 32) to number 15. And in fifteen years, it went from 16 percent of students reading at grade level to 63 percent.[1]

---

1. Seymour Fliegel, who was District 4's director of alternative schools and then deputy superintendent, narrates this journey in his book *Miracle in East Harlem*.

* * *

I went for an interview at P.S. 206 on a hot August afternoon. The principal of nearly two decades, Juana Dainis, a native of Puerto Rico and a commanding figure in four-inch heels, interviewed me, along with her assistant principal, Anna Leone.

Dainis was highly organized and genuinely cared about the children, but she was a strict disciplinarian who worked her teachers hard. If she saw the same care for the children in you, she had your back.

Dainis's pedagogical methods seemed a little old-fashioned, a sharp contrast to the more progressive and creative programs that had attracted me to District 4, but she ran a tight ship. When I got the job offer, I thought a strong structure would be good for a teacher as inexperienced as me. I accepted.

The contrast between my first year of teaching and my second couldn't have been more stark. At P.S. 206, I was given a large box of supplies, with everything from scissors to notepads. And while P.S. 262 in Brooklyn was faltering, P.S. 206 was thriving—so much so that it would be selected by a presidential task force the following year as a model school.

But despite the school's success, I faced an uphill battle in managing my class effectively. Each day felt like a constant struggle to maintain order, and I worried that I might not have the skills to succeed in this environment. After the principal fired two new teachers within weeks, I feared that I would be next. That's when I sought out the help of a sixth-grade teacher, Doris Peters, who was close with the principal.

Peters was a stickler for neatness and order, and she spent an afternoon going through and cleaning out the messy desks of my students while instructing me on ways to better manage my class. She suggested I start applying her methods on Monday, but I couldnt wait. I started the next day, a Friday.

As the school day was about to begin, I instituted the new rules. I wouldn't let the kids advance unless there was order. For every disruption, I made the kids stop and wait for better behavior. Sometimes I made them go all the way back and start over. It took twenty-five minutes to make it to the third floor, and we weren't even at our classroom yet. The kids started to balk. One student even ran down to the main office to complain.

"He's treating us like we're in the army," yelled the student.

"Good," replied the principal. "Now go back upstairs."

As the students witnessed my determination, they started to follow the rules. It was a crucial step—I needed to establish control over my classes before I could gradually hand it over to the students. Allowing young people to take control of their learning environment became a fundamental principle of HarlemLIVE.

To help with the process, I appointed some students as line monitors. I had learned this tactic in Brooklyn, but now I employed two monitors—one in front, one in back. They were effective in keeping the line orderly as we traveled the halls to the lunchroom and dismissal. This freed me from some of the friction at the start and end of each day.

Adding to the line monitors, I also assigned roles such as class librarians, trash can monitors, mailbox organizers, letters club coordinators (the group of students responsible for coordinating the organizing, enveloping, addressing, and stamping of the letters we sent in class), office monitors, and others. These assignments fostered a sense of responsibility and teamwork among the students.

There's no better way to make students invested in the classroom than to give them agency and responsibilities.

Guiding Lights

During my early struggles, I was fortunate to have the unwavering support of two remarkable women, Carolyn and Lynette. We began teaching together the same year at PS 206. In their first year there, they adopted the names Amari and Sauda after embracing the Yoruba religion, a transformation I had the privilege of celebrating with them in some of its ceremonies.

My prior teaching experiences in the Bedford Stuyvesant neighborhood of Brooklyn and substituting across the city provided initial insights into the diverse cultures of New York. Yet it was in East Harlem where I encountered a different facet of the city's diversity. Although the neighborhood had seen many changes, faint echoes of its Italian past, like the exclusive Rao's restaurant and a few enduring churches, remained.

In this environment, Amari and Sauda deepened my understanding, especially regarding the African American and Puerto Rican communities in the Wagner housing projects and nearby tenement buildings. They introduced me to new perspectives and experiences. Welcoming me warmly into their lives, they affectionately dubbed me "Moswen," reflecting my light complexion.

Together, we shared countless memorable moments, including attending the high-energy aerobics class of Gregg Washington, where celebrities like RuPaul, David Duchovny, and Jennifer Beals would often join in the excitement.

After our aerobics sessions, we dined at Dojo Restaurant in the East Village. While shopping didn't particularly interest me, I enthusiastically joined in for other outings and adventures.

Sauda, an avid reader, recruited me into her book club, where we delved into powerful works by influential authors like W. E. B. Du Bois, Malcolm X, and Assata. Amari introduced me to the film *Sankofa* (1993) by Haile Gerima, a captivating and eye-opening historical account of the Maafa, the African Holocaust. This powerful movie moved me deeply and forever changed my perspective.

Through our ongoing friendship and the profound experiences we shared, Amari and Sauda have left an indelible mark on my growth as an educator and as an individual. Their wisdom and guidance have not only shaped my teaching approach, inspiring me to foster an inclusive and compassionate learning environment, but have also transformed my personal outlook. Our paths may have diverged geographically, but our bond remains strong.

After-School Trips

In late September, 1987, just weeks after school began, I started my practice of taking small groups of students, on a rotating basis, on after-school trips to various sites throughout the city: Rockefeller Center, the World Trade

Center, the Staten Island Ferry, Chinatown, museums, and parks. By spring, many were on their second, third, or sixth(!) trip. The numbers ranged from one to nine, but most often, the trips involved five or six youth.

Although not all parents permitted their children to participate in these outings, the majority did. For me, these excursions provided an opportunity to form deeper connections with my students.

"Mr. Calton, why do you take us on these trips?" asked one student early on.

"Well, it helps me find out what interests you and get to know your parents sooner as well as your home life," I replied. "It brings us closer together as a class."

After each trip, I would accompany each child back to their apartment to ensure their safe arrival and meet with their parents, well in advance of parent-teacher conferences.

It was a risky venture, but it was worth it. For my students, it was a chance to broaden their horizons and see the world beyond their East Harlem neighborhood. And for me, it was a chance to make a real difference in their lives and connect with them in a way that I never could in the classroom.

As an educator, I believe the first question that should be put to each child is: *Who are you?* The after-school trips answered that question because they helped me understand better what ignited each student's interest.

My former student Samantha Gonzalez remembers the after-school trips well:

We went on A LOT of trips. Our parents trusted Mr. Calton. He made sure that we were safe. He was really good at connecting with us and understanding what was going on with our lives, what our parents were going through, living in poverty, struggling, and he made sure we were educated and explored New York.

*He didn't want us living in a box; he wanted us to be open-minded and to know what was out there: **opportunity***. *He would teach the history of New York City beforehand and then take us places like Lower Manhattan and the Staten Island Ferry. We learned so much on those trips! They were very exciting.* —Samantha Gonzalez

Torn Poetry

It's funny how childhood trauma can shape a person's life. Take my search for what ignited every child's passion.

My parents' divorce was hard on me, as it is on any kid. I chose to live with my dad, hoping it would make things easier. Then he started dating Laurie, who was twenty-three. I was eleven. I resented Laurie but decided to take a stab at breaking the ice.

Throughout my childhood, I enjoyed writing poetry. It was my escape, my way of expressing myself. One day, I came home from school and showed Laurie a poem that my teacher had praised.

"You didn't write this! You copied it out of a book," she declared, tearing up the paper into tiny pieces. It may seem like a small thing, but it shattered me. When you live in a home with little nurturing and much discord, your aspirations can fade away. I gave up writing poetry.

That torn-up poem could be a metaphor for how the school system often shatters the curiosity and confidence of kids. Institutional buildings and classes of twenty-five or more students can force public schools to concentrate on test scores, leaving little room for creativity.

And that's why I made it my mission to find out what ignited every child's passion. I didn't want them to feel the way I did when Laurie ripped up my poem. I wanted them to know that they were capable of great things, that they had something special to offer the world. In helping my students realize their potential, I discovered a sense of purpose and healing within myself, gradually mending the wounds from my own childhood.

Miss Liberty

On any of our trips, whether part of the official school itinerary or independently organized after-school outings, I always sought to turn every situation into a learning experience. On school-sanctioned trips, I preferred to use the New York City subway system instead of the yellow school buses with their strict time constraints.

Whenever we boarded the subway, I pretended to be unfamiliar with the route to our destination. This was a teaching strategy to engage students in leadership, problem-solving, and decision-making. Some students took on the responsibility of studying the subway map, tracking our progress, and notifying the others when we reached our stop. By doing this, I aimed to empower the students and teach them valuable life skills that they could apply outside the classroom.

During a regular school trip to the Statue of Liberty, we made use of several bedsheets weighted down by the students' backpacks to create a picnic area on the expansive grassy lawn at Liberty Island Park in New York Harbor.

While we settled in, seagulls swooped down, snatching peanut butter and jelly sandwiches from the brown-bag lunches the school had provided. Their antics caused us to race to secure what sandwiches were still remaining. The students laughed off the interruptions, losing themselves in cartwheels, games of tag, and jump rope.

However, as time passed and they gazed up at the grandeur of the statue, their curiosity to see inside intensified. This was back in the early '90s when it was easier and less restrictive to enter the statue, prior to the events of 9/11. I wearily eyed the long line of tourists waiting to enter the humongous structure. "I'm not going," I asserted. "I'm not waiting in that line. Plus, I might get claustrophobic inside the crowded statue."

"But we want to go," several kids protested.

"You all can get in if you go in smaller groups and don't act up," I said.

"We can go on our own?"

"Yes, but…"

Before I could finish the instructions, the kids ran en masse, whooping and hollering, toward the line. Minutes later, they all returned, deflated and sulking. The guards and staff had turned them away.

"It's okay," I said. "Just wait about ten minutes or so. Then go in groups of two or three, SEPARATELY. Befriend others in the line. You'll get in."

I wasn't concerned for their safety. I had experience with nearly all of them on our many after-school trips. Additionally, the island was crawling with staff, park rangers, guides, and other teachers. The only way on or off the island was by boat unless you wanted to try and swim New York Harbor.

Most of the ten- and eleven-year-olds trickled back to the entrance in smaller numbers. The vast majority made it inside. Nevertheless, as they got to different levels of the base and pedestal, students began breaking from their adopted chaperones. Horseplay and clowning ensued, and once again, little by little, they were ejected.

However, two pairs of students, Vanessa and Lisa, and Lamont and Charlie, stayed with the adults they befriended, making it higher and higher toward the top. At the last stretch, on one of the resting platforms, Vanessa and Lisa lost their chaperones and got turned around.
Lamont and Charlie stayed with their guides and reached the crown.

On the subway home, Vanessa, Lisa, Lamont, and Charlie all talked about the fascinating conversations they had with their adult guides and the interesting life stories they heard.

In class the next day, I asked them to write about which behaviors and practices resulted in some students being turned away and which techniques got Vanessa and Lisa farther than most, and Lamont and Charlie all the way to the top.

How could they apply what they learned in their daily lives? Many recognized the value of patience, listening, and forming genuine connections. Others realized that sometimes achieving a goal requires strategy rather than just enthusiasm. Their experiences at the statue became a practical lesson in perseverance, adaptability, and the importance of building meaningful relationships.

The Power of Shared Experiences

As an outsider in their community, I knew I had to work twice as hard to earn the trust of my students. That's why I took them on countless school and after-school trips—to break down the walls between us and forge a deeper connection. It was on these trips that I saw my students truly come alive, free of the constraints of peer pressure and performance anxiety. As David Brooks said in a *New York Times* article, "Teachers really teach themselves—their contagious passion for their subjects and students… Children learn from people they love, and that love in this context means willing the good of another and offering active care for the whole person."

A prime example of the success of the after-school trips for building trust and confidence was Georgie Davis. He was always quiet, never doing his homework or participating in class. But after his first trip, Georgie started doing his homework and speaking up in class. As it turned out, Georgie was a math whiz. I couldn't help but wonder—would Georgie have eventually warmed up on his own? Or did these trips help speed up that process, giving him the safe space he needed to thrive?

> **Humans are unique and diverse. Cookie-cutter curriculums and test-taking are not sufficient to engage minds. As a classroom teacher in East Harlem, I broke down the barriers of our four walls so each student could discover what hooked them.**

The Better Angels of Our Nature

Promoting such close contact with students outside of school might elicit fear in some, who perhaps think the teacher has ulterior motives. If that is a concern, vetting teachers to make sure these problems are weeded out is a better solution than making rules prohibiting what can work best. At the time, I was perhaps dismissive toward anyone who might question my actions. I'd simply say, "Speak to the kids."

I believe what Canadian cognitive psychologist Steven Pinker says in *The Better Angels of Our Nature*: that instances of wrongdoing are so hyper-publicized that it seems they are widespread, when in fact they are less frequent than one would think.[1]

Instead, let's focus on nurturing positive aspects. Let's embrace our humanity, love one another, and genuinely engage with the hearts of our youth. Let them experience failure, but in a safe environment where they can learn and grow. This sentiment brings to mind "Hey Jimmy Joe John Jim Jack," an old children's song my grandma used to play, by the American folk group the Limeliters, with lyrics in the bridge that strike a chord:

> Don't do this, don't do that,
> You might as well be a statue
> That's how children lose their spark
> But if grown-ups would take part in
> Things that children have their heart in,
> They'd never end up hiding in the dark.

Finding What Works

Amari and I used a practice to great effect: giving out point tickets to reward good behavior. The points could be used in auction for prizes every couple of weeks (stuff picked up at the dollar store or perks like skipping a homework assignment). For a new teacher learning how to manage a class of thirty kids, it was a very effective practice. But as time went on, we realized it wasn't sustainable. We couldn't keep handing out tickets forever, and we didn't want to create a culture of bribery.

In my second year, I created table groupings for students who regularly completed their homework, while those who didn't were relegated to individual seats. Students preferred sitting in groups, so they were motivated to complete their homework to earn a coveted spot at the tables.

But again, I eventually discontinued the practice. As teachers, we have to be adaptable. We need to try different things to see what works best. And sometimes, what works in one year doesn't work in the next. We have to be willing to take risks, be flexible, and keep learning. That's how we become better teachers.

---

1. Steven Pinker, *The Better Angels of Our Nature*, 2011, Viking Books.

However, the best systems are ones the teacher develops WITH the students in order to get their buy-in.

Years later, I witnessed the art of collaboratively creating systems with students used masterfully in Kathy Tolan's sixth-grade class in Harlem. At the beginning of the school year, her students delved into the history and cultures of conversation, creating a safe and respectful environment for all. She challenged me to identify her class's worst behavior problem, but I couldn't.

During class, she would read from a book, and at some point she or one of the students would say, "Say something." They would then have thirty seconds to discuss what was being read. In one discussion, some of the students were dominating the conversation, but a student pointed it out and requested a "quiet moment so some of the quieter voices can be heard." The class fell silent but remained comfortable for twenty to thirty seconds. Then one of the students who hadn't spoken up before voiced their opinion. It was an incredible experience. When students have a say in how things are run, they feel invested and engaged. And when they feel invested and engaged, they are more likely to behave responsibly and contribute positively to the classroom community.

Being a teacher is an art. You need to thread the line between being an authority figure and giving kids control of the class so they feel it's their environment. Respect goes both ways—it's a give-and-take.

Unconventional Teaching

To create a warmer and less institutional atmosphere in the classroom, I often turned off the harsh fluorescent lights, especially when reading to my students. The large windows facing the Wagner Projects across 120th Street, which provided a view of the East River, allowed plenty of natural light to fill the space.

However, when Principal Dainis brought visitors to my class at the far end of the third floor, her clicking heels on the floor would signal her approach, and she would flick on the lights before entering the room and announcing, "And this is Mr. Calton's class." Despite my unorthodox methods, Dainis was willing to tolerate them as long as she saw that I genuinely cared about my students.

I frequently called parents and made home visits to address any problems or discuss our after-school trips. As a result, I eventually became familiar with every building in the Wagner projects.

* * *

As any experienced teacher knows, it's not just about what happens in the classroom but also what lies ahead. Anticipating outcomes is a crucial skill for any educator who wants to keep their sanity intact. For example, you know that students will be excitable around Halloween as they contemplate a candy bounty.

It takes at least a year or two for a teacher to become accustomed to the myriad challenges they face throughout the year: decorating the classroom in August, assemblies, class interruptions by the administration, test preparation, post-test exhaustion, packing things away for holiday cleanings, and more. With time and experience, a teacher learns how to navigate these stressful moments, ensuring that the class continues to run smoothly.

The Writing Project at Teachers College

By the midpoint of my second year teaching at P.S. 206 in 1989, I thought I had a decent handle on things, but it wasn't until I attended a workshop that spring with Amari, Sauda, and a few others that my teaching methods underwent a dramatic transformation. The workshop was held at Hunter College, but it was part of the Reading and Writing Project founded by Lucy Calkins, which was based at Columbia University's Teachers College.

After that experience, I was hooked, and I spent the next several years attending the program's workshops and summer intensives to continue refining my teaching techniques. They taught us how to focus on students' different learning styles to create lifelong readers and writers. Their methodology was simple yet effective: mini-lessons followed by independent and small-group work, with long stretches of time dedicated to reading and writing.

I read fiction and nonfiction aloud every day, from the Rats of NIMH to *The Autobiography of Malcolm X*. Our classroom library grew so large, even the school librarian borrowed books from us. The students constructed handmade books for some of their stories, which we celebrated with publishing parties.

To encourage individual dialogues with my students about their classroom challenges, I implemented a practice of asking them to write short reflections, or "exit slips," about any problems they were having in the class or with their writing. This tactic proved to be effective and was later adopted by HarlemLIVE, where the teens wrote blog posts reflecting on their experiences and progress as well as communicating about any issues they felt needed addressing.

I allocated time in our daily routine, usually once or twice a day, for both my students and me to write in our journals. This ritual of journaling left an indelible imprint on many of my students, as they bear witness:

In my 5th grade class, I learned the power of freewriting. Mr. Calton gave us all journals, and we had to write in them every day. Some days we got writing prompts, other days a freewriting assignment. As an introvert, it was my safe space to write down and process my thoughts. Ever since, the journals have stayed with me. I have journals from middle school, high school, college, and I even keep them now. —Sharnice Jenkins

* * *

One thing I loved about my 5th grade class were the journals. Mr. Calton wrote in his journal every day, and he made sure that all of us had our own journals and that we wrote every day. The goal was to keep a log of our lives, whatever we were thinking or feeling. Writing became a tool to feel good about ourselves. It helped me express myself, and it impacted my life in a huge way. Even now I write poetry, and I'm working on a children's book. —Samantha Gonzalez

In September 2023, the Teachers College announced the dissolution of the Reading and Writing Project, a program that greatly influenced my teaching methods. While the program faced criticism, especially for its approaches to teaching early reading, its strategies for nurturing writing skills in older students transformed my classroom into a hub for literary exploration and expression.

Teaching Excellence and Innovation

By the end of my second year at P.S. 206, our school received a prestigious "school of excellence" classification from a presidential commission. As a result, Principal Dainis was promoted to deputy superintendent of District 4, and before leaving, she personally chose which teachers would teach which classes for the following year. Due to my dedication and efforts, I was assigned to teach the top fifth-grade class, which was determined by students' reading and math scores.

After Dainis left, Anna Leone served as the assistant principal for the next year until a permanent candidate was assigned. Many of the long-time teachers, including teacher/monitors, left the school or retired, which left a lack of supervision. This gave me more freedom to experiment with the curriculum. I introduced meditation sessions, formed clubs (such as law, geography, and math), and continued to organize after-school trips.

We tried to start a newspaper. The early attempts were rough, with me typing the students' stories and pasting them onto standard paper, making it look like a ransom note. It would take a few more years before we would successfully create the newspaper.

Letter Writing

I instituted a weekly assignment to students: pen two letters addressed to real people. I thought that writing a real letter to a specific person would be more interesting than writing something just for the teacher to read.

Students wrote letters to their family, friends, celebrities, and potential guest speakers. I suggested recipients—people I knew in various fields whom I thought the students might find interesting. The handwritten letters (this was before email) were due Tuesday, returned with corrections Wednesday, and ready to be sent by Friday.

When the letter writing began, I pitched that students appeal to City Hall for a solution to our treeless, blond brick school building, which baked the classrooms during the hotter months. I was amazed when, a few months later, representatives from the mayor's office came to our class to say they had received the letters and would soon be planting trees. Students learned a valuable lesson on how participating in civic life could bring results, and decades later, those trees provide great shade to the front of the building in spring and summer.

The power of bold action by young individuals would demonstrate itself once more with the HarlemLIVE youth years later, as they took up the battle with City Hall to keep the program open.

The students' letters brought to our classroom museum curators, authors, professional athletes, business professionals, and many others as guest speakers. Eventually, the kids formed a Letters and Speakers Club to coordinate communicating with, scheduling, and thanking our guests.

One of our regular visitors was Dr. Robert Gyles, head of the math curriculum for the district. The kids loved his engaging presentations and especially the calculators he gave away.

Dr. Gyles's values and goals aligned with mine, and he became my mentor. He explains:

I was with the Department of Education for thirty-six years, first as a teacher and then in administration. Richard and I connected over our dedication to teaching and commitment to service.

Richard worked in a challenging community, striving to give students experiences they lacked. Later, he started HarlemLIVE, a community-based organization. It embodied our shared philosophy: don't merely learn, but use and pass it on. —Dr. Robert Gyles

The success and impact of the letter-writing initiative showed me that students were more than capable of communicating complex ideas, and not just in the written form. Their passion for real-world interaction ignited an idea: What if these same students were given an avenue to express themselves through another medium, one that would allow them to channel their creativity, tell stories, and perhaps even transform their classroom learning into a form of art?

This thought led me to explore the realm of theatrical storytelling. I wondered, could my students take tales from the African continent, stories rich with heritage, and transform them into stage performances? Not only would it challenge them to interpret narratives, but it would also demand teamwork, problem-solving, and a blend of different talents, much like our letter-writing had done.

African Folktales: A Journey Through Theater

In my fifth year of teaching at P.S. 206 in 1991, I embarked on a new challenge to infuse my class with experiential learning: turning African folktales into theatrical productions. This endeavor was one of the most fulfilling and inspiring efforts I made as an educator.

We began in September by exploring a variety of tales from the African continent in our reading and writing groups. Every Friday, students took turns reading aloud selections until they determined which was their favorite tale. Once we had chosen the story, we studied how scripts are structured and rewrote the tale with scenes and dialogue. The readings helped us identify which students were best suited for different roles, and we held tryouts for the parts before the December holiday break. Rehearsals began early in the new year, and the performances took place at the end of February to coincide with Black History Month.

Though our inaugural play had its imperfections, with each passing year we honed our skills, elevating the quality of sets, costumes, lighting, sound, and overall presentation.

What She Gonna Do?

In the first play, *Arap Sang and the Cranes*, we cast Michael Parker, one of my most challenging students, in a leading role. Michael lived with his grandmother and younger brother, Ivan, who would later become my student as well. Michael had always been a handful, with his sharp wit and quick comebacks. Once, after I threatened to call his grandmother, he quipped, "What she gonna do? Not feed me?"

But I saw something in Michael: potential. So when we decided to do the play *Arap Sang and the Cranes*, I cast Michael in a leading role.

When the principal found out, she cornered me in the hallway, questioning my decision. "Of all the students, why cast the one who gives me countless headaches as your star?" she asked.

But in my eyes, every child, including Michael, deserved an opportunity to discover and embrace their potential. My guiding philosophy has always been to offer young minds a sense of direction, autonomy, and empowerment. Every soul craves a sense of belonging and purpose. While the precise words I used to counter the principal's concern elude me now, my conviction was clear: without purpose, how can one harbor dreams of success?

(Later in life, Michael's achievements were a testament to his potential: serving as a program director for multiple organizations and even meeting President Obama several times. He now champions a cause dedicated to eradicating gun violence.)

As time progressed, our theatrical productions evolved in depth and sophistication. Each student became an integral part of these shows, whether as actors in the limelight, backstage hands, set designers, sound and lighting technicians, publicists, or ushers. This experience underscored an essential truth: while actors might receive the most immediate recognition, every participant's role is crucial to the success of the whole production.

Sharnice Jenkins describes her involvement with one of the plays as follows:

I was supposed to be a character in Karimira and Musiguku, *but I was not able to do it. However, I got the opportunity to play a leadership role as a stage manager, and that called for the same skills I have later used as an administrator: delegating, checking in with people to make sure they had what they needed, and if they didn't, providing it to them. I've used the leadership skills I learned through that experience all the way to now. —Sharnice Jenkins*

Mr. Charles Brown: A Musical Genius

The last of our African folktale productions was a true masterpiece, thanks in part to the musical genius of Mr. Charles Brown. In the final play, Mr. Brown, our music teacher, wrote original songs for two of the female leads. He was an accomplished musician and singer, having performed in Broadway productions and on international stages, in addition to being a Vietnam veteran. When he arrived at P.S. 206 in his early fifties, some of his paperwork wasn't complete, so another teacher had to remain in the room during the first few weeks of his teaching.

Mr. Brown had a talent for delivering outlandish lines in a stern military voice that regularly had me in stitches. I remember one instance when the kids attempted to perform a new song, and Mr. Brown commented, "That sounded like a bunch of Brillo pads." I would often have to leave the class because I was laughing so hard.

Years later, I moved to an apartment in Harlem that was just around the corner from Mr. Brown. We often ran into each other and had conversations. Sometimes I would go help him with his iMac. He induced smiles and laughter in every conversation.

Tragically, Mr. Brown passed away a week before Thanksgiving in 2021 due to smoke inhalation from a fire in an apartment on the floor below his. The children of a couple of HarlemLIVE alumni covered his celebration of life, following in the footsteps of their journalist parents.

* * *

Jihan Crichlow, one of my students, played a pivotal role in the production as well. He took charge of creating a musical motif for every appearance of the lead villain in our play. His creativity added a unique and memorable dimension to our production.

Jihan recalls this experience:

Back then, I was learning basic piano at Harlem School of the Arts, exploring various sounds rather than sticking to a traditional style. My family got a Casio keyboard with lots of alternative sounds and beat-making features. Mr. Calton had faith in me to create music for the show. I was nervous but grateful for the opportunity to showcase my abilities. Having this type of experience at that time can help set the tone for your future.

In every year's production, we added a dance scene choreographed by para-professional Stephanie White. The art class and a special education class worked together to design and build the sets, while parents contributed by sewing costumes for the characters. The productions became a hit, drawing in district personnel and community members alike. For the last production, we even had evening performances and charged for admission to help cover some of the costs.

Kids eagerly engage in real-world tasks and skills ranging from designing and building sets to composing music. We discovered that students are enthusiastic and motivated to take on "adult" or "real" tasks. Classroom learning doesn't have to be limited to rows of kids memorizing material by rote. Instead, we should strive to offer diverse and plentiful opportunities for students to engage with the world outside of the classroom.

School Newspaper

In my sixth year of teaching at P.S. 206 in 1992, the district office caught wind of our on-again, off-again attempts to create a newspaper and offered us a Macintosh Classic. While I had previously led the effort to computerize

New York University's student newspaper, this was my first introduction to Apple computers, which revolutionized computing through the use of icons, drop-down menus, and mice rather than obscure commands.

The class decided on the name *Kids' Newsday* for the newsletter, and we even had access to a previously unused video camera, which we used to provide images for the publication. Although the quality wasn't great, it was sufficient for our needs.

Our newsletter included stories about class trips, assemblies, and guest speakers as well as poetry, cartoons, editorials, letters to the editor, and profiles of teachers and students. We sold the newsletter for a quarter to help cover the printing cost, which I paid out of pocket. When we required more computing power, the district allowed me to bring a few students to their offices after school.

* * *

At the end of school year, I asked to be moved up to teach sixth grade, which would allow me to continue the momentum of publishing the newsletter with my current students. In sixth grade, students changed teachers for different subjects, and I taught writing and computers. Some of my former students from fifth grade were scattered throughout the four groups that made up the entire sixth grade, which enabled them to model practices from the year before, such as writing workshops, theatrical productions, guest speakers, and after-school trips. This peer-to-peer training would later become a cornerstone of the HarlemLIVE program.

My sixth-grade students' skills developed to the point that they were able to assist in publishing a district-wide technology newsletter. The district's computer coordinator, Mark Steinberger, even organized a conference on the use of technology and invited the young publishers of *Kids' Newsday* to lead one of the workshops for teachers and students. Many of the students' previous experiences, including reporting for the newspaper, acting, and confidently navigating New York City during after-school trips, had already made them comfortable speaking in front of others.

Two students, Miriam Velez and Reggie Williams, were particularly involved in the process. Reggie recalls his experiences fondly:

I always told people that I would someday be an author or writer of some kind. Well, being in a classroom where we had sessions called writing workshops, which encouraged, nurtured, and inspired young people to use their words to accomplish goals and change the world around them, I naturally flourished into being one of the pioneers of HarlemLIVE.

A couple years before HarlemLIVE took off, Miriam and I hit the streets, talking to local businesses to get them to place ads in our school paper. Later, it helped me see that there was a world beyond my four-block neighborhood by sending me to cover different news stories around Harlem and the whole five boroughs.

Too much of education builds a false and too-safe wall between young people and reality, asking them to imagine hypothetical situations for which they may or may not have any use. I believe we must encourage students to do real things, such as public speaking, and that the biggest and most difficult step is always the first one. We should instruct and challenge our students. When they face their fear and take that first step, they gain self-confidence that will serve them well all their lives.

Sharnice Jenkins, one of my former students, attests to the lasting impact of experiential learning that goes beyond the school years:

I was part of the newspaper team, and I learned a lot of skills, like how to write a story and how to apply graphic design. These skills followed me as a student and later in my career. In high school, I created brochures, flyers, newsletters, and business cards for my teachers.

I liked the brainstorming process of thinking about your audience and about what you're trying to communicate to them, how you're trying to inspire, motivate, call to action, highlight, celebrate... These are *all ways in which you can let people know that you **see** them, you **hear** them, and you **value** them.*

As an educator, I had a website for my students and the parents so they could see what was going on in the class, and I sent a newsletter to the parents; when I moved into leadership, publishing a newsletter became a way of highlighting what was going on in the school; as a consultant right now, I often urge my clients to write a newsletter; and on a personal note, I co-lead a women's group, and we have an email newsletter that we blast out periodically to inspire women. —Sharnice Jenkins

Turning Point

In my eighth year at P.S. 206, 1994, I was living and breathing my job. With perfect attendance the year before and our class constantly in the spotlight for visitors, it should have been my shining moment. Instead, this school year would prove to be one of the most traumatic and consequential of my career and my life.

It all began with a fire in October 1994.

While I was out biking around the city, my brownstone-style apartment building was heavily damaged. I lost most of my belongings except for my vinyl record collection and a stack of journals that would come in handy later in life. Forced to find a sublet on the other side of town, I thought things couldn't get any worse.

But then my checkbook was stolen and my bank account was emptied.

And just when I thought I had hit rock bottom, the coup de grâce arrived in the form of a cease-and-desist letter from the principal.

Assigned to P.S. 206 in my fourth year, the principal had never been a big supporter of our extracurricular activities. Though she allowed us to do them, she never provided any funds and constantly questioned my methods. And then, in December, the letter arrived. It ordered me to stop taking kids on after-school trips.

In the weeks leading up to the notice, fellow sixth-grade teacher Lorett Caquias and I had been taking students in her car on Saturdays to a church soup kitchen on the Upper West Side to help feed homeless people. However, the principal feared that she or the school could be held liable in the event of an accident.

"I'm not going to lose my house due to these trips," she once said.

* * *

I stared at the principal's letter, debating whether or not to sign it. It felt like giving up a piece of myself, a crucial part of what made me a teacher. It took me a week, but I finally did sign the letter.

My hand shook as I defiantly scribbled a message in the margin: "What I do on my own time with parents' permission is my business." But I didn't want to push things too far, so I reluctantly put a halt to our after-school trips... for a time.

In January 1995, we found ourselves in dire need of paint for our upcoming school play. So, against my better judgment, I decided to break the rules and take a small group of students to what was considered the Disneyland of art supply stores, Pearl Paint. It was a multi-floor emporium with wide, creaky wood-plank floors and an endless array of artistic delights. It's unfortunate that it no longer exists.

When it was time to head downtown, two of the students canceled. Tiffany Santiago had to go somewhere with her family, and Reggie Williams got a stomachache. So, I went just with Elliot Martinez, an eleven-year-old budding artist who did most of the sketches for the play's scenery and helped construct the sets. Elliot's mom approved the outing and said we could keep the jugs of paint in their apartment since I was now staying in a distant part of town. Elliot and I would go in the morning to pick them up.

This simple trip would change the trajectory of my life. Unbeknownst to me at the time, it would also impact the lives of hundreds of young people for years to come.

Chapter 4

UNEXPECTED DETOUR: A FATEFUL TRIP

In January 1995, the trains were a mess that frigid Monday afternoon when Elliot and I went downtown to buy a few gallons of paint for our annual show. It took nearly seventy-five minutes to get from 125th Street in East Harlem to Canal Street in Lower Manhattan. This was usually a twenty-five-minute ride.

The whole time, my mind was spinning:

Something is going to go wrong. Something is going to go wrong.

For eight weeks I had obeyed the principal's edict to halt the after-school excursions; now I was breaking it.

Getting students beyond their East Harlem confines and showing them the wider world was key to my teaching, but was I now risking my job? I had never felt paranoid going on any of these trips, but I did that day. Soon, my fear would transform into panic.

We came aboveground at Canal Street and walked to Pearl Paint a few blocks away. As we arrived, they were just locking the doors. My mind screamed, "Has this scary trip been for naught?"

"Come on, Elliot, we have to get you home. This has already taken too long."

"I'm hungry," said Elliot.

Something is going to go wrong. Something is going to go wrong.

My mind couldn't stop repeating this ominous mantra.

There was a McD's between Pearl Paint and the subway, so Elliot asked if we could stop there.

"Okay, but you'll have to eat on the train."

We placed our order at the mercifully uncrowded counter, but then several uniformed cops approached. They placed a huge order for the entire station, and we were told their order would take precedence.

Something's going to go wrong. Something's going to go wrong.

After finally getting Elliot's food, we hurried toward Canal and Lafayette, where honking cars and shuffling crowds fought for space on one on New York City's busiest thoroughfares. As we bounded down the stairs, we could hear the train rumbling into the station.

Elliot raced past me, clutching his bag of food, and slid under the turnstile as the train pulled to a stop—back then, and now, kids often evade paying the fare by going under the turnstile.

I reached into my pocket for what I thought was a subway token (this was before Metro cards) and placed it in the slot.

Oh no!

It wasn't a token but rather a game slug from a previous trip to an arcade in Coney Island that I found in my pocket. As I glanced at the long line in the token booth, I momentarily lost sight of Elliot amid the crowd on the subway platform.

Was he already on the train?

Something's going to go wrong. Something's going to go wrong.

I panicked. I jumped the turnstile and raced to the platform.

"Hold it there." A white guy in jeans, an undercover cop, spread out his arms and kept me from going farther.

"The subway isn't free, Jack," said the cop.

Right then a female undercover officer joined us with Elliot at her side. She had apprehended him when his backpack got stuck on the turnstile, but I hadn't noticed.

Raising his eyebrows, the male undercover cop looked at Elliot and then back at me. Pointing to Elliot, he asked, "Is he with you?"

I nodded.

"Well, well, well. Look what we have here."

My heart sank. This didn't look good.

"We went to Pearl Paint to get paint for our school play," I said.

"Where's the paint?"

"We didn't get there in time."

"Do you always teach your kids how to jump the turnstile?"

The female cop pulled Elliot aside.

"Does your mother know you're with this guy?" she asked.

"Yes." Elliot answered confidently and matter-of-factly.

"I'll take him to headquarters and call his mom," she said, putting her arm around Elliot. "She may be facing negligence for allowing her son to be with a criminal."

She escorted him away.

The male undercover cop led me through throngs of people through an unmarked door in the Canal Street station. We found ourselves in a cramped room lit by a single flickering bulb dangling from the ceiling. The only furniture in sight was a shabby metal desk and a few metal chairs.

The officer motioned for me to take a seat and then reached into a drawer and pulled out some paperwork.

"Fill these out," he said gruffly.

The paperwork asked all manner of questions, including my level of education and any schools attended. Minutes later, a decorated sergeant showed up and looked over my answers.

"Our teachers never spent this much time with us when we were going to school," said the undercover officer, looking at me suspiciously.

I didn't know what he was getting at, but then the sergeant read my paperwork and repeated my alma mater with a sneer: "NYU to City College? NYU to City College?"

"Yes." What school did he expect me to go to on a teacher's salary?

"Put your hands behind your back," he said as he gestured to one of the officers, who proceeded to cuff me. "We're placing you under arrest." He put my paperwork down.

"No. No. No." My back slumped against the Depression-green wall, my wrists tightly pinched in cuffs behind me. My body slid to the ground, and I began to cry. The police smirked and smiled.

They took me to the transit police precinct, located at a different Canal Street subway station down the block. A family member came for Elliot, whom I'd last seen on the subway platform when I was apprehended.

Looking through my records at the police station, they noticed I had an outstanding unpaid ticket for running a light on my bicycle. The summons had been destroyed during the fire in my apartment a few months earlier.

The police scoured my journal, wondering why I had my students' names and phone numbers written in the back—numbers I needed in order to contact families about all the extracurricular activities.

While I was going through this ordeal, I would later learn, Elliot watched the events unfold, feeling a sense of guilt and despair. He recently told me, "I've never forgotten the heartbreaking mistreatment I witnessed you go through. Though young at the time, I remember it like it was yesterday. This is a man who gave so much to the community and kept a lot of us Harlem kids off the street. Stupid book bag. Stupid legal system."

With the outstanding ticket and their false suspicions, the police sent me to central booking in lower Manhattan. Being locked up overnight in the infamous Tombs prison gave me deeper insight into the dehumanizing effects of the criminal justice system.

Elliot's words still echo in my mind: "They had a problem with him running after me; imagine how much bigger a problem if he didn't keep up. Before that, I was having the best day ever. The only thing that was out of place was people placing their jobs over their humility and understanding."

I couldn't go to school the following day because the judge didn't see me until the afternoon. During my absence, the police paid a visit to the school to meet with the principal.

I phoned my father in California from a pay phone in the holding cell. He called a hotshot New York lawyer, Michael Kennedy, whom he had met during one of the whitewater rafting tours he guided down the Colorado River. Kennedy sent one of his top lawyers to represent me. It was overkill, but I didn't know that I could've called the teacher's union for representation. Plus, I didn't have their number.

I was released with "time served" and my record sealed, which meant the incident wouldn't show up on my record. It was a relief that my mentor, Dr. Gyles, continued to support me emotionally, spiritually, and professionally through this difficult period.

Elliot, with the wisdom of an adult but the clear memory of a child, ended his recollection with "So here's a quote for the book: I'm sorry I ducked that turnstile. The real criminals wore blue that day." His words were a poignant reminder of the systemic problems we faced and how they could undermine even the best of intentions.

From Burnout to Renewal

Later that week, I retrieved my mail from the post office since I was still transient following the fire. I saw the envelope stamped with the board of education's insignia. I tore open the envelope, and my eyes widened as I read the words, barely believing them: I was tenured.

The irony wasn't lost on me. The day I was handcuffed and hauled away like a common criminal was the same day the board of education had deemed me worthy of prized tenure status.

But what good was tenure if I couldn't do what I knew was right for my students? After the incident at the subway, the principal was shaken, and I knew my after-school trips were over. It was time for a change.

I made the decision to take a year's leave after the current school year ended. Some said I was crazy to leave a successful teaching position, but they didn't know what it was like to be under the principal's thumb, to be prohibited from doing what I knew was most effective. I couldn't stay in the system past my prime just for the benefits.

Teaching was hard work, and after such a stressful year, I was burned out. I had always told myself to be on the lookout for a wake-up call, a message that it was time to let go. This seemed to be that moment.

Before taking leave, the district placed a student teacher, Karen Thompson, in my class so I could impart my teaching techniques.

Thompson wrote this note after her time with our class was up:

Dear Mr. Calton,
I can't thank you enough for letting me be a part of your classroom the past three months! From the first day, you made me feel welcome and appreciated. I remember you saying, "I want you to get the most out of

this experience that you can," and because you were so willing to give me responsibility... I did.

I know you feel ready for a break from teaching and that you feel guilty for not being as committed as you have been in other years, but I have been amazed by your commitment to your students. I mean, who calls at 6:30 p.m. from a pizza place where you've taken kids after spending the past three hours working on the newspaper, and then calls again later, offering to go pick up the magazine on your bike at 7 a.m.? It is way beyond dedicated. Your students are really lucky to have such an energetic and creative teacher who will adapt African folktales into plays and put out two issues of the newspaper in one week and invite women from the Whitney Museum to speak and... the list goes on.

And I am even more amazed that you can do all this without ANY support from the school administrators!

I hope that you have a wonderful, refreshing and revitalizing break from teaching and that you find a school to teach where all your creative endeavors will be supported. More students deserve the chance to learn with you.

Again, thank you so much for your support and encouragement and trust and feedback and kindness. Working in your classroom gave me invaluable insight into what it means to be a teacher.

The Institute for Learning Technologies

In 1995, as the new school year rolled in, I found myself on a leave of absence from P.S. 206 and still under investigation for the turnstile incident. I was unsure of what the future held for me until the district's computer technology coordinator, Mark Steinberger, approached me with a job offer to introduce technology to East Harlem schools. Unfortunately, the ongoing investigation prevented me from taking the district position, although I could still substitute teach during the year.

It was then that Mark introduced me to the Institute for Learning Technologies (ILT), a group associated with Teachers College that was founded by the visionary Dr. Robbie McClintock. The organization's mission was to leverage digital technologies as a catalyst for change in education, which later proved to be the cornerstone of HarlemLIVE.

Volunteering for ILT was a transformative experience for me. The projects were diverse, ranging from the Native Web, a clearinghouse of online resources available in the early years of the World Wide Web, to wiring schools in Harlem and the Bronx with high-speed internet. I learned a lot about computer networking, troubleshooting, and emerging software programs just as the internet was about to explode.

I was surrounded by an eclectic group of imaginative individuals who were passionate about the emerging technologies. One of them was Jennifer Hogan, who would become a crucial supporter of HarlemLIVE. She saw an organization that accomplished what schools didn't: overcoming the digital divide. Bridging the digital divide was a vital objective for HL, where 90 percent of students were youth of color being taught how to create and publish on the internet.

TADA!

During my yearlong sabbatical, I stumbled upon a program called TADA!, an organization that taught theater skills to young adults and provided a platform for off-Broadway productions. Intrigued, I decided to volunteer my time. Once the staff learned of my background in theater and my previous work with kids, they offered several scholarships to some of my former students. Among those students were Reggie and Angel, who were later cast in TADA!'s evening productions. As a result, Reggie piqued the interest of a talent scout who saw potential in him for television roles.

Erica Sosa, another former student, had a breakout lead role in the last play my class produced at P.S. 206. TADA! was eager to cast her in one of their off-Broadway productions, but her parents didn't allow her to continue her involvement in the program. This recurring issue of overprotective parents hindering their children's growth and opportunities would become a source of frustration for me during my time at HarlemLIVE. Omar Parris, a talented and socially conscious writer, was another promising teen who was pulled out of the program by his mother due to concerns that his reporting and writing might get him in trouble.

* * *

Volunteering can open up a world of life-changing opportunities, from landing a job at organizations like ILT to securing scholarships for deserving students. I've found it to be an excellent way to acquire valuable expertise in fields where people might otherwise have limited exposure.

The Million Man March

Being on break from day-to-day teaching, I had the opportunity to attend the Million Man March in October 1995. The demonstration aimed to challenge negative stereotypes of Black men and unite against social and economic injustices in the African American community.[1]

I took an overnight Amtrak train and arrived early in the morning. Exhausted and self-conscious as one of the few white attendees, I tried to blend in by keeping my hoodie on as much as possible while waiting for the event to begin near the Capitol.

What resonated with me most that day was the call for attendees to create organizations and initiatives that could positively impact their communities. That idea stuck with me and was one of the inspirations behind my decision to start HarlemLIVE later on.

* * *

During my leave of absence, I embraced a diverse range of activities, including work, studies, and volunteer opportunities. To explore potential transfer schools, I took on occasional substitute teaching roles. Alongside this, I actively participated in the Reading and Writing Project at Teachers College, where I had the privilege of observing a master teacher in a sixth-grade classroom in Harlem over several days.

---

1. Million Man March National Organizing Committee (January 1996). "Million Man March Fact Sheet." In Madhubuti, Haki R., and Karenga, Maulana (eds.). *Million Man March / Day of Absence; A Commemorative Anthology; Speeches, Commentary, Photography, Poetry, Illustrations, Documents.* Chicago: Third World Press.

During a brief period, I worked part-time as a consultant for NetLive, an education start-up focused on providing high-speed internet-connectivity services to schools and educators. Interestingly, this experience served as the inspiration for the name HarlemLIVE.

Before that, in the winter of 1996, I completed a seven-week online course in Hyper Text Markup Language (HTML) at Dartmouth University. Given my computer science background from NYU, the course proved manageable, yet it equipped me with the essential skills to create basic websites.

I was thrilled at the prospect of launching an online publication that could reach a global audience. I recognized that an online publication would be an ideal platform for young people, offering them the chance to engage with the world and explore different stories. It would also provide them with a means to have their voices heard and make an immediate impact.

The Dots Connect

The notion of HarlemLIVE had taken root, but it initially faced resistance from the powers that be at ILT. Their focus was primarily on supporting ongoing projects in schools rather than starting new ventures. Nevertheless, I persisted and took the initiative to register HarlemLIVE as a business, purchasing the domain name www.harlemlive.org. I was determined to make this work even though I had no idea what I was doing.

To further support my vision, I utilized my newly acquired web design skills to create a website for a hair transplant company, earning $3,000. With these funds, I invested in an Apple 5300 PowerBook laptop and a Kodak DC40 digital camera, which became valuable tools for experimenting with various ideas for HarlemLIVE.

Step by step, the pieces of HarlemLIVE began falling into place, and I could see the vision becoming a reality.

Section B

THE STORY OF HARLEMLIVE

Angel Colon reporting

Chapter 5

FIRED UP: IGNITING A LEGACY

In the late spring of 1996, a transformative wave was on the horizon in Harlem. A collective of young individuals, former classmates from a local elementary school, stood poised to embark on an innovative endeavor. This endeavor, known as HarlemLIVE, emerged as a powerful fusion of journalism and technology, stemming from their prior engagement with a school newspaper. Though seemingly modest in its origins, HarlemLIVE carried the potential to create a lasting impact.

The organic growth of our organization was the result of several key elements coming together: my departure from traditional classroom teaching; my work with the Institute for Learning Technologies at Teachers College, which became an indispensable ally for the life of HarlemLIVE; my attendance at the Million Man March and the call to give back to one's community; my newfound skills in HTML, which were crucial for our online presence; and my enduring bonds with my former students.

Timing was also on our side. We found ourselves riding the rising wave of the internet. The mid to late '90s through the 2000s marked a period of unprecedented digital revolution—and we were right at the heart of it.

However, the main goal of HarlemLIVE went beyond creating journalists or technology experts. We used journalism as a dynamic vehicle to impart a wide range of transferable skills. These skills extended well beyond the confines of the newsroom and computer lab; they prepared our participants for diverse careers and life experiences.

Setting up interviews became exercises in **scheduling** and **organiz-ing**. **Researching** subjects evolved into a test of **critical thinking** and **analysis**. **Navigating** to and from each story cultivated resourcefulness and **adaptability**. **Interviewing** transformed into a master class in active **listening** and effective **communication**. The very act of working in teams fostered **collaboration** and **teamwork**. **Writing** articles was no longer just writing—it was **storytelling**, it was **self-expression**. **Publishing** articles online unveiled the intricacies of **technical** and **web skills**. **Editing** and **producing** video and photos unraveled the magic of **production** skills. And **presenting** work to a wide range of audiences? That involved the art of **public speaking** and **networking**.

With each completed story, slideshow, video, or presentation, the stu-dents' confidence surged as they witnessed their hard work and burgeoning abilities affirmed, making each achievement a victory.

The crucial element we wanted to give the kids was exposure to a wider world so they would expand their boundaries and find a topic, skill, or field that would kindle their enthusiasm. My ten-year trajectory as a public school teacher convinced me that experiential learning has the most profound impact on youth.

Decades after HarlemLIVE was born, the student participants haven't forgotten what they gained from their involvement. Here are a few stories in their own words:

Finding Voice and Passion

HarlemLIVE was a fantastic experience for me. I started when I was in high school and they had a small team.

It not only helped me from an academic perspective—being able to write stories, learning how to interview people, public speaking—but it *also helped me find my voice and my passions, and it fed my **curiosity**, which I think is what's important for high school students: finding out what they're curious about, exploring it, pursuing it, and then figuring it out.*

At HarlemLIVE, you could find interesting stories and topics that impacted the community and explore them, and those were things outside of the realms of the specific curriculum that you were handed at school. That not only made my writing stronger, but it also made me enjoy writing more.

The whole process of sitting down, collecting your thoughts, putting them in an outline, making sure that the paragraphs flowed correctly, that you're telling the story in a way that the reader could receive it and understand it, and getting your point across. It was a valuable skill that you could take with you wherever you wanted to go. And without being journalists, we would never have had the opportunity to meet the people we interviewed. —Nicole Schneider

Cultivating Dreams

Some of the beauty of HarlemLIVE is that you arrived pretty raw, and your dreams and desires were cultivated there. We had people go to Ivy League colleges directly because of HarlemLIVE.

One of the aspects that impacted me the most was being exposed to topics, people and places that I wouldn't have gotten to know otherwise. We worked for a while at Bloomberg's offices, and that was an amazing experience. We engaged with professionals from different walks of life, from BET to journalists. —Treniese Ladson

Meeting Pioneers

There were so many amazing experiences. Meeting so many African American pioneers in the arts as a result of covering them for the paper; going to Princeton for a week with the National Society for Black Engineers; meeting people from Microsoft; traveling in New

York because we did not just stay in Harlem, we went all over the city.
—Tameeka Mitchem

Conquering Fear

We met a ton of famous people, congressmen, people from the Ford
Foundation, millionaires. I would study how they talked, how they
moved, how they interacted, I was like, "Let me take notes." We met
a lady in the Upper West Side, Minette Coleman, and she taught us a
class on etiquette and professional behavior. We were just high school
kids, learning how to behave in the corporate world. All those experi-
ences helped me because I am not scared to talk to anyone or approach
anybody. —Johnny Alarcón

As Cynthia Simmons, a HarlemLIVE volunteer, explains:

HarlemLIVE was one of the first online magazines produced by kids,
so it was a very new idea; but because it was journalism and they
could decide what stories they were going to write, the youth got really
involved. If you thought you wanted to be an athlete, you'd find one
who'd be willing to talk to you and do a story on him or her.

Reporting a story could be a gateway to any of the interests that they
had, and the ones who were savvy learned how to use that. That's what
everyone needs: a doorway.

Unleashing Potential Through
Experiential Learning and Youth Journalism

This narrative highlights the stark disparity in educational philosophies and
teaching methodologies experienced by students across various resource
settings. Historically, students in less advantaged schools have often been
instructed to conform, follow directives, and memorize facts. In stark contrast, long-established, well-resourced private institutions have traditionally
prioritized nurturing leadership, encouraging critical thinking, promoting

self-advocacy, and fostering a culture of risk-taking. These prosperous institutions have tended to encourage students to carve their own educational paths tailored to their unique interests.[1]

However, the traditional classroom setting often falls short in inspiring students, especially those attending underfunded inner-city schools with limited access to enrichment programs. To address this lack, introducing students to diverse aspects of life beyond the classroom can spark their curiosity and foster creativity.[2]

Providing opportunities for holistic learning and exposing students to a range of real-life experiences can empower them to excel and achieve outcomes that surpass expectations. By tapping into their inherent abilities and nurturing their talents, we can cultivate a generation of empowered learners who are poised to thrive and make significant contributions to society.[3]

* * *

And what better medium than journalism to engage students, and what better canvas than the diverse and dynamic city of New York? From agriculture to theater, manufacturing to Wall Street, the city was a treasure trove of stories waiting to be told. It wasn't just a city—it was our playground. Equipped with press badges and subway passes, HarlemLIVE students navigated this urban landscape, gathering stories and experiences. The extensive public transportation system brought every corner of the city within reach. And when the stories were closer to home, students ventured out on foot or bicycle. The whole city, with its ceaseless rhythm and colorful tapestry of life, became a living, breathing classroom for our young journalists.

With a press badge and some guidance, the possibilities were limitless.

Although the HarlemLIVE model may be ideal for walkable cities with

---

1. Annette Lareau, *Unequal Childhoods: Class, Race, and Family Life*, 2003, University of California Press.

2. Eric Jensen, Teaching with Poverty in Mind: What Being Poor Does to Kids' Brains and What Schools Can Do About It, 2009, Association for Supervision and Curriculum Development.

3. Tony Wagner, The Global Achievement Gap: Why Even Our Best Schools Don't Teach the New Survival Skills Our Children Need—And What We Can Do About It, 2010, Basic Books.

good public transportation, youth-produced journalism can also be effect-ive on a smaller scale, such as covering a suburban block or an inner-city apartment building. This was demonstrated by a newsletter created by the children of HarlemLIVE alumni for the residents of my Harlem apartment building in 2019.

A local youth-created publication has the advantage of commun-ity building and fostering connection among residents. By focusing on specific neighborhoods, suburban blocks, or apartment buildings, it allows youth to explore and showcase the unique stories and voices within their immediate community. This publication becomes a platform for residents to learn about and engage with their neighbors, which fosters a sense of belonging and unity.

We were poised to further extend this concept to the buildings and blocks of each of the alumni kids when the COVID-19 pandemic brought a temporary halt to these plans.

Launching HarlemLIVE

When the idea for HarlemLIVE first started to take shape, Angel Colon, one of my former students, became a key part of its inception.

"Angel, there's this new thing called the internet. We could do our news-paper like we did in school, but for a worldwide audience."

Angel was on board, so I began contacting other former students and their parents to spread the word of our grand plan.

And so, in June of 1996, with more than a dozen students, we launched HarlemLIVE. The pioneers of the project were teens Matthew Martin, Angel Colon, Tiffany Santiago, Erica Sosa, Johnny Holmes, Reggie Williams, Aida Sanchez, and Elliot Martinez.

Hundreds of kids would follow in the years ahead. Their parents saw a positive impact.

Angel started in HarlemLIVE during middle school. He was not very outspoken, but in HarlemLIVE he got the courage to approach people publicly and interview them, and this experience gave him more confidence. He also learned a lot about computers: how to set up a website, how to do graphics… Today when I need tech help, I go to him.

New York City is not the safest place to be, but I never had any concerns about where Angel was going. I trusted Mr. Calton. I think HarlemLIVE gave my son the experience, the knowledge, and the courage to be who is. —Evelyn Colon, Angel's mother

* * *

My former students were scattered among various junior high schools, about to enter eighth grade. When we launched the organization, we didn't have an office. I would go to their apartments, where we planned stories and set out to report them. We'd return to their place to compose the pieces in their kitchen or living room, or I'd leave the laptop with them to work on stories by themselves.

The initial cohort of students had worked on the P.S. 206 newspaper, so they were already adept at basic reporting and writing. They would also be the primary teachers to any new students who joined HarlemLIVE. Peer teaching was a huge component of the program's success.

From the beginning, we called the students "staff." We had a page filled with thumbnail photos and their real names, linking to a profile page. There they wrote about their interests and perhaps also about their school or why they joined HarlemLIVE.

Most publications by youth, and certainly by any public school at that time, would only allow avatars, not real photos or names. I felt this staff page, with their real identities, was an effective tool to get the kids to feel **ownership** and **empowerment**.

For the duration of the program, we never had any problems associated with the staff page.

My philosophy leans toward expose, educate, and process rather than shielding from the outside world.

One of the first stories the kids reported was the Top Dog Amateur Night competition at Harlem's famous Apollo Theater. To the surprise of Erica Sosa and Matthew Martin, we had front-row center seats. Matthew took notes and interviewed audience members. Picture-taking wasn't allowed, but Erica discreetly moved around while taking photos anyway.

Elliot Martinez, the student who was with me when I was apprehended in the subway, and Adam Morales posted cartoons with original drawings and text; Samantha Gonzalez wrote an essay on *querencia*, the place where she felt safe and regained her strength; Reggie Williams posted his poetry; Matthew wrote about his acting lessons at TADA!; and Tiffany Santiago wrote in a humorous vein about youth fashion.

I remember going to Tiffany's family apartment across from P.S. 206 in the Wagner Projects. She lived with her triplet younger sisters, mom, and dad in a two-bedroom apartment. Sylvia, the mom, would always offer something to eat: rice, beans, chicken.

At Johnny Holmes's apartment, I'd see his younger sister, Ashley, and older brother, Lamont—the one who had made it to the top of the Statue of Liberty when I was his fifth-grade teacher a few years earlier.

For fun and practice, we took the train to Coney Island. The students created photo slideshows from the trip. They posted images taken with the digital camera and combined them with their stories on the web using software or hand-coding with HTML.

Detours & Roadblocks

As my leave of absence from the board of education drew to a close, I began considering various schools where I could continue teaching. However, my plans were abruptly halted by the P.S. 206 principal, who exercised her right to block my transfer since I was assigned to her school. Insisting that I remain at P.S. 206, she demanded that I sign documents forbidding me from taking kids on after-school excursions ever again. But I refused to sign, and as a result, she sought my dismissal on charges of insubordination.

By the time September rolled around, I was required to report daily to the administrative offices of the East Harlem school district, which were located on the fourth floor of an elementary school. Though I was idled as a classroom teacher until my case was resolved, they couldn't prevent me from working with my former students on HarlemLIVE in the afternoons and evenings.

Looking back, I realize it was a blessing in disguise that I didn't return to the classroom. Teaching would have drained all my energy, leaving nothing for HarlemLIVE, which had become my true passion.

It's ironic that I faced termination for taking kids on excursions after school, only to launch a program that heavily featured taking kids on excursions after school.

* * *

In August 1996, just a couple of weeks before I had to report to the district, I took a trip to Michigan with a friend. When I woke up the next morning in his family's guest room in Flint, I noticed something strange. The left side of my face felt numb and droopy. I had no clue what was happening to me. And what does one do in a state of shock and panic? Well, not what most would expect. Instead of rushing to a hospital, I did something a tad unconventional to distract myself: I went to Cedar Point in Ohio and rode roller coasters all day. If I was going to have a droopy face, I might as well feel the wind rushing against it on the Millennium Force!

As it turned out, I had Bell's palsy, a condition caused by a pinched nerve near the ear that causes facial muscles to become paralyzed. Despite my hopes that it would be temporary, it wasn't. I still have a crooked smile decades later, and it can sometimes appear as though I'm talking out of the side of my mouth. The experience was traumatic, but I made a vow to lose myself in the work of HarlemLIVE and not let it drag me down.

I often wonder if my stress about facing off with the Board of Education and the shame I felt about being brought up on charges was related to the onset of Bell's palsy. In September, when I reported to the district, not only was I disfigured, but I was also undergoing treatment for sun-damaged skin that left my face covered in crusted scabs. My dermatologist didn't seem too concerned about my vanity, but I must have looked like the walking dead. During the initial weeks, I felt a sense of isolation and secluded myself in an unused office.

After my skin cleared up and the district staff realized I wasn't really sick or contagious, I became more sociable. I was already familiar with many of them from when I brought my students to use their computers for the school newspaper. To integrate myself further, I started buying coffee and donuts for others and got involved in office work and celebrations. My expertise in computer issues, thanks to my part-time job at ILT at Teachers College, also came in handy, as I was able to troubleshoot and fix many of the staff's tech issues.

* * *

Despite being embroiled in a case of insubordination, which dragged on until spring, I remained stationed at the district during school hours. But with a computer and internet access at my disposal, I had ample time to focus on developing HarlemLIVE. At 3 p.m., I would either bike over to ILT/Teachers College or take the kids around the city to report stories. We'd finish up at their apartments in the early evenings, posting the pieces to the World Wide Web.

With no funding, HarlemLIVE was running solely on my dime. HarlemLIVE was not just a project for me but also a testament to the potential that lay untapped in these students. It was a mission to empower them and enable them to become active contributors to their community. As I navigated my own personal and professional challenges, I held onto the belief that every hurdle was a stepping stone to a larger purpose. With every story we posted, I was reminded of why I started HarlemLIVE and how much it mattered.

Osakwe Beale, Nicole Schneider, Kerly Suffren, Khalid Muhammad

Chapter 6

HARLEMLIVE TAKES FLIGHT

Initially, our content-publishing methodology was somewhat arbitrary and devoid of formal structure. My earlier experiences with school newspapers at both high school and college levels had familiarized me with leadership roles such as that of an editor in chief, yet it took us a couple of years to integrate such roles into our process.

Significantly, the initial cohort of students from my former school was driven by a collective zeal. However, as time passed, the students who joined us did so more intentionally. They were self-selecting, either gravitating toward us for an after-school pursuit or opting to participate through the city's Summer Youth Employment Program.

Students feel empowered when they have options and get to make their own choices. They should be given this power early and often.

With a few months of experience under our belts, the African American Day Parade became our official launchpad. This parade, held annually on the third Sunday in September, is a vibrant celebration of Black culture and community in New York City, attracting thousands to its lively display of music, dance, and unity in Harlem.

Matthew Martin, Tiffany Santiago, and Angel Colon covered the event, which featured marching bands, first responders, activists, politicians, community organizations, and the Federation of Black Cowboys—a unique group dedicated to preserving the legacy of Black cowboys and cowgirls in the American West. They often make appearances at local events, proudly displaying their equestrian skills and sharing their historical knowledge.

The parade also showcased DJs and local radio stations on their floats, as well as dancers on flatbed trucks with large speakers, all of which made for a lively and eclectic atmosphere. The parade procession, lined up on either side of Adam Clayton Powell Blvd. from 111th to 115th, offered us the chance to acquaint ourselves with a myriad of organizations and personalities. As they waited their turn to enter the avenue and head uptown, we seized the opportunity to connect with many who would later become subjects of our stories.

One group that caught Matthew's attention was the organization 100 Black Men, whose alumni included former Mayor David Dinkins and other prominent African Americans in New York City. Matthew interviewed several of their members while Tiffany and Angel took photos of the parade participants for slideshows they would create later.

At that point, our focus was on the reporting process, including writing, taking photos, and designing the pieces on the Web rather than drawing attention to the website. However, our lack of publicity for the magazine would soon change as we began to attract attention from around the globe.

The process itself was the reward, as the youth practiced new skills, witnessed the larger world around them, and learned how to collaborate effectively.

---

* * *

During the early years of HarlemLIVE, I accompanied the young reporters on every story. Together, we planned and executed our reporting. But as time passed, we had enough experienced students and adult volunteers to accompany the new recruits. Our goal was to instill in these young minds a sense of responsibility and ownership in the program, and that extended to the content they produced.

But I still went on some of the stories. It was how HarlemLIVE got started: me hitting the pavement with the teens. And it was probably how I was most effective in guiding them.

If we were at an event, I'd tell the young journalists and photographers to keep an eye out for the organizers—perhaps the people darting around the room with clipboards. They may not have had time to chat, but the young reporters could introduce themselves and ask to whom they should speak. I encouraged and nudged but for the most part tried to stay in the background. If I was next to a student and the interviewee kept addressing me with their answers, I'd politely redirect them to the youth reporter.

I consistently emphasized to the young people that their greatest advantage was their youth and that the professionalism with which they conducted themselves would only add to their appeal. People would be inclined to help, given their enthusiasm and willingness to learn.

When it came to the material they published, I always sided with the teens If adults questioned what they were putting out, the youth had the final say. They would learn from the subsequent feedback. This was their baby, and the world was watching.

At HarlemLIVE, we didn't believe in imposing strict rules on how students should participate. Instead, we gave them the freedom to explore different roles that matched their interests and skills. Whether it was reporting on local events, designing a website, taking or editing photos, or managing administrative tasks, there were always places for young people to contribute and grow.

Our philosophy was simple: provide a supportive and empowering environment where students could learn from each other and from experienced mentors. We didn't charge any fees or demand long-term commitments. If a student felt that HarlemLIVE wasn't the right fit for them, they were free to move on without any judgment or pressure.

But what truly set us apart was the sense of ownership we bestowed upon the youth. It was an essential ingredient that helped the students become more invested in the program, allowing them to develop vital leadership skills that would serve them well in the future, as Ebony Myers attests:

My entire tenure at HarlemLIVE was intricately intertwined and significant. Each experience I had at the student-centered digital publication contributed to my future goals and ultimate success. Whether it was the day I nervously stood in line to meet Russell Simmons, the time I interviewed nine strangers for "Man on the Street/Pulse of the People," or being encouraged to write an essay that won a dinner with Toni Morrison and the key to Gramercy Park.

I absorbed it all.

I remember leaving a seven- to eight-hour school day and taking the train an additional thirty minutes after work to do a different type of "work." I was full of excitement and totally committed to this after-school program that didn't put money in my pockets or give me a grade. I enjoyed it! I met other students and interacted with adults in ways I'd never encountered before HarlemLIVE. It was a genuine experience.

I felt connected on all levels, so much so that I extended an invitation to my friends Guyan and Elizabeth to join this after-school program where you got to do what you liked. There was room for everyone with all of our quirkiness.

We could do whatever we wanted with minimum helicopter supervision but with the highest expectations from the program directors. HarlemLIVE made a space for students to think, to write, to engage, to learn and, most of all, to be successful on our terms, propelling confidence levels, and developing talent that would create the next generation of leaders. —*Ebony Myers*

New Kids on the Block

From the very beginning, recruiting kids was one of our top priorities at HarlemLIVE. After all, what's a youth program without young people? We sought out organizations that already worked with teens—other youth media programs as well as counseling organizations and career training outlets. By covering their events and activities, our students learned about the opportunities these organizations provided, and sometimes we even enticed their teens to join our ranks.

Some of the early stories covered by HarlemLIVE focused on various local organizations such as the Photographic Center of Harlem, which offered training in photography for the young people; the Children's Art Carnival, an arts enrichment program; and the Hansboro Recreation Center, a city gym known for its youth swim teams.

However, our coverage wasn't confined to just these youth-oriented programs. We extended our reach to cover general-interest stories as well. These included feeding homeless people at the monumental St. John the Divine Cathedral, located in Morningside Heights, Manhattan.

Our coverage stretched to explore community gardens, profile local activists, and provide a platform for creative expression with posted poetry, essays, and editorials. Tiffany, Johnny, and I will always remember our unusual encounter with Raven Chanticleer and his eerie exhibit of wax figures depicting prominent African Americans within his Harlem brownstone.

* * *

One of HarlemLIVE's earliest stories featured the Urban Youth Bike Corps (UYBC), an after-school program that involved biking and bike repair and maintenance for teenagers. As a longtime bicycle enthusiast, I found a kindred spirit in UYBC's director, Erik Cliette, who also shared my passion for Apple computers and teaching.

The UYBC was an ideal match for HarlemLIVE, and in the years that followed, many of our students joined their bike rides throughout the city and upstate New York. We even went on trips together, like the one to Great Adventures, a Six Flags amusement park.

A few months after our partnership with UYBC began, I accompanied the group on a trip to Senegal in February 1997. During the first half of the trip, I spent a few days with Erik and the group. For the second half, I visited my former colleague from P.S. 206, Amari, who was residing in Dakar with her Senegalese husband, Modou.

HarlemLIVE published articles, poetry, and essays about the teens' experiences. Their essays were especially moving after witnessing the Door of No Return on Gorée Island, a twenty-five-minute boat ride from Dakar. The island's Maison des Esclaves, a holding place for slaves, was their last contact with the continent before being enslaved and brought to the Americas.

Two UYBC participants, Osakwe Beale and Kerly Suffren, became stars of our program. They started as writers and reporters but quickly rose to become leaders and ambassadors for HarlemLIVE. Their charisma and courage inspired others to follow in their footsteps and join our vibrant community of young creatives.

Osakwe recalls his time with UYBC and HL:

Freedom to a teenager is everything. When I reflect back on it, it's no surprise that my first taste of freedom led me to my next. That first freedom was the bike, one of my earliest mentors that taught me a simple lesson: you get out what you put in. You wanted to go further, you had to pedal longer, you wanted to go faster, then you'd better pedal harder. Don't feel like doing anything today? Cool, but that bike isn't moving either. A simple lesson but a foundational one. When I was on the bike, I had full control, full autonomy, I was free to roam the city as far as my legs would take me. My parents understood in the way that parents who have to ration out freedom to their growing teenagers did.

It almost feels natural that through my love of cycling and my participation in the Urban Youth Bike Corps, I would have my next taste of freedom: technology & the internet. For a curious person like me, it was mind-blowing.

The fateful meeting between HL and our team of "bike kids" led us to unite with a program whose name I loved from the first time I heard it; HarlemLIVE. We really felt like we were experiencing something new, like we were discovering the internet. That press badge was so many things… It was an all-access pass—it entitled you to ask questions with an expectation of time from strangers that you would never have in your daily life. It was a hero's cape we could all don and be transformed by. Between that and the grace that people show young people engaged in positive activity—"Ok, young man, I'll answer your question"—we were unstoppable. Looking back, we were fearless. We felt like we belonged, and we were there to do a job or provide an often overlooked perspective: that of young people. —*Osakwe Beale*

Chris Frierson was another member of UYBC who joined HarlemLIVE as a reporter in the fall of 1996 and eventually became a part of the video team. Throughout the life of the program, he served as a mentor to new recruits, and his commitment to the organization was unwavering. He ensured the safety of everyone during the often continuous hours at our loft and on 125th Street. He was, in fact, the longest-serving member of HarlemLIVE, even outlasting the founder! Chris's dedication went beyond his mentoring contributions; he served on the board and was the last authorized signature on the HarlemLIVE bank account in the spring of 2011. Thank you, Chris.

Shaping Futures Through HarlemLIVE

During my tenure at ILT, I capitalized on every opportunity to promote HarlemLIVE among educators and students alike. Whether it was through workshops or by leveraging the high-speed internet installations that ILT oversaw in schools, I was always on the lookout for talented and motivated young people to join our program.

One such individual was Michael Popo, a seventeen-year-old from St. Lucia whom I met while teaching an HTML class at Benjamin Banneker High School in Brooklyn. Michael was a quick study and soon became an expert in technology, helping HarlemLIVE stay at the forefront of digital innovation for many years.

In 2002, Michael was tapped by New York City's Parks Department to launch and oversee Crown Heights Live, a Brooklyn-based offshoot of HarlemLIVE. However, the project was short-lived, as Popo soon faced the same bureaucratic challenges I had encountered while working with the board of education and the city's Summer Youth Employment Program. Nevertheless, Crown Heights Live was one of the many programs across the globe inspired by HL.

Years later, while in Cape Town, South Africa, I crossed paths with a man who worked in one of the townships. To my surprise, he revealed that they had modeled their program after HarlemLIVE. It was a heartwarming and inspiring testament to the impact of our project and its ability to ignite change far beyond the boundaries of Harlem.

Michael achieved great success in his career; he went on to become a highly ranked captain in the U.S. Coast Guard, serving in their cyber unit.

* * *

Nicole Farrow (now Schneider) joined HarlemLIVE in 1997 after a story HarlemLIVE did about the International Youth Leadership Institute (IYLI), in which she was involved. She quickly rose through the ranks, becoming our second editor in chief and, as a team captain, winner of our inaugural Summer Youth Media Challenge. DeVan Hankerson, Nicole, and Osakwe Beale were among the first HarlemLIVE students to participate in an intensive two-week summer journalism program at New York University. Living on the Greenwich Village campus, they honed their skills and published their own newspaper.

Years later, Bloomberg recruited Nicole and Osakwe, who were studying at Cornell and Morehouse, respectively, to initiate the company's brand-new internship program. After graduating from college, both were hired by Bloomberg for entry-level positions. Nicole worked at the company for ten years, starting in the human resources department and ultimately rising to the position of wealth manager of the Americas.

Nicole credits HarlemLIVE for initiating her stellar career:

*After a year or so at HarlemLIVE, I was named editor in chief. It was a great experience! One of the biggest takeaways of my position was gaining more **confidence**. I also understood that maybe I didn't have the answer to every single question, or I wasn't the right person to do every single thing, but I could figure it out together with someone or we could learn together, that is, I learned the power of **collaboration**. Having such a large responsibility and working directly with adults—amazing* *educators who were taking time out of their day to help us—helped shape who I became professionally and how I was able to present myself in general.*

The crux of it was the confidence that was built into how to manage situations and different types of people while I was still a high school student.

*We also went to a journalism workshop at NYU, and it was a fantastic opportunity to learn from very smart people. It was the first time I had been away from my parents for any significant time as a teenager. **Exposure** to these great resources that I wouldn't be able to see or even know existed was crucial.*

I traveled to Italy to pick up an award with several other HarlemLIVE students. It was my first time on an airplane, let alone my first time outside of the country. It was such an honor to even be considered for a trip like that. Without HarlemLIVE, I would never have had access to such an experience.

*Giving students in high school **access** to those experiences and **opportunities** is monumental. It really helped to put us in a position of **empowerment**.*

HarlemLIVE put the stepping stones for me to get into college and shaped my professional life. —Nicole Schneider

We Are the World

During the program's tenure, a notable proportion of participants, including Michael from St. Lucia and Kerly from Haiti, were immigrants from diverse areas, including the Caribbean (e.g., Jamaica, Guadeloupe, and Trinidad), South America, and as far away as Nigeria, Côte D'Ivoire, Armenia, Russia, Myanmar, Egypt, and France. Through their hard work and perseverance, these individuals embody the spirit of hope that is at the core of the United States' founding ideals, even in the face of the nation's frequent setbacks in achieving those aspirations.

One such individual was Guyan Wilks, a Jamaican-born reporter who emerged as one of HarlemLIVE's most dedicated journalists and leaders.

Throughout HarlemLIVE's life, our teen journalists confronted numerous cases of injustice. They reported on issues ranging from the Rockefeller Drug Laws[1] to the tragic police killings of figures like Sean Bell[2] and Amadou Diallo. Our team traveled to Washington, DC, to cover the protests against the Iraq War, documented the demonstrations in Philadelphia advocating for the release of Mumia Abu-Jamal,[3] and even dispatched reporters to New Orleans to shed light on the unequal response to Hurricane Katrina.

Wilks's own account underscores the depth of experiences these young reporters faced. He recounted covering the protests that erupted after the acquittal of the officers responsible for killing Amadou Diallo,[4] a twenty-three-year-old immigrant from Guinea who was fatally shot by four NYPD officers. This acquittal led to extensive protests and public outcry.

On February 27th, 2000, I was asked to cover the protest of the not-guilty verdict for the police shooting of Amadou Diallo, the man who had been shot forty-one times by the police on February 4th, 1999. It was a crazy afternoon in Midtown Manhattan. There I was with Khalid Muhammad and Tremon Davis in the middle of 5,000 protesters marching up 5th Ave toward a wall of police in riot gear. In my head I was thinking, "This is the first time I have ever encountered a protest."

Just a few hours before that, I was in school getting the homework assignment from my math class.

It was an important experience. An experience that probably helps me deal with unexpected chaotic situations better than most people. We interviewed many people that day. The pain and anger from the protestors was so visceral… It was the first time that news I had watched on television became real to me.

That was just one example of the many times we found ourselves covering stories our parents were watching on the big networks at night.

Often big issues tend to be reserved for adults. There is a sense that it

---

1. https://en.wikipedia.org/wiki/Rockefeller_Drug_Laws

2. https://en.wikipedia.org/wiki/Shooting_of_Sean_Bell

3. https://en.wikipedia.org/wiki/Mumia_Abu-Jamal

4. https://en.wikipedia.org/wiki/Killing_of_Amadou_Diallo

would be too much to add primary races and racial profiling to the already anxiety-packed high school lives of teens. I think that exposure to big news gifted us with the opportunity to objectively look at what was affecting our communities and not just be characters in the story. Before the term "woke"[1] was trendy, the students at HarlemLIVE were living out that word every time we were sent out to ask questions about our life and times.

Some adults underestimate the civic readiness that may be dormant in teenagers. All they really need is the right setup and support.
—*Guyan Wilks*
(Read more: Essay *by Guyan Wilks and* more coverage *on HL site)*

While individual experiences, like the coverage of the protests following the acquittal of NYPD officers, enriched our journalism, the broader evolution of our program experienced an even greater influx of diversity thanks in part to our partnership with Beacon High School on Manhattan's west side. Beacon brought a steady stream of talented youth of all races and creeds as well as from every corner of the globe. Among these bright minds were Kat Vorotova of Russia and Eddie Aung of Myanmar, who served as coeditors in chief of HarlemLIVE in 2002/2003. While there are far too many Beacon alumni to name individually, I must give a special shout-out to Al-Amir Jordan, a towering 6'4" presence in our program who spent many years as a dedicated reporter and video producer. Al-Amir was a mentor to many, and his warm personality made him a beloved figure in HarlemLIVE.

---

1. Note: When "woke" is used here, it means being aware of social injustices. It's used in its older context, which originated long before its current, often pejorative, usage criticizing excessive political correctness.

Unconventional Talents: Blossoming in the Field

While our collaboration with Beacon High School introduced us to a rich mosaic of cultures and backgrounds, our association with City As School unearthed a treasure trove of unique talents right from our own backyard.

City As School, an alternative high school in New York City and a pioneer in experiential learning, was another school that contributed some uniquely gifted students to our ranks at HarlemLIVE. The school's distinctive approach to education allowed its students to engage in real-world experiences like internships at veterinarian clinics, bike shops, and, of course, our own HarlemLIVE.

One standout from City As was Justin Young, who rapidly grew beyond his initial intern role. His many hats included those of cartoonist, journalist, author, coeditor in chief, and spokesperson. Justin's commitment to HarlemLIVE was such that he even traveled with us to Rome, Italy, for an international award nomination. Keep an eye out for Justin; he'll reappear later in this HarlemLIVE story.

Kelly Koblaki was another remarkable addition from City As. With her dyed hair, expressive eyes enhanced by stylish glasses, and pierced lower lip, Kelly's unique style was hard to miss. An avid writer and reporter for HarlemLIVE, she had an endearing quirk: carrying a purple, old-school lunch box adorned with images of the singer Blondie. This wasn't your typical lunch box, though; it was her purse, and it principally held her cigarettes. The moment she opened the box, it seemed to release a century's worth of trapped smoke.

Kelly, Shem Rajoon, and I once attended the memorial for DJ Frankie Crocker, a pioneering force who dramatically transformed urban contemporary radio by introducing New York City to a unique blend of musical genres. This memorable event took place at the Riverside Church, near Columbia University, in November 2000. The event was buzzing with celebrities, and all I could do was hope that Kelly would keep her purple lunch-box purse sealed shut. Thankfully, she did. Kelly always brightened up any event she attended, not just with her unconventional purse but more so with her zest and dedication. At HarlemLIVE, we truly valued and embraced the idiosyncrasies of our students, recognizing them as the unique individuals they were.

Please, Put the Internet on My Disk

As we celebrated the quirks and eccentricities of our students from City As School, there was another youthful innocence that caught my attention in the spring of 1997, when ILT was working to install internet access for an after-school program at a middle school within Wadleigh High. The building, a landmark with a huge tower and stained-glass windows, was originally a pioneering girls' school at the turn of the twentieth century. It was during a Kodak-sponsored photography project at the school that I met eleven-year-old Trinidadian immigrant Shem Rajoon.

One day shortly after we had set up internet access, Shem approached me clutching one of the now-defunct three-inch plastic disks used for saving digital files. He spoke in a low, raspy whisper, as if telling a secret. Years later, he revealed that he had been trying to hide his Trini accent.

"Mr. Richard, could you please put the internet on my disk?" he asked me earnestly.

I couldn't help but be amused by the question—how could the entire internet fit on a floppy disk? Nevertheless, I was struck by Shem's enthusiasm, and I invited him to visit HarlemLIVE. Though he was a few years younger than the others, his eagerness and initiative made him a great fit for our program.

As Shem remembers:

I had just finished fifth grade at P.S. 113, and I was in a middle school in Wadleigh. I was walking past a door in the hallway when I saw this white guy with a laptop and a digital camera talking about the internet. I was intrigued because I'd never seen anything like that before. He told us, "This is a medium to tell your story and how you see the world in your eyes."

The technology was the bait for me, but it turned out this would become so much more.

Richard invited me to go to the basement of Columbia University to see his program, HarlemLIVE. It seemed a little sketchy to me, but one day I was playing basketball after school, and I had a moment of critical reflection.

I thought, "Here I am, going along with the routine of life, the system that I am already programmed into," because sports seemed to be the only thing that kids could do safely in our neighborhood.

I decided to do something different. I had to walk hundreds of steps through Morningside Park, which bridges Harlem and the Heights, where Columbia University is located, and where more affluent people live. Instead of playing ball, I ventured off to check out this place.

I was 11 and I had been in the States for less than a year.

When I opened the door to the basement, I saw a bunch of kids, older than me, sitting amongst cardboard boxes and typing on new Apple computers. They had a table where they would come together and bounce ideas off each other, talking about what story they would go out to cover; they would brainstorm, formulate their ideas and what answers they were trying to unearth… I had yet to experience this process of collaborating in such an open environment in a classroom. For me it was transformative.

We live in the banking system of education, where you learn something and you deposit it back; it's very transactional, and that wasn't the environment where I learned best or that felt safest mentally for me to thrive. And here was this guy pushing against the borders of education by giving kids agency and autonomy, love and trust. I found it very interesting.

I gravitated to digital photography first. I'm Trinidadian, I had a Trini accent, I was still adjusting, so I wasn't really comfortable reporting or expressing myself in writing. Graphic design was the next natural evolution for me, thinking about how to communicate this magazine by youth for youth in a multimedia age. After graphic design I got into web design, and I focused more on the operational aspect, on how to get the stories on the site, and that got me into coding.

The coding experience I got from designing this magazine online laid the foundation for my whole professional career as a product leader. I do product design for companies in the software technology space. I help them formulate their ideas and create products that align with the communities they are serving. All from my experience at HarlemLIVE!
—Shem Rajoon

The stories, backgrounds, and individual journeys of our participants emphasize the rich mosaic that was HarlemLIVE. From immigrants searching for the American dream to local youth finding their voice, HarlemLIVE wasn't just a program but a living testament to the power of diversity, resilience, and youth empowerment. Each of these narratives underscores the same truth: when given the chance, young people, regardless of their origin or background, can rise to any challenge, shape narratives, and ultimately redefine the world around them.

Chapter 7

THE ANGELS OF HARLEMLIVE

HarlemLIVE's early days were marked by resourcefulness and determination, much like my experience teaching in elementary school. Dr. Robbie McClintock played a crucial role in allowing us to be hosted on Columbia's servers, which circumvented the need to pay a commercial provider and ensured a smooth start to our web presence.

But we longed for something more, a place to call our own away from the scattered East Harlem apartments we worked in. So, I approached the situation with tact, slowly introducing one, then two, then three students to the basement lab at ILT/Teachers College. The staff was so moved by the teens' work that they granted us permission to use the lab as our first headquarters.

Originally meant to be a temporary solution, our stay at the lab was extended for over a year, lasting until the fall of 1998. During this time, we recruited more students and adult volunteers who generously offered their time to teach journalism and web skills.

A College Setting

The basement lab at Teachers College was a labyrinth of passageways snaking beneath the conglomerate of buildings. It provided us with easy access to anywhere within the college, including the cafeteria.

Having the backing of an Ivy League university brought a wealth of benefits beyond just easy access to the cafeteria. ILT provided HarlemLIVE with printing and mail services, which saved us thousands of dollars over the life of the program.

It was during this time that we leveraged our association with Teachers College to get our flyers printed at no cost. The flyer was more than just an informational pamphlet; it was our organization's fingerprint — encapsulating testimonials from alumni, our mission statement, the skills we imparted, recognitions we had received, and our broader influence both locally and internationally.

Principally taken out on stories, these flyers established a degree of legitimacy when interacting with the community. On one notable occasion, a flyer serendipitously slipped out amidst paperwork in court—an unforeseen twist that will unravel as a compelling story later on in the narrative.

We also had the use of Teachers College's auditoriums for presentations and classrooms for meetings. Later on, Columbia's graduate school of journalism provided us with invaluable mentors who taught journalism classes, edited the students' stories, or let them shadow as they covered their beats. Furthermore, Columbia's engineering school granted scholarships to Clifton Taylor and Brad Harbans for an elite summer program and helped us with a large-scale mapping project.

I was fortunate to co-teach a graduate course on emerging technologies with Brigitte Magar at Teachers College. Being part of the college community also opened up many opportunities for HarlemLIVE students to speak in front of graduate classes about their work. Our partnership with Teachers College and Columbia University played a critical role in establishing our legitimacy early on and remained a key partnership throughout the program's life span.

Anyone managing a youth nonprofit would benefit from forming strong liaisons with a college or university.

The Joys and Pranks of HarlemLIVE

While housed in the college setting, some of our youngest members, like Shem, struck up a friendship with Keith, the head chef, and for several days in a row Shem proudly showed off the free food he had charmed out of Keith and the cafeteria workers. Shem used his trademark quiet and whispery tones, the same ones he used when asking me to put the internet on his disk.

But Shem's good fortune was cut short by Malik Wilson, who had grown tired of his boasting. Malik stormed into the cafeteria, demanding free food with a loud voice, seeking the same privileges that Shem had enjoyed. As a result, the head chef immediately ceased all food giveaways. Ah, kids!

Shem was also a bit of a prankster. He had a trick where he would take a piece of paper or napkin, roll it in his palms and fingers until it became a tiny stick, and then use it to tickle Shawn Mishler, ILT's assistant director, behind the ear. Shawn, mistaking the tickling for a bug flying in his ear, would instinctively slap the side of his head to squash it. We all had a good laugh. This prank would continue throughout the life of HarlemLIVE, with one kid hitting himself so hard in an attempt to swat the imaginary bug that he fell off his chair. I can't help but wonder if today this practical joke would get us canceled.

* * *

In the late spring of 1997, my students Angel and Matthew and I had a fortuitous opportunity when we covered a Monday night reading at the Frank Silvera Writers' Workshop (TFSWW). The event took place at the Old Vic Theater on Harlem's bustling main artery, 125th Street, also known as Dr. Martin Luther King Jr. Blvd.

Established in 1973 by the likes of Morgan Freeman, Garland Lee Thompson, and others, the group had an influential director in Thompson who quickly took an interest in HarlemLIVE. He introduced us to key community leaders and arts institutions and provided historical context for the stories we covered, including the funeral of the renowned historian and professor John Henrik Clarke, and the AUDELCO[1] awards, which celebrate excellence in African-American theater in NYC.

Thanks to Garland's mentorship, members of the Silvera workshops and other community friends became invaluable advisors and mentors to HarlemLIVE. Elaine Johnson was particularly instrumental during the

---

1. https://en.wikipedia.org/wiki/AUDELCO

program's early years, while Gwendolyn McKnight brought her sons and grandchildren, who remained with HL for many years. Alfie Wade introduced the young journalists to the legendary photographer Gordon Parks before his passing. The HL advisory board, made up of Stan Ellzy, Dr. Vicky Gholson, Dave Sheppard, and others, guided us toward the Volunteer Lawyers for the Arts, who took on the arduous process and paperwork to make us a 501(c)(3) nonprofit organization, which allowed us to seek tax-deductible donations.

Numerous online resources exist to guide those interested in establishing a nonprofit organization, offering step-by-step instructions for tasks like drafting bylaws and assembling a board of directors.

Garland also showed us how to tap into funds available through local politicians. In exchange, we helped the Writers' Workshop create their first website and provided space at Teachers College to host their Saturday workshops for over a decade, as well as their Monday night readings a few years later at our sizable 125th Street location. Thanks to the influence of the TFSWW, HarlemLIVE not only gained new allies but also deepened its roots within the Harlem community.

* * *

HarlemLIVE proved to be an enriching experience for both the youth involved and the volunteers who served as their mentors. Elaine Johnson, a pivotal figure during the formative years of our program, reflects on her deep connection with HarlemLIVE and how she and many others found immense value and growth through their involvement:

> *HarlemLIVE became an oasis for me, a wonderful creative hub. I had never seen anything like it: kids taking ownership, wanting to go to a program after school. They were writing, expressing themselves, giving the community a voice on the Internet.*
>
> *It blew my mind!*
>
> *I couldn't wait to leave my office and get to HarlemLIVE. The Internet had just started, but Richard had the audacity to walk the*

streets of New York and find children and adults to support his idea of creating a newsletter.

When there were weekend assignments, I would accompany the kids as an adult supervisor. They knew how to work cameras, how to take a story and post it. They had this thing going on! Some were at-risk kids. They may have been having trouble in school, but when they came to HL, they were on it. Then they began to bring up their grades in school and become more vocal. They learned to speak out.

It was wonderful to see black and brown kids so engaged. You always heard people talking about the digital divide, but I didn't see it at HarlemLIVE. These kids were owning this thing!

It really gave me hope for humanity. I knew the youth's destiny wasn't going to be about gangbanging and all the crazy things they can get into. It was our mission to see that they become respectable and responsible adults, and they did. **They went beyond that.** *We were putting out kids who were going to be good citizens, people who knew how to vote, people who wanted to be in the community and make a difference. We changed people's destinies.*

If I were to die today, HarlemLIVE would be my saving grace; it tells me I did something of value on this Earth. —Elaine Johnson

Stop the Presses

Our early launch of an online youth media program earned us considerable attention from the media, and we quickly gained recognition as a "hot" site by Yahoo!, *USA Today*, and other major outlets. This snowballed into further press coverage from the *New York Times*, *New York Daily News*, *Village Voice*, *Time Out*, and more. Our program and young journalists even appeared on the reality show *A Walk in Their Shoes*, which sent HL student Elliot Price to a farm in Virginia and brought a farm boy to NYC to work with Shem and HarlemLIVE.

Our youth reporters were frequently invited to participate in television discussions and call-in radio programs, and HL was mentioned in several research articles and even featured in a couple of textbooks. This increased exposure attracted more adult volunteers. For instance, Angelique Anderson joined us after hearing an interview with HarlemLIVE students Angel Colon and Kerly Suffren. Anderson became a key mentor, teaching Photoshop and other advanced professional software throughout the program's life span.

Numerous volunteers served as "email editors," remotely assisting students with revising their articles for publication. Nowadays, this support could be expanded with the use of videoconferencing technology.

These mentors provided the kids with unforgettable experiences, as alum Ena Johnson explains:

> One of the beautiful things about HarlemLIVE was all the support we received from other media outlets, including but not limited to Reuters, ABC News, and popular radio stations. Guests often came by to give us seminars. I remember doing a videography project with news reporter Chris Glorioso. That was my crash course with the video-editing software Final Cut Pro and one of the most tedious tasks I had ever undertaken. I conducted an interview about sneaker culture at Atmos sneaker store, and I was to turn that video interview into a news segment, complete with B-roll and useful sound bites. Chris coached me every step of the way, through frustration and procrastination, and I made a news story! My sincerest thanks for being mentored by someone I could turn on the evening news and watch render the day's events with flawless efficiency.
> —Ena Johnson

* * *

In May 1997, my insubordination hearing concluded with a resolution in my favor. The consequences were a relatively light slap on the wrist—two weeks' pay suspension—and the reinstatement of my permission to teach. However, by then my involvement with HarlemLIVE was substantial. I was concerned that resuming teaching might not allow me the time or energy to excel in that role and continue my commitment to HarlemLIVE.

Fortunately, the district's office made me an offer, largely due to the assistance I'd been providing them with their computer needs while my insubordination case was pending. They proposed an administrative-level district job, which I was to start in September. This position involved aiding the East Harlem schools with their tech needs, a role that dovetailed well with my ongoing work at both ILT/Teachers College and HarlemLIVE.

A Soul Without a Shell

As HarlemLIVE continued to grow, it became apparent that our shared space at ILT was no longer sufficient. It was at this juncture that Dr. Robbie McClintock proposed a merger with another nonprofit program, Playing2Win (P2W), which was being revitalized by ILT and the long-standing East Harlem nonprofit Boys and Girls Harbor after a period of dormancy.

Dr. McClintock summed up the potential union perfectly, stating, "HarlemLIVE has a soul without a shell, and Playing2Win has a shell without a soul. We'd like to marry you two."

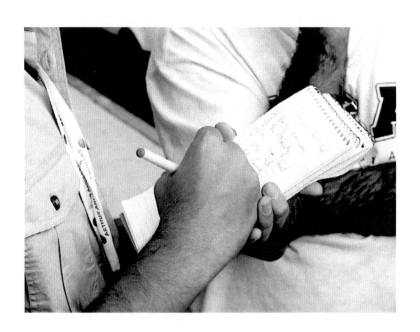

Chapter 8

BUILDING BLOCKS AND EMPOWERMENT: HOW-TO FOR HL

Moving to Playing2Win's East Harlem storefront from an obscure windowless room in the bowels of Teachers College provided HarlemLIVE more immediacy and exposure. We had use of two small offices near the entrance, but the teens would often spill out into the general gathering areas or the computer labs in the back if they weren't in use.

Anyone entering P2W was greeted by a buzz of activity, largely due to the HL kids going out on and returning from stories, working on the website, getting lessons from adult volunteers, and bantering with P2W members and Debbie Bailey at the front desk.

Years later, one of the alums recalled, "The kids looked like hip New York City kids, with hats on backward and T-shirts; they were using colorful Mac laptops and publishing on the internet instead of traditionally… At the same time they looked empowered, and the atmosphere seemed very dynamic."

Upon being hired as the director of P2W, Mara Rose proved to be an invaluable asset to HL by elevating the program to new heights and garnering recognition for its achievements.

She shares her first impressions of the program:

I was a graduate from Teachers College at Columbia University, and my advisor offered me the opportunity to run Playing2Win, which had been shut down a few years earlier; Boys Harbor, another nonprofit, wanted to reopen it under its umbrella and needed an executive director.

P2W was in a storefront in Harlem, and when I showed up I found just two large rooms full of old computers, most of which didn't even work anymore.

At the same time, Rich had a relationship with Teachers College, and at some point someone approached me and said, "Could HarlemLIVE be housed in P2W?" Our organization was re-starting, while HarlemLIVE was already thriving. Bringing them into P2W was a win/win for everybody because we immediately had life in the center.

What was challenging, and ultimately the best, was that I was really interested in clear structures, and Rich brought a very different approach to education that turned out to be refreshing and inspiring.

His passion was finding the gifts of the individual students and helping them shine, share them with the world, and encourage them to become leaders and agents of their own lives.

It was a much more expansive view than I had encountered when I worked in schools, where that is not the norm. It was messy, and yet deliberate.

As we shared the space, we found opportunities to collaborate. If a young person came in to P2W first, Rich may have seen that this youth could be part of HL; and some HL students helped with our computer classes because they had so much expertise. There was flow between the two organizations.

Rich was a rule-breaker, but he came consistently from a place of deep integrity and deep care for the students and not a lot of care for the rules that didn't serve them, or for the limitations that traditional educational environments put on learners that curtail their capacity to learn. He embodied commitment, curiosity about the students, a deep desire to build something meaningful, disregard for bureaucracy and willingness to break rules in service of what he cared about.

He also explicitly invited the students to be leaders and to make decisions. —Mara Rose

Pulse of the People

Mara Rose's insights highlight the core principles and practices that fueled our initiative. Yet, while we thrived in our collaboration with Playing2Win and under the supportive leadership of Mara, the everyday activities at HarlemLIVE truly defined our mission. These street interviews were an integral part of our program, instilling courage and honing the skills of our participants.

Central Park, just a block away from our headquarters, provided the perfect location for our person-on-the-street interviews, which we affectionately dubbed "Pulse of the People" (POP). At HarlemLIVE, we didn't hesitate to get new recruits into action, often transitioning straight from training to practice on their very first day.

Fortunately, POP interviews required little preparation. We'd initiate by asking our newbies, "What news topics interest you?" From there, we'd swiftly role-play how to introduce themselves and the organization as well as how to conduct an interview. During these exercises, I might even play the part of a tough respondent to help them learn to gracefully move on when faced with a challenging subject.

For those feeling apprehensive about approaching strangers, we might suggest they start as a photographer for their first outing. But more often than not, observing their peers navigate interviews instilled enough confidence for them to jump right in.

We'd pair our new student recruits with seasoned HarlemLIVE members or, if available, adult volunteers. This "trial by fire" was a quick way for both us and the applicant to determine if HarlemLIVE was a good fit.

The program's main objective was to provide kids with an outlet for self-expression, which stemmed from my frustration as a teacher. I observed so many talented students who lacked the space and freedom to showcase their abilities.

Rite-of-Passage

Even though the process of interviewing a stranger for the first time could be intimidating, it was a rite of passage at HarlemLIVE that enabled our students to grow beyond their comfort zones. In their own words:

HarlemLIVE opened me up socially. I'm an introvert by nature, so talking to strangers is a weird thing for me, but the second day I was there, Rich sent me out with two people to do a person-on-the-street interview. You're just asking a stranger to answer questions, and New Yorkers are naturally reticent.

It was interesting, and it forced me to come out of my shell and find my own way. Once you get people to give you amazing answers, a lot of assumptions drop, so it ended up being a really fun thing to do, but it also forced me to not be so shy, to speak up a little bit more.

HarlemLIVE definitely informed my leadership. It made me more aware of my ability to go out and get the things I want. *—* *Tameeka Mitchem*

* * *

HarlemLIVE had a tremendous impact on my life outlook and my journey to self-actualization. I came in as a wet-behind-the-ears high schooler. My naiveté was humored with good nature. I felt seen. More than that, I felt nurtured. Richard worked full-time to coax us out of our comfort zones and off into the world to use our voices, to have the audacity to ask anyone questions or for a moment of their time. This built in me a confidence that I would take into adulthood: the ability to walk in any room with my head high, not feeling inferior but compelled to work the room; the ability to ask and, at times, demand information, respect or my just due.

I always considered myself shy or an introvert, but none of that mattered because we all had to head out into the streets, hand out pamphlets, and let the world know who we were and what we were cooking up.
—Ena Johnson

Newbie Card

Over time, we established systematic procedures for onboarding new participants. Anyone who showed interest, particularly those with an inquisitive mind and enthusiastic spirit, were encouraged to apply through a straightforward application form. As a program, we seldom turned anyone away.

Upon completing the application and interview process, we presented each newcomer with a "Newbie" card. This card served as a roadmap for their initial days at HarlemLIVE. It was a comprehensive checklist of tasks and abilities designed to help the newbies navigate their first steps within the program and ensure their quick integration into our operations. This included tasks like creating a digital folder for their work, taking a headshot for their press badge, and capturing a picture of themselves working in the office. The card also stressed familiarizing themselves with office equipment and procedures, such as using the phone, cameras, calendars, and mentor lists, and emphasized taking responsibility for the maintenance of the space.

Prior to embarking on any reporting assignment, our team always referred to a comprehensive checklist. This list ensured they were prepared with essentials such as contact information, press badges, HarlemLIVE flyers, notepads, pens, cameras, and charged batteries.

After outlining the tools at their disposal, we would often encourage them to dive into personal projects. On his first day, I asked Kelvin Christie to write his profile.

"What should I write about?" he inquired.

"Write about anything you want," I replied.

"I've never heard that before," he responded with amazement.

Given this newfound freedom, Kelvin began to express himself through various forms of writing, including poetry, essays, and stories. Though Kelvin was a transient residing at Covenant House, a shelter for homeless youth, he found a sense of belonging and a platform for his voice at HarlemLIVE.

His first piece was an essay detailing his institutionalized life experiences up to that point. HarlemLIVE served as a springboard for Kelvin's academic pursuits. He went on to earn four master's degrees—in biomedical science, psychology, mental health counseling, and healthcare law and policy—before embarking on his doctorate. Kelvin's story stands as a testament to the transformative potential of programs like HarlemLIVE.

A Powerful Piece of Plastic

Wearing a press badge and being supported by peers was a significant boost for the newbies' learning at HL. We printed four badges per 8½" x 11" card stock, laminated them for durability, and then separated them. Each badge had a hole punched at the top for attaching to a chain or colored lanyard, allowing students to wear them professionally around their necks.

We'd tell students that the press badge alerted anyone with whom they spoke to understand that the intent was for publication and thus they were protected by the US Constitution's First Amendment inherent rights.

These badges represented more than just plastic and lamination—they symbolized doors opening to new opportunities and experiences that many of our students hadn't previously imagined. Hear it directly from some of them and our partners as they share their stories:

*The press passes were really important. Once you put a press pass on, you have access to people in a different way. The students got invited into spaces they might not otherwise have had access to, and they had an official role to play. That was part of their **empowerment**.*

Rich did a really great job finding role models—people of color whom the students could interview and see themselves reflected in to create that sense of potential and of all the amazing options for their lives. —Mara Rose

* * *

*My niche became reporting. I started doing "person-on-the-street" interviews, going out with Khalid, who held the tape recorder. I would make up the questions, ask them, and write the stories. We were **empowered**. Rich told us, "You're kids, so use that to your advantage."*

*When we saw **Russell Simmons**, we didn't have to stand in line because we had press badges and we got **access**. —Ebony Myers*

* * *

*The first major story I went on was when **Michael Jackson** came to Harlem. We had press badges and, literally, you just showed the press badge and they let you walk right in. Till this day it still amazes me. There were cops everywhere, barricades, people standing outside, but we showed our press badge, and we had **access**, no questions asked. — Reuben Quansah*

* * *

*One of the most meaningful stories I was on was the shooting of **Amadou Diallo**.*

*When black people or people of color die at the hands of their supposed guardians and protectors, it creates a cognitive dissonance. I was 12 or 13 when this happened, and I was afraid to cover the story. I'd never been in a crime scene before, but **we took our press badges as an oath to tell the authentic stories of our community** and I had to live up to it.*

I was terrified, but I thought, "His family needs to hear how the community thinks about this as opposed to seeing an outside reflection of this experience, which is how we often see the world."

So we went there, and I remember seeing the bullet holes on the door; it brought reality back to me: "This is the environment I live in." —Shem Rajoon

HarlemLIVE Legacy: Second-Generation Journalists

Flash forward to 2022. HL alumni Gisely Colón López, Ena Johnson, and Shaunetta Gibson were at the Harlem School of the Arts for a function celebrating the life of music teacher Charles S. Brown, mentioned earlier, who taught with me at P.S. 206. Shaunetta was with her children, Ohjani and Brian, and Ena with her daughter, Taylor. These second-generation HL youth covered the event with the press badges we made for them. Taylor, twelve, recorded with a digital video camera set on a tripod, checking the sound and changing the location depending on the speaker or the performance. Ohjani, fourteen, mingled throughout the large room beyond the entrance of the building with notepad and pen in hand, conducting interviews. Brian, ten, moved around the perimeter of the room taking pictures.

I called Brian over and whispered in his ear that with his press badge, he could get as close as he wanted and to just be respectful. Off he went, taking close-up shots of those being interviewed and of the performers and speakers while cheerfully introducing himself to the attendees.

Sometimes young people just need to be given permission to do their best.

See Chapter 18: Creating Youth Journalists, for practical steps in getting students going.

Story Tickets

In order to effectively manage our stories, we created Story Tickets that evolved over time but consistently captured key information such as the story subject, intended section of the website, assigned students, advising adults, and dates and locations of interviews.

To keep the Story Tickets organized, we mounted five folder pockets on a wall for easy access and efficient tracking:

1. Potential stories: This folder housed story ideas and upcoming events that had not yet been scheduled or assigned.
2. Scheduled stories: This folder contained stories for which interviews had been arranged and students had been provisionally assigned.

3. Reported stories / Stories in editing process: This folder contained stories for which reporting had been completed and the writers were in the process of composing the story. We often paper-clipped other pertinent information to the Story Sheet that pertained to the subject.

4. Ready for publication: This folder contained stories that were edited and ready to be posted on the website.

5. Stories to be archived: This folder contained stories that had run their course and were no longer current but that we wished to preserve for future reference.

We experimented with digital methods of tracking stories, but sometimes old-fashioned, hands-on methods proved to be the most effective. Visitors to our office could instantly see the status of each story, including how many were being worked on and their progress toward publication. We also utilized an online calendar that allowed remote access to upcoming stories. In addition, we had a large whiteboard for daily announcements, which we later supplemented with blog posts. We provided cardboard mailboxes reminiscent of those found in classrooms for our dedicated youth and adult volunteers to store their notes and papers in.

Chat Apps

In our formative years, we often turned to AOL Instant Messenger (AIM) for communication. Before the ubiquity of smartphones, AIM was a widely-used and practical social networking tool. Its interface showcased a floating window on a computer screen, listing contacts who were online and ready to chat. Users could also establish chat rooms for virtual group discussions. Even though AIM has since been phased out, it was an indispensable tool of its time.

Below, you'll find snippets from various AIM chats over the years. In this first excerpt, a student discusses a school report. We had previously asked the HL teens to craft stories about their schools in any manner they preferred – be it a student profile, an overview of a popular class, a piece on the school band, and so on.

Kwame de Afrique:hey, it's Kwami... just wanted to let you know I sent the final copy of my school report to Danya... and I should be able to come in either tomorrow or Friday, I've been busy with all this college stuff, and it's been crazy

Kwame de Afrique:how've ya been?

HarlemLive:*cool. you should come by on Wednesdays, we do college counseling*

Kwame de Afrique:yeah? okay, I'ma be there next week

HarlemLive:i think next week it's gonna be at Columbia w/ a guest speaker but just to help you get things finished

Kwame de Afrique:great...

HarlemLive:*if you're by on Friday, there'll be the same advisors there to see where u at in the process*

HarlemLive:*you come up w/ any ideas for the music section?*

* * *

HarlemLive:*I told Shem...*

Mrosemrose:*What?*

HarlemLive:*that most of the responsibility would fall on him next month and that he should go to his teachers and see if he could get a jump on next semester, so he doesn't get behind in his work at the start of the semester in feb*

HarlemLive:*well...*

HarlemLive:*he's been coming late, like 5 pm everyday, cuz he did just that... and he's getting a head start... i bet the teachers must be blown away*

HarlemLive:*that a student would take that initiative*

Mrosemrose:*That's very cool. He is so great. Has he been getting good grades at CPESS?*

HarlemLive:*yes, he's been doing really well.*

* * *

AIM Chat with Melvin Johnson re: video production:

HarlemLive:dd u look at any of the video of you
InternMoney:yeah i saw it
HarlemLive:you should edit it down to some snippets
InternMoney:thats what i'm gonna do
HarlemLive:have one of the interns log the tape
InternMoney:i'm gonna have to show them another way of doing it cause Al-Amir does it the long way
InternMoney:he told me how he does it
InternMoney:and I told him a quicker way
HarlemLive:ok, cool
HarlemLive:tell him to pass it on

Back in the day, AIM was our go-to tool for staying connected, sharing ideas, and keeping up-to-date on what was happening at the office. Nowadays, there are even more powerful and versatile text chat apps available, like Discord, Telegram, and many others, which offer features such as screen and file sharing, voice and video calls, and extensive customization options. These apps are used for a wide variety of communication purposes, from business and education to socializing and gaming.

The Youth Do It Themselves

Students assigned to or initiating a story were responsible for arranging the appointments and conducting the interviews. Administrative work could also be assigned to a student, which allowed for complete autonomy in the process. Adults only served as coaches and didn't interfere with the work of the youth.

However, this approach sparked disagreement with a community advisor who believed that adults should make initial contact to alert potential interviewees about the incoming call from our youth. I strongly disagreed with this notion, as it would give the students a false impression of the real world where adults don't always "play nice."

We prepared new students with role-play scenarios and even developed a script, much like those used in call centers, to help them navigate the calls. One exceptional student, Jerlena Rhodes, was able to efficiently set up a month's worth of stories through her phone calls.

Veteran HarlemLIVE students also handled the intake and interviewing of new recruits. Despite the immense responsibility, students thrived in this environment.

In their own words:

I was a junior in high school when I found out about HarlemLIVE through a flyer that talked about a youth media organization. I worked in my school newspaper, and I wanted to be a journalist, so I decided to travel from Brooklyn to Harlem to find out more about this program. I was involved ever since.

I loved the fact that everything was done by the students: the writing, the videos, putting together the website, even keeping the office clean. Everybody had duties. We were responsible for ourselves, so we were also responsible for each other.

Initially I started in HarlemLIVE as a writer, and later I dealt more with video because I took a class on documentary filmmaking. Being able to actually shoot and edit video helped me refine my skills. Interviewing people on the streets was a little nerve-racking, but it really helped me later in life when I had to cold-call or stop people for stories as a professional reporter.

*Sometimes we ran our story ideas by the adult mentors, but for the most part we had **autonomy** and could do whatever stories we felt were right, so that helped us develop a sense of editorial discernment.*
—Aisha Al-Muslim

* * *

I was 16, in Junior High, and starting to focus on college research. I needed a computer, and I saw an advertisement for Playing2Win. Once I went there, I realized that P2W held computer classes, but there was this other group of kids from HarlemLIVE, and it looked like they were doing something interesting, so I ended up on that side. Rich was managing the space, but it seemed like **the kids ran the show, and I liked how that felt***.*

To pursue news stories, we had to go all around the city, and getting to know New York was a draw because I was from the Bronx. Rich would send two to three people together, so it felt safe, comfortable, and natural. At some point I stopped being scared to approach people; interviewing became something I looked forward to doing. It was low key, low pressure.

Rich didn't force anyone to do anything or micromanage us. It was very different from school. He always encouraged us. He definitely had boundaries, and disrespect would not be tolerated, but he gave students independence to be, to do, and to make mistakes. He would say, "You are a kid. The worst that you can get is a 'No' or a 'Get out,' and then you find another way to report the story." When we finally got to approach the person we would interview, we had to make sure that we were ready.

Being ready for opportunity when it comes was another lesson that I learned through HarlemLIVE. *—Ebony Myers*

* * *

To ensure comprehensive training, we created checklists for our learning areas, including journalism, photography, web design, tech, and administrative roles. Each checklist, like the newbie card mentioned earlier, had several tasks and steps in mastering each track.

These checklists were used by newbies and veteran students alike, with experienced students taking on most of the training responsibilities. The checklists allowed them to progress at their own pace while still receiving structured guidance.

Peer teaching, a fundamental aspect of HL, arose out of necessity, as we didn't have a paid staff. This approach also allowed for a deeper understanding and internalization of skills and processes.

Furthermore, we were fortunate to have a continuous flow of professionals volunteering their time to teach industry standards such as Photoshop and Final Cut Pro. Our students also had the opportunity to learn from journalists who demonstrated interview and camera techniques as well as public speakers who taught how to deliver engaging presentations.

Public Speaking

At seventeen, I was the youngest participant when my father enrolled me in a San Francisco–based Dale Carnegie class on public speaking. The course taught me a valuable rule: speak only about the things you have earned the right to talk about.

At HarlemLIVE, once a teen had spent a few weeks immersed in producing an aspect of the youth-led online magazine, they could easily stand in front of an audience, speak about their work, and ask for questions. It was a straightforward formula to get them started.

HarlemLIVE's youth were frequently asked to participate in panels or visit colleges to discuss their work. High school presentations were an essential recruiting method that also provided them with unique experiences. For example, they presented in front of several classes at a high school within NYC's notorious Rikers Island prison.

It's safe to say that any young person who spent time at HarlemLIVE was not intimidated about speaking in public, as they explain:

I was reserved and afraid to speak in public. I second-guessed myself even if I knew what I was talking about. At HarlemLIVE, though, we did a lot of public speaking. We traveled to many different places to talk about the program, the work we did, and the impact it had. For example, we went to Vermont to present our work to students from Georgia, Pakistan, and other countries, and to learn from them.

That was one of the best things for me because that's what I do now in my job: I sit on panels, journals and conventions, and I present our program to the interns. —Aisha Al-Muslim, Senior Editor for Internships at the Wall Street Journal

* * *

*You got great public speaking skills at HarlemLIVE, without even realizing it. I participated in presentations at Columbia College. Maybe you were struggling with imposter syndrome, but you were being forced to speak to these graduate students who were clearly more educated than you but interested in what you had to say. That builds **confidence**, and it has helped me stand out in job interviews. I've had to do group interviews in competition with seven or eight other people. Being able to assert myself, being able to feel the room, and having the confidence of knowing what the audience wants are all skills that I cultivated at HarlemLIVE —Treniese Ladson*

* * *

*HarlemLIVE shaped me in a profound way, and it continues to serve my life even today. I came in as a writer, but I also quickly became one of the main public faces of HarlemLIVE. I was always on panels and conferences talking about the future of media, and I was the only kid on the panel. All that gave me a lot of early **exposure**, which allowed me to grow my **confidence**.*

*It gave me a really positive outlet at a time when a lot of things had been turned upside down in my life. At HarlemLIVE I could safely be me, and it instilled in me a sense of **empowerment, encouragement**, and **self-esteem**. To be able to figure out complex problems with nothing but an adult saying to you, "You can do this" is something that stays with you for life. —Danya Steele*

* * *

As an English as a Second Language student, I overcame my fear of approaching strangers, interviewing them, and synthesizing that information into an article thanks to HarlemLIVE. I also got over my fear of public speaking. These skills were tremendously helpful in my career as a strategy consultant in my early 20s, and then as an entrepreneur. Since

HarlemLIVE, I did not shy away from speaking opportunities—whether it was to speak on panels, appear as a guest on podcasts, or give keynotes.
—Kat Vorotova-Dey

* * *

HarlemLIVE's model let people know that youth could be empowered, but it's not what most people do. The adults are the ones who are doing most of these things. The kids are doing some of it, but it's the adults, not the kids who are presenting to organizations about who they are and what they are accomplishing. Maybe you meet the kids, but they're not the ones doing the pitch. And HL kids always were. —Cynthia Simmons

Exposure to Diverse Settings

At HarlemLIVE, we believed that exposure to different settings and circumstances was essential for all students, regardless of their area of interest. We encouraged our techies and web designers to go on stories, too.

Our program provided an unparalleled chance for students to interview prominent individuals across a wide range of fields. These included not only the editor in chief of various magazines, cast members of the *Lion King* on Broadway, and artists and offices of DC Comics, but also musicians, rappers, former and future presidents, celebrities, famous authors, and dignitaries. In addition, students had the opportunity to visit a plethora of events and locales, such as movie sets, television studios, media headquarters, openings, sporting events, award shows, book signings, and functions with the mayor. All these opportunities were magnified by our location in New York City, widely recognized as the media capital of the world.

One memorable moment was when first-day reporter Mike Wills returned from a story involving the Reverend Al Sharpton and his National Action Network.

"I just met Michael Jackson," he said with an awestruck, glassy-eyed look.

We jokingly told him he might as well quit on his first day because it was unlikely anything could top that experience.

Our program's focus on action-oriented learning provided students with unique opportunities to explore their interests and engage with influential individuals, which they greatly appreciated. In their words:

The attitude at HL was always "What are you doing in the office? Get out of here and go report on the streets, go be in action. Use your youth to your advantage. It's going to be tough for people to turn you down because you are young and doing positive things." I was 16 at the time.

*That was such a good culture because it was **dynamic**. You could turn into a story anything you wanted to know, and you got in everywhere because you had a press badge. It was rewarding because I could be myself, express my strengths, and it helped me grow because you had all these professionals coming in and teaching you skills. —Danya Steele*

* * *

During the summer, Rich keep pushing me to take the bike and go do some reporting. If you were idle in the office, he would be like, "Hey, what are you doing? Why are you still here? Get out, go see this." And that pushed people to go out and when they came back, they had awesome stories, and I helped upload them on the website.

To be honest, I came from Queens, and I was scared. I didn't ride my bike on the street, I rode it on the sidewalk, but Rich pushed me to get on with it. And what's unique about HarlemLIVE is that there was a buddy system, so I was always with someone, and they were teaching me how to do it.

Clifton was one of the first ones to take me out and explain to me how to approach people. "You know, people love kindness; always smile, even though they've not given the right answer." And then I learned how to use the camera well, how to turn on the mike… All of that was brand new to me. So I was like, "Okay, let me go ahead and get myself out of my comfort zone and see if I like it."

That's when I started reporting, doing person-on-the-street, taking the Picture of the Day. I remember that was a thing. —Johnny Alarcón

Clickable Map of Harlem

The sections of HarlemLIVE's magazine evolved over time but were generally categorized as Community (organizations, parks, businesses, events), Arts-Culture (music, theater, dance, sports), Writing-Art (memoir, poetry, artwork), and HLWorks (HL covering itself at award ceremonies, trips, and activities). Later, we added new sections such as Life in the City, International, She Thang, Health, and Education/Schools.

One of our most significant projects was the Clickable Map of Harlem, where we sent students to photograph and document every block of Harlem—multiple times. They captured churches, schools, restaurants, parks, landmarks, and more. This project was a precursor to Google Maps, and Columbia University even got involved by having some of their engineering students assist in building the Flash interface. The project caught the attention of AOL Time Warner, which provided funding.

Once the section of the website was up, users could click on different blocks and see what existed in those locations. People in the Harlem community began to recognize and approach the HarlemLIVE team, curious about why they were taking photographs. The project taught the youth many technical skills and helped the reporters and photographers gain more knowledge of the neighborhood, which assisted them in scoping out future stories.

Although we invested years into the Clickable Map of Harlem and had it posted on our website for a while, the emergence of Google Maps in 2005 and the subsequent obsolescence of the Flash platform, which we were using, forced us to abandon the project. However, we did not consider the project a failure, and we ensured that participating students understood the value of their efforts.

Frankie was one of them:

Long before Google Maps and Street View, there were no maps with photography of neighborhoods. I was tasked with HarlemLIVE's first attempt at creating a clickable map of Harlem. People from all over the world would be able to see how Harlem looked, block by block.

Little did I know I was in over my head. In order to build the clickable map, I had to learn Flash, and I was struggling. Rich always guided me in the right direction and told me to keep hacking away at it.

Over a year passed by, and I never formally launched the clickable map project. I was overwhelmed, and I gave up. This is something I think about until this day. But in reconnecting with Rich, he reminded me it was about the process too, not just the end point.

At that time, technology wasn't necessarily adopted by the black community; it was considered a "white" thing to do. HarlemLIVE gave me proof that people that looked like me and came from my background could share the same passion. Oftentimes, all it takes is other people believing in you for you to believe in yourself.

HarlemLIVE gave me the confidence that I should and deserved to work in tech. I recently raised 3.5 million dollars in seed funding for a metabolic health start-up that I founded called Measured. —Frankie Brannon

Think Different

HarlemLIVE accomplished an impressive amount during its formative years despite having limited funding and no paid staff. For the first five years, we were fortunate to receive space, utilities, and phone services. Any funding we obtained was allocated toward acquiring high-quality cameras, supplies, and Apple computers.

The Apple brand played an integral role in shaping the culture of HarlemLIVE. Personally, I drew inspiration from Steve Jobs, who was only five years older than me, and his visionary leadership. The MacOS platform, in my opinion, was more user-friendly and better suited for fostering creativity compared to Windows.

In June 1996, when HarlemLIVE was established, Apple was on the verge of bankruptcy. There were apprehensions among some parents about training the youth on an operating system that could soon become obsolete. However, within six months of HarlemLIVE's inception, Steve Jobs returned to Apple and introduced the groundbreaking "Think Different" campaign and the iMac computer.

The educational philosophy of HarlemLIVE was perfectly in sync with the "Think Different" campaign, and we embraced it by incorporating several logos from the campaign into the bottom of our stories for many years. The students' press badges enabled them to attend the annual Apple Expo at the Jacob Javits Convention Center, and they even gave a successful presentation at the Apple Soho store theater, which was the first Apple retail store in Manhattan.

With Apple's rising popularity, several alumni of HarlemLIVE found part-time jobs providing technical assistance to new Mac users. One of them even became the head of technology at City College, in part because of his extensive knowledge of MacOS, which he and many others acquired through their training at HarlemLIVE.

Osakwe Beale can attest:

Rich was a staunch Apple supporter and advocate long before it was the cool thing or before Apple spent billions in marketing to convert the masses. He introduced us to an all-Mac world, and as a result, all of us had a new skill set.

* * *

The website flourished as it showcased an abundance of creative content ranging from memoirs, poetry, and essays to personal interviews with people from all walks of life. It also featured numerous stories and events from the local community and beyond in New York City. Writing for HarlemLIVE proved to be a profoundly immersive experience for our teens and supported them in surpassing their previous writing endeavors.

Let's hear from a couple of the students to understand why:

I never quite got the same feeling writing for my high school newspaper or my college newspaper that I got writing for HarlemLIVE. HL had quite a few things going for it that those entities didn't.

Number One: *They trusted us to share our points of view of the times we were living in and the environments that we were living in using our own voices.*

Number Two: The school newspapers only covered their bubbles. Our motley crew of talent was being empowered to cover the best city in the world.

Number Three: They never sent you out alone. They always paired you up with other teens and one adult. Each member of that unit who was sent out knew their role and did it well.

Number Four: Something about the whole HL project felt like an "us versus the world" kind of vibe. We never had enough money. We always needed more support. We always needed more equipment. We always felt like we could use a grant or two. We didn't look into readership or site numbers, but I always felt like we were competing for attention. I naively thought that good content was the only thing we needed to beat other publications, so in my head I always thought that one more story meant we gained ten more readers. I enjoyed that feeling, though. To me, feeling like the underdog helped me to want to do better for the team each time. —Guyan Wilks

* * *

An impactful aspect of HarlemLIVE was learning that your voice can matter at such a young age. As a young person, you had an opportunity to express your opinion. If you came with an interest, you could write an article about it.

One of my first articles for the magazine was about sex and the role that it played in advertisement for women. Another time I wrote an article about a women's professional football league, and the title was "Women and Pigskins Are No Longer in the Kitchen." After the article was on the site for a while, Richard told me that someone in Australia had read the article and gave it accolades. It was shocking to realize, "Oh, wow, we have a voice, and it is far-reaching."

We were young people full of energy and opinions, and we had a safe way to channel those opinions and engage the community.

Even if you are shy or an introvert, when you're interviewing strangers for a piece, sometimes even celebrities, it's either show up or get embarrassed, so you rise to the occasion. It builds your confidence because you're constantly being stretched to try new things. —Treniese Ladson

Melvin Johnson

Chapter 9

CROWNING ACHIEVEMENTS

During the spring of 1999, Tameeka Mitchem, a self-assured and energetic seventeen-year-old, joined HarlemLIVE and took on the role of editor in chief. As someone with experience in both college and high school journalism, I recognized that this was a pivotal leadership position for any publication. Nevertheless, no one had previously appeared willing to assume the responsibility, and I did not want to impose it on anyone.

Tameeka's arrival was a pivotal moment for HarlemLIVE. As the first EIC, she brought her own unique ideas and energy to the publication, instituting several procedures that became HL traditions. These included roundtable discussions on current events, regular editorial meetings, a section focused on women's perspectives called She Thang, and fun trips and movie nights to build camaraderie among the staff.

Tameeka was motivated to give girls a stronger role in the publication, and she worked tirelessly to ensure that their voices were heard. Her ideas for the publication were born out of a desire to create a platform for young women to express themselves and to be taken seriously as journalists.

Overall, Tameeka's tenure as the first editor in chief of HarlemLIVE was instrumental in shaping the publication.

Tameeka explains why she was so motivated to give girls a stronger role in the publication and how she came up with her ideas:

I joined with HarlemLIVE because I was in my senior year in high school, and I needed more community activities for my college application. I found out about this online magazine, and I thought it was interesting.

I saw where their address was in Harlem and that they were looking for writers. I'd always loved English and I was always a writer, but I wasn't really a journalist. At the time, though, I was a huge fan of magazines, and I read a lot of political magazines. I emailed them with my AOL email.

One of the HL students, Osakwe, was on Messenger (AOL), and he messaged me right away. We started conversing, and he said, "Oh, you've got to come in…"

So I ended up going the very next day, and pretty much after that, I was locked in.

I thought it was an amazing program. Rich was super exciting and very engaged with everyone. He was always pushing us to go out and report, but there wasn't a structure of how to run the magazine from the top down. Maybe I was a bossy kid, but after a couple of weeks I said, "Hey, maybe we could have a little bit more structure and specific positions."

I could see people who were interested in some topics and others whose skill set wasn't so much on reporting, but they were really good at being organized or at other roles. I went home, looked at the masthead in my VIBE *magazine, and researched different positions and their job responsibilities. Then I analyzed where different kids would fit best. I could see, "Oh, this person is really great at getting people to come in, or that person is really great at talking to folks and getting interviews."*

There were a couple of sit-downs with Rich to talk about the direction for the program and to set a structure. Once we did, it was important to establish regular editorial meetings.

One of my favorite movies was All the President's Men, *and a huge part of that film happens in the* Washington Post. *You would see the journalists in editorial meetings, and the editor in chief would ask what they were working on, so I knew that was how you run a newspaper. I started an editorial meeting because we needed to plan out our content more.*

HarlemLIVE was a unique, amazing experience, but it was a little limited in the sense that it was mostly boys because it was around technology and computers, and boys had gotten into computers early to play video games. They were the ones coming and staying, while the girls flowed in and out. We had some steady girls eventually, like Jerlena, Danya, and Nicole, but at the beginning I often wondered why I was the only girl or why there would be two girls and eight boys. I started She Thang, a section focused on women's perspectives, to attract more female contributors.

At that age, 15/16, you're interested in serious topics, but you're also interested in music, dating, movies, makeup, and beauty, and none of that was being addressed because a large part of our goal was covering Harlem. I thought that if we had a specific section on the site that women could choose to focus on, we could recruit more females. I called the section She Thang.

We did music reviews, book reviews, we covered female artists, we did person-on-the-street interviews specifically with women subjects, we talked about relationships, we talked about beauty. We wanted to make it about things that girls would normally chat about. I think that having a female perspective going on made women more interested because they felt they could contribute, and they saw themselves.
—Tameeka Mitchem

Honored by a King

Six months into our residency at Playing2Win, we enrolled in an international competition called the Global Bangemann Challenge. Winners would be announced in Stockholm, Sweden, at the prestigious Great Hall, where most Nobel Prizes are awarded. Our category was media. As East Harlem youth were part of HarlemLIVE, my district job, where I continued to work from 8 a.m. to 3 p.m., allowed me the flexibility to make the trip.

The organizers sponsored the airfare for me and three teens: Angel Colon, Osakwe, and Jerlena, while Khalid Muhammad's mother paid for her photographer son to join the experience. In addition to attending the ceremony, HL students were scheduled to conduct a workshop and give a talk to a large audience.

THE STORY OF HARLEMLIVE

We kicked off the trip on a high note by traveling to the airport in a limousine, as suggested by Khalid's mom. We arrived in Stockholm by train and walked through the city with our luggage, trying to find our hotel. At one point, while waiting in a lobby, one of the kids accidentally knocked over Angel's luggage, causing him to do a headstand. We couldn't help but laugh out loud.

After checking in, taking a quick nap, and refreshing ourselves, we met Ulla, our host and guide during our stay. A Swedish TV crew who were doing a story about HarlemLIVE followed our every move as we toured the city.

Ulla told me that if we were to win, I was to go alone up the steps of the Great Hall to accept the award from the King of Sweden. When it was announced that HL tied for first place, the kids and I looked at each other with huge smiles as the crowd cheered and a huge screen blinked HARLEMLIVE!

I went against Ulla's instructions and sent Angel up to shake the king's hand and receive our award. HarlemLIVE youth became the youngest winners of the international contest, and Angel had the honor of being the only young person to greet the king.

Angel Colon: Pillar of HarlemLIVE

Angel was the only original student from P.S. 206 who remained with HarlemLIVE until there was enough momentum and additional youth to carry the program forward. He possessed an affable personality, a quick wit, and exceptional listening skills, all of which made him a natural at reporting and engaging his interview subjects. These same qualities also facilitated the recruitment of new students. During the program's first two years, Angel wrote and reported nearly half of the stories. Without Angel, there likely wouldn't have been a HarlemLIVE.

The day after our victory in Stockholm was announced, a newspaper article featured a subhead that Angel had provided to the reporter: "My school assumed I was playing hooky, not receiving an award from a king."

From Angel's article on the website about the trip:

"Feeling like underdogs, we overcame the odds and won in our category, Culture and Media. Before we received the award, we were very busy attending dinners and going on photo shoots. Then things just got crazy. The day after the ceremony, we saw ourselves in magazines and cover pages of local newspapers. Receiving a lot of "fame" was not too bad for me because I love attention, but all the reporting and taking pictures does get a bit tiring after a while. We went to several places in Sweden in which we were congratulated for our achievements. It felt good knowing everyone noticed our work in a different part of the world."

HarlemLIVE taught me how to listen and to keep my eyes open. Most of all, it taught me how to MOVE! It took me out of the hood and showed me how to move in any hood. I was able to take on the world. I might not be flawless, but I'm certainly fearless because of HarlemLIVE.
—Angel Colon

Winning Reasons

During a grand dinner for all the competitors at the Great Hall, we had the opportunity to sit close to the judges, who praised HarlemLIVE for several reasons that made our project stand out from the rest. These reasons included:

1. Our project engaged various members of the community, as students interacted with them to produce content.
2. We maintained an updated website, with each visit showcasing new work in progress.
3. Our team brought to fruition what had previously been mostly academic discussions of the potential of technology.
4. Unlike most web magazines published by large corporations, HarlemLIVE was a community-driven product that gave voice to the people.
5. Perhaps most crucially, our youth were actively involved in all aspects of the project.

* * *

The morning after the award ceremony, we were pleasantly surprised to see ourselves on the cover of the Stockholm daily newspaper. As we walked to an internet cafe, passersby across the street recognized us and yelled out "HarlemLIVE!" At the cafe, we updated the website and announced our victory. It was how the staff back in New York found out about our win. When we called Angel's parents and siblings in the States, they were screaming with excitement. It was an exhilarating time for us.

However, the trip ended on a different note. Khalid was detained for several hours at JFK airport and treated as a potential terrorist because his name was the same as that of a controversial political activist. Ms. Muhammad, Khalid's mother, had to make a special trip to the airport due to his detainment and was also questioned for hours.

Additionally, the Stockholm newspaper's coverage of HarlemLIVE and its origins caused a stir when it labeled the principal of my former school as a villain for forbidding the after-school trips that were instrumental in forming the program. The article prompted the principal to threaten me and the district with a lawsuit for slander. As an administrator in the district, I was viewed as the principal's colleague, and the superintendent cautioned that the article could lead to my demotion back to the classroom, suggesting that I didn't understand my role as a district leader.

Despite the potential fallout, HarlemLIVE had already gained significant momentum, which prompted me to resign from the board of education. While a union representative warned that my resignation could make it challenging to return to the system, citing my jumping the turnstile and subsequent arrest, I was fortunate enough to secure a part-time position with ILT under an existing grant, which allowed me to continue tending to the digital needs of schools. Although the salary was lower than what I had earned as a tenured teacher, this opportunity enabled HarlemLIVE to continue. Jen Hogan of ILT explains:

As Associate Director of the Institute for Learning Technologies, I always did my best to get whatever funding I could to HarlemLIVE and to support them.

To me, the most appealing aspect of HarlemLIVE was that it was fully committed to equity and excellence, which were the guiding principles of ILT's work.

HarlemLIVE strove to encourage youth, mostly youth of color, and organize them in an interesting journalistic endeavor; the students were not only knowledge consumers but also producers of knowledge, using their voices creatively in different mediums. They had the opportunity to author something and were put in situations where they had to converse with or interview adults; this gave them a tremendous amount of skill building and confidence. It fed their human development, in addition to their education.

It was such a pleasure to watch these youth, who didn't have a lot of opportunities, being so professional; they were given much responsibility and trust, and you saw them grow and take this incredibly mature ownership of the project of the HarlemLIVE newspaper. There was certainly some pride in how innovative and cool it was, but in general the kids were just fully engaged in the work. It was a net positive cultural vibe.
—*Jennifer Hogan*

* * *

While some members of HarlemLIVE were in Sweden, another group of students traveled to Washington, DC, to receive honors for the program's induction into the Smithsonian Institution Archives.

Ebony Myers describes the experience as truly memorable for the students:

I went to Washington, DC, with Kerly and Elaine to accept an honor in the Smithsonian. I hadn't ever left the state before for a trip like that, other than going with family to South Carolina. To get dressed up and go in a limo… just knowing that those doors were open, that we could go to D.C. and do this big thing was something different.

Eventually I learned to open my mind and take risks, to do new things. I recently became a Fulbright Distinguished Teacher and lived a year in Finland with my three kids. If it weren't for HarlemLIVE, I

wouldn't have had the confidence to even apply, especially as a black person; I would have stayed in my little box in the Bronx, but HarlemLIVE gave me the sense that I could do anything because it provided those experiences of being in spaces that you would not ordinarily be in.
—*Ebony Myers*

HarlemLIVE's appeal grew with the addition of charismatic and captivating teens like Tameeka and Melvin.

A Powerhouse

In the fall of 1999, it was a dreary Sunday in the Bronx. Melvin Johnson and his older sister, Wanda, decided to grab a meal at the IHOP on 233rd Street. On their way back, they stopped at a Rite Aid nearby. Wanda couldn't recall exactly what they needed, but she remembered Melvin getting distracted by the magazine section.

He picked up a copy of *The Source* magazine, flipping through the pages with interest. He turned to Wanda, holding the magazine out. "Wanda, can you buy this for me?" he asked, his eyes pleading.

Wanda sighed, looking at her brother with an arched brow. "Money's tight, Mel. Can't you get it off the street? If I buy it here, I'll have to pay full price, plus tax."

"C'mon. Don't be so cheap. Don't be like that." His gaze fell back on the magazine with longing in his eyes.

She hesitated but then relented.

"Alright, fine. But listen, Melvin," she pointed a warning finger at him, "if I buy this magazine, you have to promise me you're going to read it from cover to cover. Don't waste my money."

He nodded eagerly. "I will—I promise."

True to his word, Melvin dove into the magazine the moment they got in the car. By the evening, he had come across an article about HarlemLIVE's Michael Popo. Excited, he asked Wanda about reaching out to them. Wanda, never having read the article, agreed without a second thought, willing to support her brother in whatever way she could. That small act of support marked the beginning of a journey neither of them could have anticipated at the time—a journey that would change Melvin's life as well as the trajectory of HarlemLIVE.

* * *

Throughout his life, Melvin was a chameleon who could connect with anyone, from a chief executive officer to a street hustler. Born in the Bronx in the early '80s, he could have ended up being a gang member, given the environment. However, his story didn't turn out that way, and he exceeded expectations, according to his friends and family.

Melvin was a natural, charismatic public speaker, and he would be a powerhouse for the life of HarlemLIVE. He didn't fully realize this until early into his tenure when he was asked to come along with Osakwe and others to Teachers College to speak in front of a graduate class. Osakwe had been doing this for a couple of years, so it was no sweat to do these gigs. But Melvin was a nervous wreck.

Osakwe said, "Melvin was so scared, he made me nervous."

Melvin and Osakwe received a standing ovation that evening. It would be the first of many for Melvin.

Melvin became HarlemLIVE's primary spokesperson, advocate, and father figure, and he also represented HarlemLIVE on a trip to Italy for an international competition. Additionally, he was heavily involved in web development and video production, which later earned him the nickname "The Shooter" due to his exceptional skills behind the camera when he went on to do it professionally. When he watched TV shows like *The Wire*, his main focus was the cinematography. Melvin also served on HL's board of directors and helped direct the program for a time.

Mel maintained ties with alumni throughout the years and encouraged them in all their endeavors. When alumna Odie Santiago was defending her doctorate in sociology in 2020, she credited Melvin for encouraging her and providing a sounding board for ideas. The defense committee members were taken by how immersed Odie was in her subject matter about homelessness in New York City, which she attributed to her days reporting at HL.

* * *

Despite living with sickle cell anemia and fighting the disease for years, Melvin became a passionate advocate, using his platform to educate others and raise awareness about the condition. He even developed a podcast for that purpose. In one of his last social media posts, Melvin went viral discussing the coronavirus pandemic and data that showed African Americans contracting COVID-19 and dying at an alarming rate.

In late 2019 and into 2020, Melvin spearheaded a documentary project about HarlemLIVE alumni, conducting nearly a dozen interviews. Tragically, in April 2020, he passed away due to complications from sickle cell just as the pandemic hit and hospitals were overwhelmed.

He is survived by his three children: sons Harlem and Justice and daughter Pharaoh. Melvin's loss was felt deeply by all who knew him. He will be remembered as a driven, generous, and intelligent young man who made a profound impact on HarlemLIVE and beyond.

HarlemLIVE's appeal grew with the addition of charismatic and captivating teens like Tameeka and Melvin.

When in Rome

In December 2000, while the US was anxiously awaiting the final outcome of the George Bush–Al Gore presidential election, HarlemLIVE sent a group of eight students—Nicole Schneider, Jianna Caines, Melvin Johnson, Enita Okodiko, Obatunji McKnight, Oscar Peralta, Michael Popo, and Justin Young—to Rome, Italy, to accept honors in another international contest.

To make the trip possible, Harlem's Abyssinian Development Corporation and other donors contributed funds. In the months leading up to the departure, the team had to ensure that all students had their passports.

Michael Popo, who was a few years older than most of the students and always exuded an abundance of confidence, insisted that he did not need help getting his documentation together, as he had a St. Lucian passport.

"I am a British citizen. I can go anywhere!"

The team took him at his word and didn't press the issue any further. Elaine Johnson and I chaperoned the group on the nine-hour flight to Rome, and Editor in Chief Nicole Farrow and Melvin Johnson led the group in making a presentation, attending an award ceremony, and demonstrating their work for several days at a booth in a large conference hall.

Upon arriving in Rome, customs authorities informed Popo that, as a St. Lucian, he would need a visa to enter Italy. Upon closer inspection, they also realized that his passport had expired, and he was sent back to the US. It was a sore loss for the team as they struggled to get all of their tech up and running in the early days of Wi-Fi availability. "British citizen," my ass!

Despite the setback, it was a great trip overall. The students frequented an internet cafe nearby with their cameras, laptops, and wires, uploading photos and posting new stories on the HarlemLIVE website. The cafe patrons were amazed by the students' tech skills, with some exclaiming, "We didn't know computers did all that!"

A Perfect Record

HarlemLIVE is a testament to what is achievable when you empower young people with trust and responsibility. Over the course of fourteen years running the program, the organization experienced no tragedies, scandals, or injuries despite the fact that our teens went out on countless assignments, reporting, writing, biking, and traveling both domestically and internationally.

There were many years when our older alumni and teenagers ran the office themselves 24/7 and produced events that were large enough to disrupt traffic. Yet no incidents occurred. There were never any police reports, hospital visits, or major mishaps.

HarlemLIVE created a sense of community among its participants, comprised of adults who cared and young people who were engaged. Many of our alumni have gone on to become leaders in their respective fields, proving that exposure to the real world, acquiring new skills, and building self-confidence foster the development of individuals who are not afraid to be proactive about their life choices and direction.

As Mara Rose explains, access and opportunity were key elements to bring out the best in the kids. So was a certain degree of chaos.

People now talk about creating opportunities for youth to authentically fail or succeed, and that's what Rich did. He created real-life situations. It wasn't a sanitized educational curriculum. His creative approach to designing, engaging, and structuring a very multidisciplinary experience was about all of the skills and knowledge you can develop when you're building a real thing.

He believed these young people would do what they said they were going to do—they would show up and treat the space with respect. We had a lot of expensive equipment, but he entrusted the youth in ways that maybe society was not trusting them. He was also very comfortable with some degree of chaos, and within that chaos came beauty and creativity. It encouraged the students to step up and create order, and to identify opportunities with a lot of confidence and power. It was like an organic creature that self-managed itself.

Kids were coming and going all the time, zipping out to cover a story, coming back; they often stayed very late at night working on things; it was a safe space for them to hang out in. The office was always crowded and teeming with activity. It was vibrant. Access and opportunity were at the center. —Mara Rose

* * *

It was in this bustling environment, where youthful energy met guidance and opportunity, that stories like Bryan's emerged.

They gave me the keys to the office.

At a very young age, I had major responsibilities and handled them while still balancing school and the overall NYC teenage experience. Being exposed to such responsibility at a very young age has allowed me to not fear any obstacles or challenges in my way. I invite the challenges often and work well if not better under pressure. I'm able to handle all the responsibilities in my life and still find my calm and balance. I fear I would not have this mindset if it weren't for HarlemLIVE.

You amazing folks also sent me to Vermont with Mera Beckford and Shem Rajoon as tech ambassadors to help teach and inspire teenagers from the former Soviet Union. It was a very surreal experience coming from the Bronx and ultimately an honor. I remember at our introductions with the students, I gave my backstory, and I shared an inspirational story of my mother that left everyone in tears.

I'm grateful for my short experience at HarlemLIVE, but in that small time, HarlemLIVE has prepared me for the world.
—Bryan Michael Conforme

From Tameeka's charm to the unexpected lessons in Rome, HarlemLIVE continued to write its story, with every chapter reflecting not just the growth of an organization, but the maturation of countless young lives forever changed by it.

Team leaders for the inaugural Summer Youth Media Challenge: Nicole Schneider, Michael Lynch, Oscar Peralta, Jassie Harris

Chapter 10

RISING TO THE CHALLENGE: A SUMMER OF YOUTH MEDIA

In 1998, HarlemLIVE began participating in the Summer Youth Employment Program (SYEP), a city initiative providing jobs to teens for seven weeks in the summer. At many of these job sites, teens supervised kids in "camps" on blocked-off city streets or did office work, filing papers. HarlemLIVE, on the other hand, was an educational program where young people would be paid to learn.

When SYEP first got started, we were able to get most of our regularly attending year-round youth into the program. Now, with the help of the program, they were paid for a few weeks in the summer.

However, SYEP quickly grew in size and popularity. Starting in 2000, the city began using a lottery system. Not all HarlemLIVE teens would get in. They could still participate, just not get paid.

Several umbrella agencies receiving funds to administer SYEP had to find sites for the increased number of youth. Fearing diminished attendance over the summer, I impulsively agreed to their request to admit an additional two dozen youth to HL.

What was I thinking? How were we to take on so many teens with an all-volunteer staff and minuscule funding? These kids would be totally new and need training to become journalists, photographers, web designers, administrators, and public speakers. What tactics would work to keep this large group engaged?

Channeling the current zeitgeist (the first season of *Survivor* aired that summer), a competition came to mind. It took a couple of weeks of intense preparation to put it together: thinking up tasks, producing a binder with guides and guidelines, mapping out a schedule, coordinating equitable use of equipment, deciding on a point system, scheduling classes taught by adult volunteers or alumni, and more.

I was nervous before presenting it to the students. What if they pooh-poohed the whole idea? What if it met with disinterest, yawns, and groans!?

I was floored when I saw how quickly and seriously they took to it. Reuben Quansah explains:

> *Despite any anxiety Rich may have felt while presenting the Media Challenge to us as teenagers, it did not transfer over to our experience. In fact, Rich approached our engagement as if we were already skilled professionals in our respective roles. The team leaders for the competition were given the freedom to make it what we wanted it to be, and Rich trusted us to do so. I was able to create a collaborative and competitive effort with my team, and HarlemLIVE provided opportunities for any student who wanted to engage. However, the unspoken prerequisite was to always do your best. With the support of skilled adults, physical resources, and personal autonomy, the environment made it easy for us to compete and collaborate at a higher caliber while doing our best. It was fun! —Reuben Quansah*

Let the Games Begin

On the inaugural day of "summer work," we kicked things off with ice-breaking activities and trust games. Armed with sandwiches, water bottles, balls, blindfolds, and other items, we led the teens on a walk to Central Park. The first year was skillfully coordinated by former middle school teacher Monique Lee, who expertly modeled best practices. In subsequent years, alumni mostly took up the mantle.

After several hours of trust games, we randomly assigned the teens to teams and sent them on a two-day scavenger hunt throughout the city. The items they sought foreshadowed places they'd need to know for the upcoming competition: Manhattan Neighborhood Network (where they would take advanced video production classes), city and federal court buildings (where they'd cover court cases for stories), bike shops (in case they needed repairs or air for their tires), and headquarters of magazines and broadcast news shows (where they would later set up site tours for their team). They also had to find items online and demonstrate adeptness using various virtual tools and internet services.

After observing how the youth applied themselves during the scavenger hunt, alumni, adult volunteers, and I reviewed their applications and formed balanced teams on the basis of their interests, skills, and personal dynamics. The competition consisted of which team could earn the most points by producing the most and best content for the online magazine, taking the best pictures, editing the best video, making the best presentations, and completing the most classes.

Once the teams were formed, we provided them with a comprehensive binder filled with guides, schedules of classes, subway train passes, and other support materials. They needed to complete a menu of various types of assignments and stories. Teams received broad outlines but had the freedom to choose how to complete assignments. We gave them the "what" (such as person-on-the-street interviews or stories on youth organizations and cultural institutions), but they made the "who" and "how" decisions.

Each team also had to come up with a team name, team colors, a leader, a coleader, and members assigned to do reporting, video production, administration, photography, and marketing. We gave them a list of available adult volunteers and alumni from which they were required to adopt two or three as advisors.

We also established mini challenges, such as who could pass out the most flyers in a busy section of the city or, after giving each team a small budget, deciding how to fix up a portion of the office. If one team was struggling, we would break them up and divide the students among the remaining teams. Teams also organized mini fundraisers, like a dinner or raffle. Mind you, this was years before *The Apprentice* ever aired, but our competitions somewhat foreshadowed their tactics.

Individual contests were also held for best writing, video, photography, blogging, and more. This way, if an outstanding student ended up on a losing team, they could still be recognized for their work. We solicited and received numerous donations as prizes, including bikes, iPods, and cash.

Each team received a card-stock "report card" that the youth coordinators (some veteran HL members who were not part of the contest but helped manage it) filled in each week with a tally of points. A prominent bar graph was updated and displayed in the office so teams could visualize how they were doing.

* * *

Competition isn't always seen as an effective means of educating youth; some argue that kids should be motivated by a desire to learn for its own sake. However, I was faced with the daunting task of keeping a large group of teens engaged and had to come up with a creative solution quickly. Research supports the idea that healthy competition can help focus and motivate young people to achieve at a higher level.[1]

Despite the competitive aspect of the program, we also emphasized the importance of collaboration and teamwork. We made sure the young people engaged in many collective activities that reinforced the idea that, in the end, we were all still part of the same family.

Goofs!

Teams were not only awarded points for their achievements but could also lose points for any errors, referred to as "Goof Points." These mistakes could range from improperly checking out equipment to failing to charge camera batteries or riding a bike without a helmet. However, each team was given a limited number of Goof Waivers to subtract a few demerits as a way to acknowledge that everyone makes mistakes.

The final week of the competition featured last-minute challenges and culminated in a presentation in front of a panel of judges held in one of the

---

1. "The Upside of Rivalry: Higher Motivation, Better Performance." APS: Association for Psychological Science, September 2014; https://www.psychologicalscience.org/news/minds-business/the-up-side-of-rivalry-higher-motivation-better-performance.html

grand classrooms at Teachers College. Distinguished journalists like ABC's Ron Claiborne served as judges. In subsequent years, teams did smaller weekly presentations leading up to the finale, which allowed them to hone their skills over the course of the summer.

This is a clip of Jessica Batson presenting at Teachers College at her team's final presentation: https://www.youtube.com/watch?v=FmabSQjSD1A

The Talking Drum

Following the intense summer competition, we held an eagerly anticipated award ceremony to celebrate the hard work and achievements of our members. Family members, community members, and adult advisors all gathered to witness the revealing of the winning team as well as to view some of their standout work. In addition to this, we announced the new editors in chief for the upcoming year. The event was not without some lighthearted moments, as we included a song or dance performance and shared some comical outtakes from the summer madness, often featuring the flyer dissemination contest.

This AIM chat with team leader Jessica Batson took place the night before an award ceremony:

HarlemLive: u excited?
Penny15033: yeah. i'm nervous too though
HarlemLive: it's fun and u did great so no matter what, u gotta feel good
Penny15033: yeah i'm happy with myself, but i'm nervous for my team
HarlemLive: it's cool it's so close
HarlemLive: i really have no idea yet who's winning cuz we have a lot of checking and counting still to do
Penny15033: ok. you know who i'll hoping will be the victor
HarlemLive: is your family aware of what's been going on?

Penny15033: kind of. they know all about the challenge, and the ceremony. they don't know how tense it's gotten, though.

At the ceremony, we held a drum ceremony and awarded all new members a necklace with a drum pendant. These unique pendants were brought all the way from Dakar by a Senegalese family living in my apartment building. It was our way of congratulating the teens for making it through a grueling summer.

The drum pendant was particularly meaningful, as it had become the symbol of HarlemLIVE shortly after its founding in 1996. The talking drum was one of the earliest forms of mass communication, while the internet and the World Wide Web represented the latest. The pendant symbolized the connection between the past and the present, and the importance of communication and storytelling across generations.

* * *

Here are a few alumni remembering the intense summers at HL:

In my first summer competition, we started with an orientation. We met everyone at a nearby park in Manhattan, and we had lots of snacks and drinks. We did some icebreakers and group games so we could get to know each other. From there, we were broken into groups and given some tasks to do for the next two days.

I loved it. We got to know each other, and I'm still friends with the ten people that were in my team. It was a competition, and we were enticed by the prizes we got at the end of the summer, which were donated items and could include an iPod or even a MacBook. —Johnny Alarcón

* * *

The summer competition was like an adventure: going on different stories, building with my team, even connecting with the leaders of the other teams because we leaders had our own unique challenges of trying to rally our team members, finding out who wanted to do what.

Some people wanted to record, some people wanted to write, some people didn't want to do either. We built our relationship around that competition, and some of those folks are still my friends today. It was a great experience. —Reuben Quansah

* * *

I absolutely enjoyed the HarlemLIVE summers. It had everything I love all coming together. I knew I was going to have the opportunity to write a lot, to explore the city, to work with a steady team of people, to compete against other teams and to be paid in the process.

The first year, I was a member of Nicole Farrow's team. We won that competition. The second year, I led my own team. We tied for first place with another team. It was so much fun because the whole project accomplished many things in a short span of time.

The object of the competition was to churn out as much quality content as possible. I loved to write stories, and I enjoyed churning out content. If you didn't like the stories available from the topics file, then your team had to come up with story ideas of their own.

I remember coming up with a story about the underground performers in the subway. We didn't have a specific place to go for that story. I simply told the team we would head to 14th Street / Union Square and also Times Square. Sure enough, we ran into singers, dancers, and a steel pan drummer. It was really good to work with other talented youth.

As team captain, I was responsible for getting everyone motivated to do stories. I often led by example. We also had to give a final presentation to the judges about the experience we had. I made sure our final presentation in front of the judges was as polished as it could be.

Leading the team the second summer empowered me to see myself as someone who could lead teams in other arenas. It was an important life lesson and skill to obtain. I later would run for multiple student body government positions and became a manager at multiple jobs because I'd been empowered to see myself as a leader.

I can still recall the lessons on accountability, setting an agenda, time management, and recognizing strengths and weaknesses that I learned from leading a Summer Youth Competition team at HarlemLIVE. I draw from those experiences all the time. —Guyan Wilks

* * *

The summer competition at HarlemLIVE was a content gold mine, producing so much material that we didn't publish everything at once. The wall pocket designated for "Stories Ready for Posting" was jam-packed, and we had enough quality content to last us until mid-October, which proved useful, as September was typically a slower month for us, with the students readjusting to their school year.

The inaugural Media Challenge was a resounding success and quickly became the crown jewel of the HarlemLIVE program.

The Bureaucracy of It All

As our summer competition grew in size and popularity, we relied on the city's Summer Youth Employment Program (SYEP) to ensure that we had enough youth participating to create a robust competition. However, navigating the bureaucracy of the city's program proved to be a challenge and a source of frustration for us. It was a stark reminder of why I left my job as a public school teacher to start a groundbreaking project like HarlemLIVE.

In our initial year of involvement with SYEP, we encountered a troubling incident involving a young girl who suffered from kleptomania. Sadly, she began to steal from the teachers with whom we shared the basement of Teachers College. It took a significant amount of persuasion and persistence on our part to convince SYEP to take her back. What was even more disheartening was that the program transferred her to a different agency without any repercussions, which allowed her to continue to steal. This incident underscored that while our mission was to engage and educate youth, we couldn't ignore the broader complexities and challenges that some young people faced.

* * *

Fortunately, theft had never been an issue at HarlemLIVE. Despite possessing valuable equipment and regularly self-supervising, the young people took it upon themselves to safeguard the program.

* * *

Fast-forward to 2002, one of the SYEP administrative agencies asked if we'd take on a new student several weeks into the summer. Even though this child was being reassigned, like the kleptomaniac, I didn't think to ask why he was being transferred from his previous job. I failed to recognize this red flag. The second red flag I ignored was a personal essay he wrote called "Next Stop: Insanity." In the last line of the essay, he wrote:

"Well, I know one thing. I'm crazier than people or I think and because of that, my power will always be limitless."

A stark reminder of our earlier experience with the kleptomaniac came when, three days before the award ceremony, this kid decided he'd make his team win by deleting ALL of the photos of the two opposing teams from the server, which was not backed up yet.

The student never returned after that day. The other two teams were devastated. Some of the deleted photos included encounters with Michael Jackson as well as many photos from the entire first half of 2002. This event served as a valuable lesson about the need to be more vigilant when taking on new students and the importance of ensuring that important data is frequently backed up.

Despite these challenges, the vast majority of the youth we welcomed each summer were exceptional and brought an amazing energy to the program, a testament to the resilience and determination that HarlemLIVE fostered among its participants.

* * *

We made a strong effort to encourage Summer Youth Employment participants to attend classes at our offices before the paid program began. While
we couldn't force them, we explained in interviews that HL was different
from other SYEP programs and offered rewarding experiences and transferable skills. We wanted teens who were passionate about HL and saw it as
more than just a job.

Here, Troy Robateau elaborates:

*I was introduced to HarlemLIVE through the Summer Youth
Employment Program. Being from Brooklyn, I didn't know what to
expect, but I knew they provided services like journalism, photography,
and videography. Taking the position to learn and make money was the
best choice I have ever made in my life.*

*Rich told us that this could "just" be a job or something we could
enjoy doing and use as a stepping stone in life. I was introduced to Chris
Frierson, who would teach me everything I needed to learn, from holding the camera, using tripods, learning features to make the picture better, using a green screen, editing, and so much more.*

*I was weirded out when Rich said, "Okay, guys, we're going to have
teams do MOS (Man On The Street)." I was scared. Raynale, Catalino,
Rhonesha and I took to the streets to find people to interview. It was so
much fun, and it built my confidence and courage.*

*In my second year, HarlemLIVE had us take speech classes, which
improved the way I talk and pronounce words. I gained a lot of strength
and support to be able to make calls to people in the industry to allow me
to interview them. I spoke to a guy from California who wanted to fly
out and be a part of my project, "Hip-Hop History," which was the name
of my video. I won the best video for the contest we had, and I knew from
that day nothing would stop me.*

* * *

Some teens from the summer program stayed on, working through the school year without pay alongside other volunteer youth who were deeply committed to HL. For these teens, HarlemLIVE became a second family. Keisean Marshall, for example, continued with HL for several years after his first summer in 2004. He mainly wrote stories about the entertainment business and has since become a successful television producer, having worked for top-rated shows such as Dr. Phil and Tamron Hall.

Keisean sat for an interview in 2020 with Melvin Johnson and related the following:

HarlemLIVE was transformative. It taught me that I was capable. I learned how to write. I learned how to talk to people, how to approach people on a whim. It taught me how to edit, how to shoot, and all aspects of using the camera. It gave me my first steps in what I'm doing now. I loved going to HarlemLIVE. I knew it was bettering my life down the line. —Keisean Marshall

A clip of the interview is here: https://www.youtube.com/watch?v=rp5AhlbIApE

Despite the challenges we faced with SYEP and the bureaucracy it entailed, we also had to deal with certain aspects of the program that were less than ideal.

Dealing with the Challenges

Participating in SYEP had its share of annoyances, such as their requirement that all students attend a week of classes that often took place in large school auditoriums with no air-conditioning. These classes often instructed over a hundred disinterested teens on appropriate dress codes and how to conduct themselves at work. While the city taught youth about skills in theory, our participants were actively living and practicing those skills.

The classes were a nightmare for us since our team members were gone for a week, which complicated our coordination efforts. We fought tooth and nail to get our kids exempted, but it was not always successful. Sometimes we had the city send someone to our site to instruct the teens.

Despite these challenges, we were able to keep a large group of diverse kids highly engaged by providing them with real-world job experiences, including scheduling, interviewing, writing, and taking classes.

Looking back, I believe that a better model would be to raise the money ourselves for summer stipends, which would allow us to guarantee spots for any youth who participated during the school year and avoid the bureaucracy associated with the city program.

A Social Conscience

Even as we navigated the bureaucracy of SYEP, we never lost sight of our mission to foster a social conscience among our participants. One compelling example of this happened in August 2001, at the conclusion of the second Summer Youth Media Challenge, Danya Steele, a talented and dynamic sixteen-year-old who would later grace the cover of *Teen People* magazine as one of their "Twenty Teens Who'll Change the World," was appointed our editor in chief. With her assertive personality, she earned the nickname "Damn Ya" from Treniese Ladson, one of her colleagues at HarlemLIVE. Danya was a creative powerhouse who overflowed with ideas for captivating stories.

One of her most memorable pieces was about homeless teens. Here are her own words about the experience:

One day I was at home, and there was a social-political commentary program called Street Soldiers *on Hot 97, which was a very popular hip-hop radio station for young people at the time. They were talking about homeless teenagers. As a teen myself, I wondered, "Wow, there's homeless kids?" I had never even thought of that. My wheels started turning.*

The very next day I went into HarlemLIVE and I pitched the story to the staff, trying to recruit people for reporting from the vantage point of teens. We came up with the idea of going undercover, pretending to be homeless to see how services for homeless teens operated and how people treated them.

I recruited Justin Young and Rocky Kabir as "homeless" teens, and we created a project plan: where they were going to go panhandle on New York City. They got in "costume," and I set out with my cameraman, Jonathan Kua, who had the camera in a duffel bag, filming from down low. We were acting as if we were just walking behind them.

There were several things I wanted to show. One was how people treated them—who would help them and give them money. And the other was the Covenant House, which is an organization that serves homeless teens. The two reporters undercover as homeless had to go through the intake process to see what it was like, what services were they providing, and what needed to be improved.

We learned a lot of things from that experience. First of all, we realized not all homeless teens look homeless; because they're teenagers, they might not have been homeless for that long, and they still care about what they look like and are trying to keep up appearances. I also learned, sadly, that around that area a lot of girls are preyed upon by pimps and men who want to exploit young, vulnerable women. It impacted me. All these experiences helped me see that I had strong communication skills and that I cared about social issues.

* * *

Throughout this chapter, we've explored the HarlemLIVE Summer Media Challenge—from its inception to the challenges it faced and the impact it had on the participants. In upcoming chapters, we find out what happened when the youth took on City Hall.

Chapter 11

EVOLUTION

In the wake of the 9/11 terrorist attacks, one may question whether the heartbreaking pain of that day diminished the conflicts and struggles of people's everyday lives. Were any divorces, firings, evictions, or even murders interrupted? Did the tragedy inspire a period of compassion, forgiveness, and understanding?

At HarlemLIVE, the answer was yes. Only a few days before the attacks, an altercation almost brought an end to my time with the program I had founded. However, as if fate had intervened, the tragedy of 9/11 put a halt to it.

New Management

HarlemLIVE was soaring to new heights, but the mood at the Playing2Win offices was growing increasingly tense.

The previous year, I had overlooked a few incidents that now seemed like red flags. The umbrella nonprofit overseeing Playing2Win, Boys and Girls Harbor (now SCAN-Harbor), was seeking more control as both HL and P2W gained success and positive press. Mara Rose, P2W's director and a staunch ally of HL, resigned in the spring of 2001, citing concerns about autonomy.

Initially, Boys Harbor offered me the opportunity to manage P2W. However, administrative work did not interest me. When I declined, they inquired if HarlemLIVE could merge with their organization despite the fact that HarlemLIVE was its own 501(c)(3) nonprofit. Once again, I turned down their offer.

The new administration of P2W commissioned a report that concluded that HarlemLIVE was not on an optimal path and that I was not leading it in the "right" direction.

In August, during a technology-related event, one of HarlemLIVE's adult volunteers overheard a P2W teacher mention that HarlemLIVE would have new management in place by October. As I was preoccupied with the Summer Media Challenge and committed to the program's success, I overlooked these hints, whereas HarlemLIVE's advisors grew increasingly apprehensive about the new management's motives.

Despite the concerns and speculations, it turned out that none of it mattered in the face of the global upheaval that would occur just a few weeks later.

Where's Elliot?

On September 8, 2001, Playing2Win was gearing up to promote their new class offerings that fall by sending volunteers to canvass the nearby housing projects with flyers. Meanwhile, I had arranged to meet Elliot Price and Khalid Muhammad to cover several events and block parties in Harlem.

Khalid, our photographer, arrived early, and I instructed him to get everything ready while I left for a meeting to enroll Clifton Taylor's brother, Jason, in an outdoor education program in Colorado. But when I returned, Khalid had not made any preparations and instead was editing a wedding video for one of the administrators at P2W.

"Stop that and let's go," I said. "Where's Elliot?"

"He's in the back, helping Playing2Win."

When I made my way to the lab in the back to get Elliot, I was met with unexpected news: management had reassigned him to help P2W that day.

"But we have stories scheduled," I protested.

It didn't matter. In what they deemed an "editorial decision," P2W had canceled our stories, requesting that HL lend a hand at their center instead. We occupied their offices rent-free and had been warned about the need to contribute more to their programs. While I understood this, I refused to compromise on this particular day. With no backup plan, I insisted that Elliot come with Khalid and me to report on the scheduled events.

A heated argument ensued, but ultimately the three of us set out on our bikes. Hours later, we returned, posted our content, and then left. Both Playing2Win and HarlemLIVE were closed on Sunday.

* * *

HL advisors Garland Thompson and Alfie Wade strongly urged me to attend the inaugural meeting of the Harlem Arts Alliance, headed by Voza Rivers, on Monday, September 10. The alliance aimed to be an umbrella organization for scores of Harlem artists and nonprofits, providing them with a collective voice to raise funding and political clout. By attending, we made HarlemLIVE a founding member of the alliance.

After the meeting, I made my way to HarlemLIVE's offices. As I arrived, the manager from Saturday's altercation approached me, requesting to speak privately. I set down the materials I had collected from the meeting on a table, feeling a sense of unease. I had no idea what this meeting was about, but I sensed that it could be ominous.

"On Saturday you disrespected me and embarrassed me in front of my new staff and the youth. You'll need to take a break from HarlemLIVE for at least a couple of weeks or longer. Other adults will be put in charge. Today is your last day."

I was stunned. It was a clear sign of a takeover, and I couldn't imagine life without the program I had poured my heart and soul into for the past five years.

My hands trembled as I dialed Elaine Johnson, one of HarlemLIVE's board members and youth mentors, at her job.

"You stay there," said Elaine. "I'm going to call the other advisors."

By late afternoon, Garland, Alfie, Elaine, and others showed up, determined to fight the looming threat. When Playing2Win was about to close, we gathered our things and continued the meeting at the lab of ILT/Teachers College, where we still had access. We talked about writing letters to the press, politicians, and others. It got late, and we left without having done anything concrete.

I went home, but I couldn't sleep. I couldn't shake the feeling of uncertainty about what the next day would bring. While I had bounced back from difficult situations in the past, such as being ousted from my first year of teaching in Brooklyn and being arrested in the subway station, I didn't know if I could handle the prospect of HarlemLIVE being taken away from me.

I was filled with questions. Should I even try to go to the office the next morning? Would I be denied entry? What kind of conflicts would HarlemLIVE and I be facing in the days, weeks, and months to come?

* * *

The next morning, I was jolted awake by my roommate. I stumbled into his room, where the TV showed breaking news: a small plane had crashed into the World Trade Center. It seemed impossible. The sky was crystal clear.

Then the unthinkable happened. Another plane hit.

Terrorists.

Without hesitation, I jumped on my bike and pedaled down the block to the P2W offices, where I watched in horror as events unfolded on a small TV in one of HL's offices. No one stopped me or even spoke to me.

After a few minutes, I rode my bike a few blocks over to CPESS high school, where Shem and several HL students were enrolled. When I arrived, the halls were silent. All the students were sequestered in their classrooms. The administration had decided to keep everyone in the dark until more information was available.

On Borrowed Time

The terrorist attack on our country had a profound impact on the world, and it also had an unexpected effect on me and HarlemLIVE. Despite the chaos and devastation, the plans to displace me from the program were effectively derailed, which allowed me to continue my work with the teens.

The very next day after the attack, I, along with Editor in Chief Danya Steele and reporter Rocky Kabir, rode the HL bikes to Lower Manhattan to cover the scene. Though we couldn't make it all the way to ground zero, our press badges and Danya's "Damn Ya!" energy helped us get farther than the public was allowed.

It was eye-opening to see all the blocks between 14th Street and Houston, river to river, become one gigantic pedestrian mall. No car movement was allowed besides first responders, and they mainly used the roads on the far west side of Manhattan. It served as a reminder of how cities can be humanized when people interact with each other on the streets without the isolating shells of their cars. Today, there is a growing worldwide movement toward more walkable cities that aren't centered around the automobile, which for many decades has segregated people and communities.

The atmosphere was somber, and we witnessed firsthand the resilience of New Yorkers as they came together to mourn, support each other, and rebuild. Makeshift memorials with flowers, candles, and photographs were set up throughout the area. It was a powerful and moving experience that deeply affected all of us at HarlemLIVE.

In the following days, other HarlemLIVE reporters covered the memorials and collective grief downtown through essays, poetry, and photo essays. HarlemLIVE was on the story.

However, as time passed, our situation at P2W grew increasingly challenging.

To the Closet

Two weeks after the tragedy, P2W took over our offices, forcing us into a cramped space resembling a walk-in closet that couldn't accommodate all our equipment, far from the entrance. We were also denied access to the alarm passcode and now had to comply with P2W's hours of operation. In a moment of crisis-induced mania, I suggested going virtual and starting "Virtual HarlemLIVE." However, I soon realized that this wouldn't work, as the program was too complex and depended on constant face-to-face collaboration. We needed a new physical space to continue operating effectively.

But where? And how?

* * *

It was a bleak October when my father, who had extensive experience in real estate, flew to New York to help us find a new location for HarlemLIVE. Once again, Dad was stepping in to "save the day." Despite his mesothelioma diagnosis three years prior and the fact that he was undergoing chemotherapy, he was putting up a good fight.

Dad and alum Melvin Johnson began canvassing Harlem to search for a new home for our program. I'll never forget when Melvin returned to our office after spending several days with my father.

"Your dad is WAY cooler than you," said Melvin.

Whereas I tended to be reserved and socially awkward, my father was a natural at charm and charisma, able to finesse difficult situations with ease. As a warehouse manager, he could connect with both management and workers, making them feel supported and represented. He was fearless and inventive, sneaking into China before relations had normalized in the early 1970s and traveling to Iran under a false name with a passport claiming he was importing peaches.

But his passion for adventure didn't end there. After learning the craft of whitewater rafting with us in tow on the Stanislaus River in California, he went on to become a professional guide on the Colorado River. He put us in dangerous situations to teach us about fear and our ability to survive, proving that we could trust him to find a way out.

Once at Lake Mohave, he even had us get out of the boat as he sped off, shouting, "Swim to the shore!"

Despite inheriting some of his qualities, I never quite learned to move through the world as he did or develop his unique set of people skills. I found him to be an enigmatic figure, often overbearing, which was one of the reasons I moved across the country at the first opportunity.

* * *

We found a promising but dilapidated space above one of the several Manna buffet-style restaurants, this one on Frederick Douglass Boulevard two doors north of 125th Street. Being above a restaurant, it was littered with dead rats and would need gutting. Despite its condition, I believed we could make it work.

However, we grew queasy after learning someone was murdered there a couple of years earlier.

Fortunately, the real estate agent had another option for us: a 2,400-square-foot loft just around the corner. The loft, located on the third floor of a walk-up, was situated above a nail salon on the second and a clothing store at street level. On the fourth floor, there was an elderly piano teacher, and on the fifth floor, a music studio.

The building, nearly a century old, was situated on Harlem's main corridor, 125th Street, and was only half a block away from the world-famous Apollo Theater. Although the space was a single large room that had been unused for over a decade, I knew this was it—the new home of HarlemLIVE.

But, as with any project of this magnitude, challenges lay ahead. We needed to find a way to pay for rent and renovations, to transform this single large room into a multifunction space that would serve our needs. But I was undeterred—after all, if there was one thing that HarlemLIVE had taught me, it was that where there is passion and determination, there is always a way forward.

* * *

In early December 2001, another shoe dropped when ILT announced that the funding source for my salary was running out. Despite having worked with ILT for two years since leaving the board of education, my position would be terminated within a few months due to a lack of funds. Once again, the new management at P2W saw this as an opportunity to pressure me into withdrawing from running HarlemLIVE.

Fortunately, my living expenses were low at the time. I shared a rent-controlled sublet apartment with roommates and was able to cover my rent, utilities, and groceries by doing some tech consulting and teaching jobs on the side. However, I had to rely on credit cards to make ends meet, and this eventually led to substantial debt.

* * *

Despite the challenges, HarlemLIVE continued to thrive. HL mentor Stan Ellzy and I drove two van loads of teens to Syracuse University's S.I. Newhouse School of Communications, a top-rated journalism school, to broaden their horizons. This venture was organized by EIC Danya Steele.

We continued to produce stories and gain more exposure. Some of our team members had the opportunity to go on trips and learn from industry professionals. For instance, a group of kids traveled to Connecticut to learn about web technology from Sonalysts, a company that worked with the US Department of Defense. Additionally, Michael Rosenbaum, who worked for Oprah's Oxygen Network, gave the teens tips on camera and editing techniques and granted them a tour of their offices in Chelsea.

But our time at P2W was clearly limited. The new closet-like space was so small, we had students work from home on computers, twenty years before that became a regular thing with the pandemic.

They Think Danya Is an Adult

In mid-December, the Pew Charitable Trust Fund sponsored a conference on youth communication and technology in Milwaukee. Heavyweights from dot-com companies such as AOL Time Warner attended, and innovative digital projects from across the globe were invited to participate, including HarlemLIVE, a pioneer in the field.

A week before the conference, while I was entering our office, or rather, our closet, HL board member and mentor Elaine Johnson approached me with a startling revelation.

"Rich, look at this." Elaine handed me some papers and documents. "They think Danya is an adult!"

I looked them over and agreed. I called the coordinators of the conference, and they confirmed that after talking at length with Danya over the phone, reading her detailed emails, and seeing she had the title of editor in chief, they assumed she HAD to be an adult instead of a seventeen-year-old.

To allay Elaine's concerns about Danya traveling alone, the conference coordinators offered to provide me with lodging and admission, but I had to pay my own airfare. Danya flew out on Thursday. I charged my airfare to my credit card and flew out on Friday.

It was an oddly warm December in New York City, and I forgot my coat before flying to Chicago and renting a car for the ninety-minute drive to Milwaukee. I had to buy a new winter jacket at a department store upon arrival.

Despite the frigid temperatures, it was a pleasure to attend the conference and meet innovators from all over the world. However, my frustration with the lack of funding for HarlemLIVE boiled over during a gathering on the second day of the conference. I passionately expressed my disbelief that despite our success in winning awards and being featured on TV and written up in numerous publications, we were still struggling to find sufficient funding.

After the meeting, Michele Sacconaghi of AOL Time Warner approached us and offered to have breakfast with us the following day. Over breakfast, she said she was captivated by HarlemLIVE, Danya, and my passion for the program. She announced that AOL Time Warner would donate $10,000 to HarlemLIVE, which was later increased to $25,000.

We had money to move!

Phenomenal Women

Getting the lease for the space on 125th Street was a challenge, but our board member Evelyn Cunningham made it happen. She had connections with Eugene Giscombe of Giscombe & Henderson, the managing agent of the loft we wanted to call home.

Evelyn, a pioneering Black female journalist of the 1940s and 1950s, stood over six feet tall in heels and had a remarkable history, having worked with prominent figures such as Israeli Prime Minister Golda Meir, New York Governor Nelson Rockefeller, and Richard Parsons, executive director of AOL Time Warner. Without her support, it's doubtful that Giscombe would have taken us seriously. He was initially hesitant to grant a lease to a "hippy surfer" from California running a program with teens.

But the loft needed major renovations and wouldn't be ready until the end of April. Playing2Win wanted us out yesterday.

Fortunately, one of our volunteers, Nina Siegal, a *New York Times* reporter who now works in Amsterdam, stepped in to help. Nina was deeply invested in our mission, having taught journalism classes at HarlemLIVE and being inspired by the students.

> *The HarlemLIVE youth were incredibly motivated and always had great ideas. My job was just to steer them a little in this direction or that direction, but they were very creative and driven. It was one of my best life experiences to be a part of HarlemLIVE. —Nina Siegal*

Nina at one point left her position at the *New York Times* to join a newly formed general news team at the fledgling Bloomberg News and sent out a note to colleagues in search of a space for HarlemLIVE. To her surprise, her boss offered space in Bloomberg's headquarters, then on Park Avenue at 59th Street, until our loft was ready. Our residency at Bloomberg began just after Michael Bloomberg, who founded the company, became the mayor of New York City.

Once again, it was the women of HarlemLIVE who came to our rescue. Nina played a key role in securing a temporary space for us, while Djvonne David helped us get housed in ILT's lab, and Pat Nicholson and Glenna Ross became lifelong supporters. Teachers Oni Hutchinson, Monique Lee, Abiodun Harris, and many others were instrumental in their work with the youth. Board members Elaine Johnson and Dr. Grace Hughes guided me through the early years of HL. Cynthia Simmons generously contributed her time, resources, and insight for many years.

These and other phenomenal women made HarlemLIVE not only possible, but feasible. Their contributions and support will always be remembered and appreciated. While these phenomenal women were making strides in securing HarlemLIVE's future, our situation at Playing2Win was taking a turn for the dramatic.

Like the Cat in the Hat

We chose to keep mum about our wonderful new 2,400-square-foot space and Bloomberg's incredible offer to host us until the loft renovations were completed. We planned the move for a Saturday in mid-February and arranged for a rental van to transport our equipment and supplies to Bloomberg. The rest of our stuff would be put into storage until our move to 125th Street.

On a Tuesday, four days before HarlemLIVE's surprise departure, a meeting was held in one of the labs at Playing2Win. I was sitting near the entrance when Robert North, one of the directors of Boys Harbor, came to speak to me.

"Richard, have you guys made any progress on getting a new space? When are you moving?"

"Oh, I don't know, maybe late March," I said flippantly, knowing we were actually moving out that weekend. North grew somewhat agitated.

"We need to know if you're making progress. We've let you guys remain rent-free long enough."

"Okay, we're working on it," I said half-heartedly.

Perhaps my dismissive attitude was upsetting because two days later, we were handed a hefty eviction notice accompanied by nearly five hundred pages of supporting documents. The eviction was delivered both through mail and by hand to our office-closet, with additional copies sent to my apartment and the staff at ILT/Teachers College.

Playing2Win and Boys Harbor might have been bracing for us to be upset with histrionic behavior. Instead, we acted amused and delighted. The HL kids made copies of the front page of the eviction notice and circulated it among everyone at P2W. Arguably the most popular program at the center and the one touted in Boys Harbor's pitches to funders, HarlemLIVE was being evicted.

Management was puzzled.

Two days later, on Saturday morning, a few of us arrived early while classes were getting underway in the labs. Debbie, the receptionist, quickly realized what was happening and alerted the directors by phone. However, no one was available to come by, having been caught off guard by our unexpected move.

One of the directors phoned a program assistant, who rushed to P2W.

But like the mother arriving home to her panicked kids in Dr. Seuss's classic, as the assistant arrived, we—including Michael Popo, Katrina Vorotova, Elliot Price, Danya Steele, Jason Taylor, Charles Chavis, HL advisor Stan Ellzy, and myself—had just finished packing up our things and were out of there.

Just like *The Cat in the Hat.*

With our old space now a memory, we set our sights on an exciting new beginning. Eagerly anticipating the fresh start, we geared up for the unfolding chapter that awaited us on the 45th Floor of Bloomberg LLC.

* * *

Being welcomed into the corporate headquarters of the growing media conglomerate Bloomberg LLC was a fantastic and nurturing turn of events for HarlemLIVE. The high school teens, dressed in their street clothes—jeans, hoodies, and perhaps do-rags—were all given 24/7 security passes to the heavily guarded office building. For the next two months, they had residency on the forty-fifth floor, which allowed them to work and collaborate in a professional environment.

Nina's connections at Bloomberg proved to be invaluable, as she invited several experienced journalists from the Metro team to teach classes at HarlemLIVE. Among these professionals were Antonio Olivo (now a journalist at the *Washington Post*), Glenn Thrush (currently working at the *New York Times*), Maite Junco (now affiliated with the City University of New York), Liz Willen (currently serving as editor in chief of the *Hechinger Report*), and Patrick Cole (now working at Bloomberg). Additionally, students had the opportunity to learn from experts in radio and TV production at Bloomberg, further enhancing their education and skill set.

Our temporary residency at Bloomberg was a dream come true. We were granted access to a large classroom that was normally used to teach employees how to use the specialized software and computer systems for analyzing and trading in the financial markets. The space featured four tiers of long tables that rose toward the back, with floor-to-ceiling windows offering stunning views of the 59th Street Bridge leading to Queens and the elevated tramway to Roosevelt Island.

A small stage was situated in front of the room, complete with a giant whiteboard and a descending projection screen. Just outside our new classroom/office, we had the added bonus of a twenty-four-hour security guard as well as a kitchen stocked with all-you-can-eat snacks, drinks, and meals, including fresh fruits and veggies daily.

Our students quickly got to work, pushing aside the Bloomberg terminals to make room for our iMacs and iBooks. With the help of our techies, Michael Popo and Clifton Taylor, we worked with Bloomberg engineers to bypass some of their network security, which allowed us to continue uploading files and updating our website.

While the students were enthusiastically seizing the opportunities provided by Bloomberg, behind the scenes the need for balanced organizational leadership was becoming apparent.

Two People

During our eight-week residency at Bloomberg, my longtime friend Margot, a seasoned administrator who managed various branches of Shakespeare and Company bookstores in Manhattan and had previously visited my class in Bed-Stuy, stepped in to handle the day-to-day operations of HarlemLIVE. Her organizational skills were essential to the success of our program during this time, as I tended to shy away from administrative duties and focused more on programmatic aspects.

Unfortunately, finding a good administrative partner had always been a challenge for me and was one of my chief downfalls in running HarlemLIVE. The capable ones we found either left too soon or came on board too late in the life of the program. Cynthia Simmons, who later filled this gap for a few years, recognized the importance of having a strong administrative partner:

When you start an organization, you're really supposed to have two people: one who focuses on the program, the creative aspect—that was Rich—and one who manages the money, the nuts and bolts of administrative and budgetary aspects. Rich never had that second per-son. I think he didn't even know when he started the program that he needed it. He would have somebody who came in for a year or so and then leave. —*Cynthia Simmons, HL volunteer*

* * *

We left Harlem behind for a few weeks, venturing out to cover stories across the city and continuing our person-on-the-street interviews in the bustling streets of Midtown Manhattan. Our tech-savvy students were given the rare opportunity to learn from the best, as Bloomberg engineers took them under their wing to guide them through the intricacies of the company's large computer network. In fact, Bloomberg even went the extra mile by dis-patching trainers to teach our teens how to master the Bloomberg terminals in a specialized classroom.

After being cramped in a tiny closet for months and reeling from the aftermath of the 9/11 tragedy, things were finally beginning to look up for HarlemLIVE. Amid the chaos and setbacks, HarlemLIVE was finding its footing once again. The resilience of our crew made it clear that this was just the beginning.

Chapter 12

A CREATIVE SANCTUARY

As soon as I laid eyes on the raw loft space on 125th Street, I knew it was home. The wide, worn wood plank floors and six massive wooden pillars dividing the space in half exuded a rustic charm that was hard to resist. Despite the space needing a lot of work, I had no doubt we could make it spectacular.

To help us realize our vision, we hired Arturo, a licensed contractor who was recommended by someone my dad knew. Arturo installed an abundance of electrical outlets to accommodate all the tech we would be using, and he also hung long-necked incandescent light fixtures from the fourteen-foot old-fashioned pressed-tin ceilings. We refused to settle for the institutional fluorescent lighting that seemed to plague other spaces. In addition to these changes, we also covered the frayed and splintered original wood floors with wood tile and constructed a half wall in the back to provide privacy for the two bathrooms. The video team used this wall as a backdrop for a green screen, which allowed for digital effects to be added later.

Although we had hoped to incorporate healthy cooking and eating into our program at the new space, we encountered some obstacles. The kitchen was fully equipped, but it was never operable. We weren't able to get the gas approved, and we didn't have the funds to switch over to electricity, nor did we have enough money to pay the utility bills if we were to connect the stove and hot water heater. So, we made do with a microwave and hotplate to cook and heat water for mopping the spacious area. As much as we wanted to prioritize healthy eating, it would have to wait.

Fortune Smiles on HarlemLIVE

As we settled into our new loft in late April 2002, we faced the reality of having zero furniture. We were prepared to sit on the floor or milk crates until we found something better. As if by divine fortune, something came along that first week.

Our friends at AOL Time Warner reached out to us with an irresistible opportunity. They had a basement filled with fairly new office furniture that they needed to dispose of by the evening. We had to act fast. We rented a van and made several trips between 125th Street and their Midtown office.

The effort was well worth it. The furniture we acquired that day was enough to furnish the entire loft. We had eight two-person workstation tables, couches, area rugs, file cabinets, a glass-topped dining room table, a large wooden conference table, and even a podium that was perfect for our events. It was amazing how timing and good fortune seemed to be on our side.

Designating Specific Areas

With the addition of furniture, we were able to designate specific areas within our space. Upon entering, there was a sign-in desk equipped with pamphlets, event flyers, and occasionally flowers to greet visitors. The metal entrance door always slammed shut, loudly announcing the arrival or departure of anyone who entered or exited. Adjacent to the entrance, we created a small area to store bikes used for errands and stories. Centered between the front windows overlooking busy 125th Street was our lounge area: two couches and a rug nestled between large palms and several ferns.

Moving beyond the sign-in desk and to the right of the entrance, we created a library complete with chairs, another couch, and several wooden bookshelves. Nearly six-foot-tall white metal cabinets were used to separate the library from twelve workstations, including video editing and administrative areas. Opposite the entrance and toward the far wall, we placed our conference table with a ficus tree and decorative metal-and-cloth standing screens, which provided a sense of privacy for meetings and classes.

The rear of our space, with windows facing 126th Street, we designated the kitchen and dining areas. On days with favorable weather, we opened the windows in both the back and front to create a pleasant cross breeze. However, this sometimes resulted in the metal-and-cloth room dividers being blown down and slamming onto the wood tile floors, which made a loud gunshot sound. It startled us every time.

In the far back corner of the space, a door opened onto a large fire escape and led to the roof. The balcony-sized fire escape and roof were often used by students for photo shoots and hangouts.

We intentionally left the large area sandwiched between the conference table in front and the half wall concealing the bathrooms barren to provide ample space for meetings and events. For these occasions, we purchased folding chairs and stacked them against the wall with the podium when not in use.

On occasion, videographer Anthony Henry brought his skates and turned the open area into a one-person roller rink, adding a unique touch to our versatile space.

Bringing the Space to Life

The raw loft space on 125th Street truly came to life with the addition of the bright wood floors and oversized tropical plants that my resourceful dad had transported all the way from Florida. Their presence brought a sense of dramatic vibrancy to the space, making it feel alive and inviting. To add to the whimsy, we hung three disco mirror balls and spotlights in the meeting area and strung a hammock between two of the massive wooden pillars. We even adopted HL videographer Sean Van Bryan's pet iguana at one point.

Thanks to the hard work of Popo, Clifton, and other team members, we were able to get the space wired and online within just one day of moving in. It was a warm and welcoming environment, reminiscent of a one-room schoolhouse filled with endless creative toys and tools for interactive and multilevel learning, all in the heart of Harlem. The space was designed to celebrate and respect the youth who would be using it, and we were thrilled with the result.

I think young people should feel incredible about their surroundings. They should be in a place that is safe, comfortable, and fun. A place to feel valued and trusted. But make them responsible.

Instilling Responsibility and Ownership

To encourage accountability and a sense of ownership among our group, we implemented a chore board. This simple yet effective tool consisted of a sheet of paper on a clipboard with spaces to write names and corresponding duties.

The first person to arrive was designated as the monitor, and it was their responsibility to survey the space and create a list of assignments, such as emptying the trash, watering plants, cleaning the kitchen, and organizing workstations. As other students arrived, the monitor would assign them a task from the list.

If the first person was unable to perform monitoring duties or had to leave early, they would pass the responsibility to the next incoming student, and they would be assigned a task from the list like everyone else.

The monitor was also responsible for ensuring that everyone followed through with their assigned tasks. By taking on this role, they learned the importance of accountability and responsibility, which were crucial values in our youth-led organization.

Growth and Success at HarlemLIVE

HarlemLIVE was now well-equipped to thrive in its new and exciting home on 125th Street. During the inaugural Summer Media Challenge held at this location, Tameeka Mitchem, a former participant and editor in chief, was hired with a stipend to assist in running the program while on break between her sophomore and junior years of college.

In early November, we had a successful open house / housewarming party to show off the space. Local politicians, the founder of Black

Planet (a pioneering social networking site specifically tailored toward the African American community), the editor in chief of the *Amsterdam News*, and other notables from the tech world and the Harlem community attended.

Alumni and current staff regularly hosted visiting groups from around the country and abroad to explain how they produced their youth-led magazine. On Monday evenings, we hosted readings headed by Garland Thompson and the Frank Silvera Writers' Workshop. By the second year in the loft, we began having talent shows, lectures, poetry slams, and fundraisers.

Reuben Quansah, one of the new recruits for our first summer at 125th, remembers:

A friend of mine told me I should go to HarlemLIVE. I was a senior in high school and very busy, but I finally decided to go one day. I walked in, and it looked like a newsroom: there were kids literally working. I met Rich, and he told me I should come back around in the summertime when they did a competition, and I said I would check it out.

When I went back, Rich remembered me, and he said, "Oh, so you want to be part of this competition?" And I said, "Sure." And he replied, "Ok, in about five minutes you're going to have to give a speech about what you would do if you were to run a team." He just threw me into the deep end. I and two other people gave a speech, and then there was a vote. They liked my speech, and I ended up being editor in chief for one of the teams for the summer competition.

I'm from the Bronx, but I learned a lot about Harlem that summer. That's something you won't get in a classroom. It was really defining for me. I was learning, I was having fun, I was engaged, I was with people I enjoyed, and I was building with them as a young person.
—Reuben Quansah, program manager for NYC Men Teach

As Miriam Plotinsky says:

"When we surrender rigidity and learn to trust our kids, we realize how little control we had to begin with and how much talent we are brushing aside."[1]

Learning and Growing Through Challenges

With complete control over our space and the guidance of seasoned alumni like Michael Popo, Chris Frierson, Tameeka Mitchem, Melvin Johnson, Danya Steele, and others, we enjoyed the freedom to set our own hours. Our doors were often open around the clock in order to host gaming nights and marathon card games. Justin Young, after winning at Spades, would get up on the conference table and perform Pee-wee Herman's tequila dance, affectionately nicknamed "Justin's sexy dance" by the teens.

Though most of the youth ranged in age from fourteen to seventeen, some were as young as eleven, while others were in their early twenties. In 2003, an older participant from another youth media program who shot video at a poetry slam downtown took an interest in HarlemLIVE and began to frequent our space. After several weeks, he began bringing alcohol into the loft, and our youth noticed and took action.

A snippet from their AIM chat reveals the teens' responsibility and accountability:

DS:	"Did you know this new guy is bringing alcohol into the space?"
MW:	"What?! He needs to be suspended. We can't risk HL shutting down."

And so it went. They quashed bad behavior on their own. They were trusted and thus invested. They had ownership and protected the program, from the office where it happened to the stories they posted on the site.

---

1. Miriam Plotinsky, (@MirPloMCPS) "The Incredible Benefits of Letting Students Drive Their Own Learning," *Edsurge*, October 3, 2019, https://www.edsurge.com/news/2019-10-03-the-incredible-benefits-of-letting-students-drive-their-own-learning/

Embracing Big Opportunities

This sense of ownership resonated with the students, who learned to take risks and go big:

I became HarlemLIVE's editor in chief at 17 years old, overseeing a newsroom of 50+ teens reporting all over New York City.

While preparing for college, I noticed that many of my peers were not applying. Our newsroom was filled largely with inner-city youth who were often extremely gifted yet lacked backgrounds to prepare them for the futures they deserved. I responded by launching our organization's first-ever college tour because I thought, "What better way to get over the trepidation of applying to an elite university?" I called that initiative the Ivory Tower Project. I had no budget and a tiny team—two or three other kids and maybe one advisor. We needed a bus, but the quotes to rent it were ridiculously expensive. I also had to pay the driver, the hotel, and the meals. What to do? This was my plan:

#1: I successfully pitched and secured media placements across local radio and print to recruit tour applicants, in and outside our newsroom.

#2: Interest established, I asked our donors for help. Some donated, but progress was slow. $14K for the bus—the best quote I found—was still expensive. Pre-social media? I needed to think smart.

#3: A prime-time CNN producer had asked me to contact them sometime; they wanted to feature me. I felt shy about that but saw a strategic benefit to leveraging CNN to entice a bus company to sponsor us. CNN sent me a formal letter of interest. I told the bus company we'd happily mention them on-air as sponsors before millions: valuable publicity. My pitch worked. The bus company cut their price by 71%+. I returned to our donor base, saying we needed just "40 Angels" to donate $100. Within minutes, I got my funding; our tour was secured! We succeeded through clear communications strategy and creativity.

Rich created a space where experiences like that were even possible. As a 17-year-old, I was given free rein to create a project of value (so valuable that it was still impressive when I talked about it in a job interview I had as recently as 2022) and that helped me see myself as "able." Because, of course, if I can do that at age 17—what am I capable of now?

HarlemLIVE was a wildly creative, supportive space of virtually anything the teens could think of. That sense of "you can do anything you wish, and you are creative and smart enough to figure it out" has been a great character-development tool that has remained with me well after age 17. —Danya Steele

Blackout 2003: A Moment of Resilience and Unity

On August 14, 2003, a devastating power outage swept through the Northeastern and Midwestern regions of the United States. The root cause was traced back to a software bug in a company called FirstEnergy that caused overloads in transmissions, resulting in a widespread blackout that left millions without electricity.

True to their HarlemLIVE spirit, the students sprang into action immediately. With public transportation disrupted and the streets dark and dangerous without traffic lights, some students chose to stay in the office overnight. Others ventured out into the city to report on the situation. Here are some stories from that wild day and night:

One of my fondest memories of HarlemLIVE is the blackout. I was in KFC on 125th Street and 8th Ave., waiting for my meal, and boom. Everything went out at KFC. Then we heard beep, beep, beep, because the traffic lights were out, and cars were honking.

We had this beautiful 2,400-square-foot loft office that was home base for a long time. I ran up to the office, and everybody was kind of hanging out, thinking we just had a shortage or maybe the electricity bill was overdue, which wasn't strange to us, so they didn't react immediately. When I came upstairs, I told them, "It's a blackout. The streets are going crazy."

We made two teams really quick, one to cover the East Side and one the West Side. We went up and down on 125th Street with digital video pro cameras showing all the chaos and the stores shutting down. There were the longest lines to get items out of the corner grocery stores (bodegas). The beauty shop kept going. They moved their chairs to the sidewalk so they could still work on their clients. People were committed.

[That evening]... we went down to Times Square on bicycles. That was something about HarlemLIVE—we always kept bicycles available so you could go out on stories. A bunch of us rode down to 42nd Street and Times Square, and it was crazy. People were sitting on the streets, just hanging out. There were large crowds, and the vendors were making a killing: $10 for a frank, $12 for a pretzel. We scoured the area and got tons of footage of us doing interviews, getting people's reactions and their experiences.

History happens in journalism, and you're able to participate in it in a more in-depth way than just as a citizen. You learn more and learn how to navigate it and how to move people. HarlemLIVE taught us how to create a narrative and document all the details. *—Melvin Johnson*

☀ ☀ ☀

During the blackout of August 2003, I had to spend the night in the loft because I lived far and I couldn't go home. There were no trains running, and it was just crazy in the street. I was the only girl with a group of guys: AlAmir Jordan, who was a big guy like a teddy bear, one of my best friends, Shem, and Curtis Jackson, who worked on video. I felt protected because they were like my brothers; we were family. It would have been scarier having to go outside, so the fact that I was able to wait till the next day was great. It took three buses to get home the next morning, but I finally made it. —Aisha Al-Muslim

Chapter 13

THE STRUGGLE

Finding enough resources for computers, cameras, bike repairs, trips, food, and other expenses was always a challenge since the program was started on a whim without funding. Becoming a nonprofit organization was not on my radar when starting HarlemLIVE, but that's where we ended up. Thankfully, the ILT staff, community members, and countless adult volunteers were always willing to lend a helping hand when they saw the positive impact our program had on the children.

Becoming independent in our new loft was a challenging transition, as we were solely responsible for costs and overhead such as phone, electricity, Wi-Fi, rent, and equipment. While Pat Nicholson, my former colleague at ILT, generously provided us with financial resources to hire a development person to write grants, unfortunately the hired person was unable to secure any funding.

Show Me the Money

Despite our best efforts, grants and funding were hard to come by for HarlemLIVE. We relied heavily on our contacts to secure financial support. Through Nina Siegal's introduction to Bloomberg, we were granted patronage from 2004 to 2009, receiving $25,000 annually with a simple request for an annual activity report in return. The Bloomberg team also invited our youth to their annual holiday party for all the youth programs they funded.

In 2004, HarlemLIVE was anonymously nominated for a Union Square Award funded by the Tide (not the soap) Foundation, which awarded us two $25,000 grants, one in 2006 and one in 2008. We also got that same amount from Pat Nicholson of ILT. Pat and Cynthia Simmons were our two largest individual donors, but even alum Melvin Johnson came through once with $600 when we were having trouble paying the electric bill. Other than that, not a lot of funding came.

Sometimes the stress of scrounging to pay rent led me to make poor decisions. HL lost a couple of opportunities to have creative young adults who wanted to work in our loft and mentor our youth. However, since we needed to pay rent, I foolishly insisted that these groups contribute financially for the privilege of using the loft. They weren't able to do it, so HL teens missed those learning opportunities.

No Dress Code

When I stopped receiving a salary from ILT shortly after HarlemLIVE left Playing2Win in early 2002, I had to further reduce my personal expenses. Instead of wearing a collared shirt, I switched to a white T-shirt every day—a habit that has stuck with me ever since. I kept collared shirts and ties in a wardrobe at the back of the loft for special guests or events, but HarlemLIVE never had a dress code. I found dress codes to be mostly pretentious and uncomfortable, especially when riding bikes or casually writing stories.

However, I did wonder if not having a dress code was doing a disservice to the kids. Was I giving them the impression that they could wear jeans and a T-shirt to any office?

Interestingly, over the past couple of decades, offices have been moving away from strict dress codes. Dress-down Fridays were the first step, but as the world has evolved, especially post-pandemic, many workplaces have become more relaxed about what constitutes appropriate work attire, moving away from the traditional suit and tie. It seems that perhaps HarlemLIVE was ahead of the curve.

* * *

I was willing to run HarlemLIVE on a volunteer basis because it gave me the freedom to operate the program without any constraints. For the better part of a decade, we had a loosely formed board of directors that consisted of friends of the program rather than heavyweight fundraisers, which worked well for us. They trusted us to run the program as we saw fit and didn't interfere with our methods.

HarlemLIVE had established itself in the community, and we received several grants from local politicians ranging from $3,000 to $5,000. We used a portion of this funding to buy NYC's municipal liability insurance, which was necessary to secure our lease on 125th Street. When we were based in ILT or P2W spaces, we were covered by their liability insurance policies.

Once on our own, no private insurance would touch us. No paid staff? No sexual harassment training of this nonexistent staff? You send kids out every day? Without adults? ON BIKES?!!! Any insurance company would be like, "NO. NO. And HELL, NO!!!!"

If insurance in your state works as it does in NYC, consider getting funding from local politicians to be able to buy into the municipal liability insurance for a nominal percentage of your grant. Trying to get private insurance for liability involving a teen program could be problematic.

Wrap It Up

During the holiday season, we wrapped books for tips at a Barnes and Noble bookstore on East 86th, a tradition that continued for a few years. The event not only raised about $2,000 for HarlemLIVE but also provided a fun opportunity for our community of adult mentors and advisors to join in with the kids. It was a great way to build camaraderie among the group.

Moreover, the event gave the affluent Upper East Side community a chance to learn about HarlemLIVE and the important work we were doing. The youth had numerous opportunities to interact with interesting individuals, such as when Justin Young engaged in a conversation with Michael Eisner, then CEO of Disney. These encounters were valuable experiences that helped the participants develop their communication and networking skills. Justin wrote about the book-wrapping experience in an article posted on the site at the time (circa 2002):

After devoting an entire weekend to wrapping books, I gained a level of humility never before achieved by this lowly kid from the Bronx. I experienced the customers—their moods, quirks, and sometimes odd behavior. I experienced the customers' children—their screaming, playing, and mouth-gaping fascination with Scotch tape. But it was all taken with a grain of salt, and by the end of the day I could truly say that I enjoyed myself. I got the opportunity to mingle with new and interesting people, I experienced my first paper cut, and I did it all with a sense of meaning and purpose. —Justin Young

An Angel Appears

In 2002, the Clark Foundation sponsored a two-year partnership between Harlem and the Foundation Center. As part of this program, Development Consultant Michelle Hodges was assigned to HarlemLIVE to help us create a strategy to secure future support. The goal of the program was to build the capacity of selected small to midsize nonprofits.

After Michelle's time with us ended, she introduced us to Cynthia Simmons, who became our development volunteer. Initially, Cynthia wasn't enthusiastic about the idea, but she ended up leading several important projects for HarlemLIVE. She shared her reasons for her initial reluctance:

I thought the website was fabulous, but I was resistant because what I had seen with white directors of programs that catered primarily to minority youth did not make me happy. It took a while for me to set up an appointment. At the time, HarlemLIVE was in this fabulous loft space on 125th Street.

*When I got there, I saw kids coming in, going to a computer station, and doing whatever it was they were supposed to do. They were completely and totally **self-motivated**. And then Rich got there, and he was the most unassuming person. It was clear that HarlemLIVE was not a way for him to promote himself, so I started volunteering, going to the loft a few times a week for about two years, until I moved out of New York. I still helped sporadically. I interfaced a lot with Gisely, a high school student who was running the office like a pro. —Cynthia Simmons*

As we reveled in the success of Cynthia's winning us the Bloomberg grant, a new, unexpected challenge reared its head.

Eviction

Scores of selfless individuals offered their help to HarlemLIVE over the years. Without their help, we couldn't have done what we did. However, there were always some with ulterior motives, ranging from opportunistic behavior to more nefarious intentions.

It was 2004, and we were two years into our lease when we fell behind on rent. Thankfully, our first $25,000 Bloomberg grant came through just in time. We immediately informed Giscombe and Henderson, our property management company, of our intention to pay off our arrears. But they remained unresponsive to our calls, which left us feeling uneasy. Desperate to remedy the situation, I sent a $10,000 certified check to them, but still no reply.

Then in late April 2004, a call from Gisely Colon, our dedicated alumna and longest-serving administrator, shook me to the core.

"Rich, the doors have different padlocks, and there's an eviction notice on the door."

Evicted.

For a brief moment, a sense of relief washed over me. After all, the youth media program that I had impulsively started in 1996, which had ridden the wave of the internet's emergence, was now over. Despite my love for HarlemLIVE, the constant bureaucratic challenges and lack of financial stability had taken a significant toll on me, causing chronic stomach pain. It was a weight off my shoulders.

But then, in my mind, I could hear the resounding chorus of the kids saying "Not."

"I Want This Cleared Up!"

In hindsight, it all seemed like a calculated move by the property management firm, one that almost cost HarlemLIVE everything. They sent eviction notices, disguised under the innocuous "ABC Corporation," to our address, but we never saw them. The notices were delivered by hand or mail, but every time someone tried to deliver them, the guy running the hat-and-T-shirt business on the ground floor, Al, claimed no such corporation existed. The management firm was covered legally, but it was clear they didn't want us to receive these notices.

It wasn't until the doors were padlocked shut and an eviction notice was taped on our door that we realized what was going on.

With our base of operations shut down, we had to scramble to maintain some semblance of normalcy. I walked Gisely, a junior in high school, and web editor, Ashley Covington, over to Teachers College and ILT's third-floor offices to set up shop. Robbie McClintock and others weren't happy about us crashing their offices, but I assured them it was just for a few days.

I made a desperate call to our board chair, Robin Bell-Stevens, who, like her friend and HL board member Evelyn Cunningham, knew Eugene Giscombe, the head of the management company. Giscombe told Robin not to worry—we could work something out. He instructed Robin to tell me NOT to show up to court on Friday, as we were instructed to do in the eviction notice taped to our door. This was the FINAL court hearing dealing with our eviction since we were no-shows the previous times, but we didn't know this.

However, two days before the court date, I bumped into Mark, who ran the music studio two floors above us and had his own battles with the landlord. He urged me to ignore Giscombe's offer to work things out and to make sure I attended the hearing.

Perplexed but more willing to trust Mark, whose son, Allan Marshall, participated in HL, I showed up at the courthouse on Friday as instructed. Always wanting to expose the youth to all aspects of running the organization, I took alum Shem Rajoon and a good friend who was visiting from Florida.

It was late Friday morning. The judge stated that we needed legal counsel, so she couldn't pass judgment. She set a new hearing for the following Wednesday at 9:30 a.m.

I asked if it was okay to gain access so some of the students could get their books and portfolio materials they needed for college interviews.

"I can do that," replied the judge. "When do you want access? Monday?"

"Can we go today?"

The judge allowed us to go at 4 p.m. that Friday afternoon. I asked if we could also water our plants.

"By all means. Water your plants, get the kids' books and anything else you need."

As the judge handled a folder with our paperwork, a HarlemLIVE flyer slipped out. She took a moment to read about the program and its amazing youth.

The judge extended her arm toward me while holding the flyer and asked, "Is this the program?"

I nodded.

The judge then pointed her extended arm to the management lawyer.

"Have you seen this?"

The lawyer answered nervously, "Oh, I don't really know who they are." He took the flyer, glanced at it, and handed it back to the judge.

"Yeah, it looks like a good program." He seemed anxious to leave.

The judge replied vehemently, "I want this cleared up!"

Outside the courtroom, the lawyer for management took me aside and confided that if we hadn't shown up, we would have lost everything. The space, our belongings, the equipment... EVERYTHING.

* * *

I found and paid a lawyer $300 to represent us in court the following Wednesday. I explained to the judge that we had fallen behind on the rent, which we tried to pay after we received the Bloomberg grant, but that Giscombe's office had been unresponsive. I showed the judge a copy of the $10,000 certified check we had mailed—demonstrating a good faith effort—and documentation that Giscombe had cashed it.

The judge was having none of Giscombe's shenanigans. Her decisive intervention gave us an unexpected reprieve from Giscombe's obstructive actions. She ordered us to come to an agreement for repaying the arrears and demanded we be readmitted to our loft immediately so HarlemLIVE could continue operations.

We would survive and continue to thrive in our wonderful loft in the heart of Harlem.

Chapter 14

REBOOT

Coming back from the brink of demise breathed new life into us. In May of 2004, alumni Melvin, Justin, Danya, Shem, Enita Okodiko, and others visited high schools throughout the city to recruit for our Summer Media Challenge. We were thrilled with the response to our recruitment drive. Dozens of students came in for interviews, eager to be a part of our program. We declared June Newbie Month, with Gisely Colon doing a bang-up job of scheduling a wealth of classes taught by alumni and outside professionals.

We welcomed a diverse group of talented and passionate youth that summer. Tracey Casseus went on to create a health section for the online magazine. Brad Harbans, who attended the renowned Bronx High School of Science, became our main techie for many years (he now runs tech for all of City College). Johnny Alarcón, a passionate member of HL for several years, was crucial later when we fought City Hall and is now a head techie at Baruch College in Manhattan.

Mera Beckford started as a reporter and writer before taking on administrative duties and becoming office manager. Kevin Benoit, sixteen, who was named editor in chief after leading the winning team that summer, began publishing his own magazine, *Parlé*, at the same time and is still publishing it today.

These incredible youth gave me the strength and the inspiration to soldier on.

* * *

Three weeks into June, aka Newbie Month, an older Trinidadian couple came to the loft with their young teenage daughter, Lea. It was Brad Harbans's mom, dad, and younger sister. They entered the loft and looked around, perplexed, curious, and somewhat in awe.

"We had to see where Brad was," Brad's mom said.

For years, Brad came home after school and sequestered himself in his room. Now he was at HL for hours and hours every day.

His sister, Lea, signed up.

The magnetism of the HL program and this dramatic space was demonstrated later that year, in mid-November. A heavy snowstorm took officials by surprise, and schools were officially still open. A little before noon, an administrative monitor for some of our school interns appeared in the loft. Her jaw nearly hit the floor.

"Oh, my," she said. "Your interns are here!"

At every one of the other internship sites, all the teens stayed home that snowy day.

Expanding the Content

Not only did we get more youth, but the breadth of the program also expanded.

Mara Rose paid us a visit with some colleagues who introduced the kids to **blogging**. Blog posts became a regular and important feature of the program as another outlet for youth expression as well as to help the organizers determine the progress of both individuals and teams.

During the summer challenges, team members took turns blogging daily. We had individual and team awards for the best blog posts. Many of the posts from those summers are still online. HL admin students and I also had a general blog where we posted announcements and addressed the teams collectively throughout the summer instead of calling meetings.

We also started some **podcasts**, but those never became regular. However, several alumni, like Catalino Rodriguez, currently host their own podcasts.

Video production increased substantially in the following years after alum Neruda Williams encouraged us to take advantage of the free studios, training, and equipment available through the Manhattan Neighborhood Network, a community-based nonprofit that operates cutting-edge media production and education facilities.

Editor in Chief Kevin Benoit took the lead in organizing several **poetry slams** as well as fashion and talent shows at both HL's loft and other venues. He was able to secure food, prizes, judges, and clothing from top designers for these events.

Pivoting from Kevin's dynamic engagement with creative events, another crucial contributor at HarlemLIVE was adult mentor Cynthia Simmons. Her approach centered on innovative projects and institutional development, which added a new dimension to the organization's resurgence.

The first was HL Designs, a venture led by three of HarlemLIVE's more experienced members: Shem, Justin, and Melvin. This initiative allowed them to engage with the community, take on web design projects, and learn firsthand the dynamics of running a business.

The second project formalized the organization's path to college. Aware of HarlemLIVE's impressive success rate with its members going on to higher education, Cynthia saw the value in making this a more structured part of the program. Each student planning to apply to college was paired with a volunteer mentor who assisted them with their applications.

Simmons also leveraged her grant-writing skills to secure funding for HarlemLIVE. Small grants, mostly from local politicians, kept the program afloat. However, Cynthia was also forward-thinking and ambitious—she aimed to secure more substantial funding through a capacity-building grant. She understood that demonstrating fiscal responsibility on a larger scale would be a significant asset to HarlemLIVE's credibility and sustainability.

Global Connections

In three consecutive years, from 2003 to 2005, Project Harmony invited four HarlemLIVE youth to Vermont as technology ambassadors for young participants from former Soviet Union countries. The program, called the Future Leaders Exchange (FLEX) Program, was funded by the US State Department and took place in Burlington, Vermont.

Each HL student stayed with a different host family and led workshops to train the exchange students so they could create a web magazine upon their return to their home countries.

Project Harmony program manager Abigail Marks praised the HL youth, stating, "They made significant contributions to our workshop and inspired many of our participants. They conducted themselves with incredible professionalism."

Darya Zolotova, a participant from Russia, remarked, "HarlemLIVE broadened my perspective of the world. The teens achieved so much."

In his reflections on the trip to Vermont, HL student Eddie Aung shared his experience using AIM:

> ***tausilon:*** *my host family was really great*
> ***tausilon:*** *so kind*
> ***tausilon:*** *their house is like 4 times bigger than hl*
> ***tausilon:*** *we had a great time watching movies and talking with ppl*
> ***tausilon:*** *we learned new dances, diff cultures*
> ***tausilon:*** *the trip was a life changing experience*
> ***tausilon:*** *we gave inspiration to the students*
> ***tausilon:*** *we were like celebrities*
> ***tausilon:*** *i feel so great right now*
> ***tausilon:*** *the cool thing is that all the students are top students back in their country*

Some Chaperone

Shem Rajoon, a seventeen-year-old alum, served as a chaperone when we sent the first group of teens in the spring of 2003. He repeated this role in 2004 and 2005, but each time with a different twist. Shem had a fear of flying, as he and his younger sister, Valene (also an HL alum), experienced a harrowing flight with lots of turbulence when they immigrated to the U.S. from their native Trinidad to join their mom in New York. So the first year, Shem took a bus while the teens flew.

Some chaperone!

The second year, Shem successfully convinced the new trio of students to go with him on the bus. It was just a domestic flight, but it turns out Shem was also fearful of flying because he was unsure of his legal status to remain in the US.

When the last year of the three-year program approached, Shem came to me:

"Rich, I want to do Project Harmony again."

"Then this time you will have to fly."

Shem finally flew and overcame his childhood trauma.

A Good Vibe

In addition to more youth and expanded content, we had more adult volunteers as well. Nina Siegal organized over a dozen professionals who began making their way uptown on a regular basis, schooling the teens on finding sources, interviewing techniques, writing leads, and mentoring the teens one-on-one with their stories.

Raqiyah Mays, a radio personality on popular FM hip-hop station Hot 97, taught journalism, video production, web design, and public speaking. Columbia's journalism school sent mentors from their graduate journalism school and would sometimes have youth shadow them on their stories.

Raqiyah remembers:

I became an advisor and a mentor at HarlemLIVE, teaching journalism classes, specifically how to interview: how to prepare, how to break the ice, how to dress, how to ask the hard questions, how to be a woman in this business. In a word, how to be professional so they could be taken seriously and get the best answers.

Since I had started in the hip hop business, the kids always wanted to know how to approach artists, so I would give them advice on who to call, what to say, and I told them they had to follow up with an email. Follow-up is everything because in this business, you really have to hunt people down.

Sometimes they could approach artists at a public event, so I gave them advice on what to say, for example: "Hi, I'm such and such from

HarlemLIVE, I'm 14 years old, we have a paper, and we'd love to interview you."

I was impressed that the kids were interviewing community officials and community advocates because it's not an easy interview at all. When you talk to those types of people, the higher they are up the ladder, the harder they can be at times to talk to unless you find somebody that sees themselves in you.

The kids at HarlemLIVE really wanted to learn. I loved their energy, their vibe. It was a voracious, really smart group of youth that asked a lot of questions and wanted to do something positive for the community by sharing its stories. I loved that.

Their office was always busy and loud. There was music playing, there were kids in one corner tinkering on a computer, or somebody tinkering with the camera, others just over here talking, or some sitting in the front row of a class to get the information and knowledge that they needed. It was a vibrant atmosphere.

HarlemLIVE produced kids that went to Cornell and other great colleges and did really amazing things. These are kids who are now creating TV shows in L.A., who are CEOs and founders of their own businesses and have their own websites, who are getting sponsorships and thriving.

They are visionaries. —Raqiyah Mays

The Phillips Effect: Elevating HarlemLIVE

In late 2005, a new member joined HarlemLIVE's board: David Phillips, the executive director of the Elie Wiesel Foundation, who would become its chair in 2007. David had an impressive stature and a global perspective, having worked with or for nations across the globe. His name carried weight, his connections were substantial, and his leadership style was magnetic, which made him an appealing figure to our contacts at Bloomberg.

At first, I had reservations about placing the organization advocating for people of color in the hands of a white male. However, after years of striving, this shift felt like an opportunity for a breakthrough.

David initiated a speaker series that proved to be a standout feature of his tenure, drawing notable journalists, educators, and leaders to address HarlemLIVE students every couple of months. We even had the privilege of a visit from Marion Wiesel, Elie's wife.

In 2007, the Elie Wiesel Foundation honored Oprah Winfrey at the Waldorf Astoria. David ensured that we were part of that event, securing over a dozen tickets for HarlemLIVE. Our table was far from Oprah's, but the kids were allowed to mingle closer during intermissions. The youth were thrilled to have the opportunity to meet Sidney Poitier, Barbara Walters, and other luminaries. The buzz in the office the next day was palpable as Kareem called everyone he knew to share the news about "our dinner with Oprah."

Under David's leadership, the board expanded with members adept at securing the funding HarlemLIVE needed. Unfortunately, the newfound stability lasted only until the onset of the Great Recession in late 2008. However, thanks to the aid of Cynthia Simmons and David's resourcefulness, we managed to secure a two-year grant from the Ford Foundation just before the financial crisis hit.

Unforgettable Experiences

The opportunities and exposure awarded to the youth just kept coming.

One night the students got to interview former President Bill Clinton. On another story, Democratic strategist Donna Brazile was signing her book *Cooking with Grease* at Barnes and Noble. Brazile was so taken by the questions and conduct of reporters Maya Williams and Ty Carlton that she arranged for them plus HL reporter Janelle Jemmott and adult mentor Kody Emmanuel, a journalist from Haiti, to attend the 2004 National Democratic Convention. There, they hobnobbed with all the bigwigs, including Illinois senator and future president Barack Obama.

Janelle Jemmott remembers:

As a teenager, having the experience of attending the 2004 Democratic National Convention was a memorable one. I was surrounded by politicians and musicians and entertainers whose work and career

I followed and admired. I was able to interview Rev. Al Sharpton, Atlanta Mayor Shirley Franklin, and BET and NBC news anchor Jacque Reid.

We also got to meet Illinois US Senator Barack Obama. But more special than being in the room was having the privilege to interview them and, on one occasion, even break bread with them. However, there was one moment that left an indelible impact on my outlook.

I remember vividly riding the escalator and seeing rapper and activist Andre 3000 and the way I went into a frenzy to be so close to one of my favorite artists. After coaching from Kody and Maya, I went over to one of the booths in the venue hall and asked for an interview. To my disappointment, his bodyguard abruptly turned me away and said he was not giving any interviews.

I was a bit disappointed but was determined to try again after the BET reporter told me I wouldn't get the interview because all of the major news outlets were waiting for the same thing. I took it as a challenge, and I mustered up all the power and Outkast lyrics in my body and made sure he knew I was there for an interview—and then I got the personal invitation from Andre 3000 to ask my questions.

This singular moment impressed on me that people will sometimes think less of me for whatever reason—my age, gender, race, affiliation, etc.—which is fine. However, I can either internalize it and let their words discourage me, or I can internalize it and let them empower me. In that moment, I chose to let my gifts answer for me, and it is something I have done repeatedly over the years.

I will always cherish my time at HarlemLIVE—the opportunities and the life lessons it offered me. I am so grateful for the role it had in my life. —Janelle Jemmott

Diverse Encounters

Other students share stories about how they were able to access opportunities they may not have otherwise encountered:

I got to meet Ossie Davis and Maya Angelou. I interviewed Jay-Z. We interviewed Tara Phillips of the NY WNBA Lady Liberty team. I got tickets to the game. Through HarlemLIVE, I got connected to internship opportunities working at different financial institutions while I was in college. I can't talk highly enough about HarlemLIVE and its impact in my life. —Reuben Quansah

* * *

There are few opportunities at the high school level that allow students to be placed outside their regularly scheduled programs. A normal day in the life of an inner-city teen would consist of waking up, going to school, maybe playing for a school team or being involved in a chess club. Then they'd go home and have dinner. A day in the life of a HarlemLIVE staff writer would consist of all the things I mentioned plus gearing up to cover a protest against police shootings or covering the New York City mayoral race. HarlemLIVE did an incredible job of placing you in scenarios you otherwise wouldn't encounter without their support for your curiosity. —Guyan Wilks

* * *

Rich said, "I'm going to keep the lights on and create an experiential learning environment for you all; you will brainstorm ideas, and write stories, and work on your public speaking..." He created opportunities and instilled in us this philosophy of "figuring it out" when we ran into an obstacle. Once I was trying to get a photo of former mayor Dinkins, and I couldn't reach him because he was surrounded by photographers. At one point he had to get something from his trunk; when he opened it, I jumped into it and took the photo. That resourcefulness was very restorative. —Shem Rajoon

I Got This

One night in September 2005, Angel Colon passed by HL headquarters on 125th and called me while I was in California visiting my dying father. "Hey, Rich. What's happening at HL?"

"Oh, I think there's a poetry slam there tonight," I said.

"Half the block is cordoned off by the cops, there's doormen and security downstairs and a long line out the door."

While I don't recall my response to Angel, I do remember feeling a sense of pride that we had never experienced any incidents requiring police or hospital visits despite the various activities and events our youth engaged in.

It felt as though we had a guardian angel watching over us.

It turns out Editor in Chief Kevin Benoit had notified the police beforehand, as he expected high attendance. Community Affairs, a division of the police department, worked with Kevin to set up barricades and increase patrol. They agreed not to enter our building unless requested.

Kevin had a mantra: "I got this."

We've grown so cautious in this litigious society, we're fearful of doing those things that are perhaps most growth-inducing and powerful, and instead we produce mediocrity. HL was not fearful and produced excellence.

---

* * *

As HarlemLIVE approached its milestone tenth anniversary, we were cruising smoothly until City Hall threatened to put a stop to us. But due to the fiery determination of our youth, they weren't going to let that happen without a fight.

HarlemLIVE on the set of ABC TV's LIve with Regis and Kelly

Chapter 15

FIGHTING CITY HALL

Two weeks into our annual Media Challenge in July 2006, the city declared HarlemLIVE to be an unsafe working environment for students participating in their Summer Youth Employment Program (SYEP). This was HL's eighth year participating in SYEP, which added about two dozen paid teens to our regular year-round volunteer students.

The city's order meant our newly minted and trained reporters, web designers, techies, and public speakers would have to quit HarlemLIVE and be reassigned to other work sites, which would put a halt to production of our world-renowned youth magazine.

* * *

Weeks earlier, a gravel-voiced city bureaucrat had come for an inspection visit. She noticed some cracked plaster in the stairwell leading up to our third-floor loft. Her report made it sound as though the building was about to collapse. It wasn't. Regardless, we were warned to get it fixed, or else.

This was the "or else."

This blow from the city couldn't have come at a worse time. It was HarlemLIVE's tenth anniversary. The culminating ceremony for our annual Summer Youth Media Challenge was to be held on the set of ABC Television's *Live with Regis and Kelly*. Winners would be revealed, prizes given out, new editors announced, and all participating teens would receive their drum necklace for making it through the demanding seven-week contest. It now seemed HL's tenth anniversary would be a huge disappointment.

* * *

During that summer, we recruited eighteen-year-old Kamal Muhammad, younger brother of alumnus Khalid, to manage the newsroom. Kamal successfully consulted with team members, managed city agencies, handled paperwork, and resolved team disputes, among other responsibilities. While I taught classes, mentored students going on stories, and did what it took to make ends meet, Kamal took care of everything else. However, Kamal's new role would soon be put to the test.

In response to the city's report, which deemed our building unsafe due to the cracked plaster and a slightly loose doorknob, Kamal persistently urged the building's management, Giscombe/Henderson, to carry out the necessary repairs. However, our relationship with them had been tense ever since we successfully thwarted their attempt to evict us two years prior.

Finally, management sent workers to repair the plaster but were instructed to fix only up to the second-floor nail salon. The Spanish-speaking workers told HL web designer Johnny Alarcón that Giscombe instructed them NOT to fix the part of the hall leading to HarlemLIVE's office. When we tried to have our own contractors fix the plaster, management threatened to nullify our lease.

On a Wednesday in mid-July, Johnny confronted an official from the Department of Youth and Cultural Development (DYCD) during his visit, explaining that relocating SYEP students would disrupt their progress. "The stakes are high," he contended. "Relocating us means we lose four crucial days of work, and all the parents have been informed about the situation."

Taken aback, the official questioned, "Your parents were okay with that?" He demanded, "Who else's parents were okay with that? I want this on tape!"

In response, one of the youth gestured toward a fellow student, diligently recording the confrontation with a digital camera. "It's already on tape, sir. Everything is being recorded."

The youth were then quick to inform the official that they hadn't received any communication about this issue from the agencies. The official seemed to be caught off guard by this revelation, as indicated by a big "Wow!"

"We don't want to be relocated to a site where our only job is to monitor children at play. There's no other place like HarlemLIVE," a female reporter asserted.

Her peers echoed her sentiment, noting they had been uninformed until Kamal had taken the initiative to draft and send a letter to their parents. The letter had garnered unanimous support from the parents, who expressed their preference for their children to remain at HarlemLIVE.

Kamal highlighted the evident dissonance within the SYEP. On one hand, officials were warning him that HarlemLIVE was on the verge of being considered unviable; on the other hand, he was getting inquiries asking if they could accommodate more students.

The official ordered all the students to report to their respective administrating agencies for SYEP the next morning. Kamal then received phone calls from these agencies reinforcing the directive. Strikingly, no written communication—no official letters or faxes—was received by Kamal or any of the students.

* * *

The kids were livid. Shem and other alumni converged in the meeting area with the summer teens, who refused to respect the city's order to quit HarlemLIVE. They wanted to fight the decision. For nearly two hours, they contemplated what to do before finally deciding to storm the offices of the DYCD the next day. The department was a few blocks from City Hall in downtown Manhattan.

Caught up in their enthusiasm, I agreed to go with them to "storm City Hall." I immediately told Kamal to contact the *Amsterdam News*, a local Harlem publication with offices just around the corner. They promptly dispatched a reporter, which ensured that the story would break in the next morning's weekly issue, even before we set foot downtown. Concurrently, Aisha reached out to Chris Glorioso, a mentor and TV reporter, about the situation. He took the initiative to contact both the building management and city authorities.

* * *

By morning, I was despondent. After further consideration, I realized how pointless and ridiculous this was. We'd never get past security! I couldn't decide if I would actually go. Shem Rajoon, then twenty-one, talked to me in the back of the loft. "Rich, you gotta go!"

Shem recalls:

> I remember when we had to defend HarlemLIVE when DYCD was trying to shut the doors on us. I had a lot of struggles to confront in my life, and those moments were like, "Do I want to go back to the street, or do I want to take a stand and fight for something I believe in?" I decided that I loved this place and I was going to rally up team members and rally up the staff. To help us get through security at DYCD, I'd use theater, act as if we were a classroom visiting the place.
>
> You are the Department of Youth and Community Development, and you want to close a youth community program? They weren't seeing that, because they were into "the politics of helping" our community as opposed to actually helping our community. —Shem Rajoon

* * *

I checked the freestanding cabinet, pondering what attire would be suitable for storming the offices of a city agency. While we waited for everyone to gather, Kamal and a couple of reporters ventured with cameras to confront the staff at Giscombe in their offices on the east side of 125th. Once they returned, we were ready.

With seventeen of the teenage reporters, photographers, web designers, administrators, and graphic artists assembled, along with three of HarlemLIVE's most dedicated alums, we descended the three flights and walked one block over to St. Nicholas Avenue to catch the A train downtown.

The mood was somber. Uncertainty hung in the air.

Once out of the Wall Street subway station, I led the twenty youth through the narrow streets of Lower Manhattan to an administrative office building a few blocks away. We entered the building and proceeded toward the back, where we had to sign in.

The security guards instructed me to just sign once for the entire group.

I was dumbfounded. (Years later I realized that they probably thought we were a school group, not a mob there to protest the city's actions.)

We packed two large elevators to the fourth floor and to the DYCD's glass-enclosed reception area. The receptionist nervously made phone calls informing her superiors that a mob of determined teens was in their lobby.

Several minutes later, a woman—the deputy commissioner of DYCD, who was dressed in a gray vest, white blouse, and low heels, and was flanked by three taller staff members—pushed through the lobby's double glass doors.

"Who's in charge here?"

The deputy commissioner was clutching a copy of that morning's *Amsterdam News*, which had broken the story that her agency was trying to end our summer program.

I raised my hand, the only middle aged person among the group of young Latino and African American youth.

"Come with me." The deputy commissioner turned and motioned for her staff and me to follow down a long, narrow hallway leading to various nondescript offices. She poked her head into one, where a woman sat behind a desk with a huge mound of papers and files.

"I need this office," barked the commissioner.

The woman's eyes widened upon seeing the agency's second-in-command. She tossed papers around before scurrying out of the office and running nervously down the hall.

The deputy commissioner led me in with her people. She slammed the door. Without saying a word, she glared into my eyes while walking slowly toward me like a cat stalking its prey.

When she was within inches of my nose, she said, "How daaaaaare you! Who do you think you are bringing these teens to disrupt my staff and offices unannounced?"

Her words hung in the air, tension thickening around us. From past experiences, I knew when dealing with cops and school principals that it's best to let people in positions of authority have their say, agree, and speak as little as possible.

"We never heard of HarlemLIVE until this morning," added one of her assistants.

I briefly argued that the city was overreacting and urged them to speak to one of the students about the program's impact.

"Fine! Bring me one."

The deputy commissioner put the newspaper down on the desk as I turned and headed out of the office. I knew I'd bring back one of HL's three star alumni—Shem, Aisha, or Kamal—but which one?

"Actually..." said the deputy commissioner.

I turned toward her at the doorway.

"Bring me three!"

Yes! I did an invisible fist pump in my head. I knew I had a winning hand.

The deputy and her staff waited as I went to get Aisha, Shem, and Kamal. Within minutes of speaking with the DYCD officials, they won the government officials' hearts with their impassioned defense of the program and their engaging, professional manner.

Meanwhile, as we made our case in the office, other DYCD officials had escorted the remaining teens to a conference room on the third floor. There, the teens faced a barrage of questions. Undeterred, they passionately defended their participation in the program, pleading for its continuation.

"We're interviewing the mayor, interviewing CEOs, learning web design and video editing, while our friends in other Summer Youth Employment jobs are picking up garbage in parks, supervising young kids at play, filing papers, or just sitting idle."

The deputy commissioner guided me, the three alums, and her colleagues to the conference room. After the officials had finished questioning the teens, they gathered for a brief discussion before addressing us.

"We're going to come tomorrow to see your space," they announced.

Whereas the mood coming downtown was somber, going back it was jubilant. Filled with a sense of joyous vindication, the kids made music and danced on the subway. We felt victorious, the atmosphere festive. Yet despite our triumph, we knew our work wasn't over.

* * *

"Emergencia, emergencia!" I left frantic messages with Arturo, the Dominican contractor who had renovated the raw loft space several years earlier. We needed him to come fix anything that DYCD might feel was a bit off.

The youth and I figuratively took the place apart and put it back together, making sure it was spotless and up to snuff. The doorknob leading into the space was a little loose; Arturo tightened it. The wood tiles under the twelve-foot tropical plants were warped from water spills. HL videographer Troy Robateau, who knew something about woodwork, fixed them. Others mopped, organized the work areas, cleaned the bathrooms, and straightened the library.

At the same time, the building management, shamed by the reports in the local news outlets and contacted by DYCD, finally sent workers to repair the exposed brick and broken plaster on the walls leading to the third floor. Their refusal to fix this earlier had instigated the entire crisis.

* * *

By the next morning, the kids who had boldly defied the city's edict trickled in. They had chosen to risk their pay, courageously preferring to disobey rather than be reassigned to other workplaces. As the morning wore on, the tension built up in anticipation of the deputy commissioner's visit.

At about 10:30 AM, the deputy commissioner showed up with about eight staff and some lawyers and began looking around while students showed off some of their work and the large loft space. Twenty minutes later, I overheard one staffer say to the deputy commissioner, "It looks good to me."

Before they left, they once more admonished me for the previous day's disruption and promised to make a decision soon.

A couple of hours later, a fax was sent to all the administrative offices. HarlemLIVE was deemed safe, and the students could return as part of the Summer Youth Employment Program. Our Media Challenge could continue and, in less than a month, they'd be on the set of ABC Television's *Live with Regis and Kelly*, speaking about the iconic moment in the life of HarlemLIVE when they used their power and their voices to fight City Hall.

And they won!

Nana Poku helps with sprucing up our drab surroundings

Chapter 16

THERE'LL BE OTHERS

The tumultuous events of summer 2006 were far from over. After our confrontation with City Hall, we faced a new challenge. Our five-year tenancy at the loft was drawing to a close, and the property owners intended to raze it to make way for new development.

Board member Paul Dunn stepped in and connected us with Urban Home Ownership Corporation, a nonprofit that provided housing to families in need. They offered a small community center space in the basement of a building not far from our headquarters. While it was a much less appealing space than our beloved loft, we knew we could make it our own.

Plus, it was (conditionally) free!

Although it was hard to say goodbye to our amazing space, moving to the new location was the right decision. With the money saved on rent, we were able to hire alums Gisely and Melvin to run the program, paying salaries for the first time ever.

* * *

Our new spot was on a quiet residential block filled mostly with brownstones. Yet, our new base was in a bit of a different setting, housed in a larger, twelve-unit prewar building. We had churches situated to the east and the west of us and a community garden down the block.

To access our space, we had to enter through a locked black mesh metal gate on the far left side of the building. The gate had an overhanging metal plate by the lock that, if you weren't careful, could cost you a finger or two, or at least require a Band-Aid or three. Once through the gate, you turned to the right and went down metal stairs. From there, a concrete walkway wrapped around the perimeter of the building. Our basement entrance was in the back.

A participant from the city's summer youth employment program wrote this blog about her first day:

> *My first day at HarlemLIVE was really not what I would have expected. I came to Harlem thinking I was going to a large skyscraper-like building, to be surrounded by businessmen. Instead, I found myself going down the stairs to a basement-like facility. The first thing going through my mind was, "I hope I don't get murdered." Then, as I walked down the steel staircase and down the enclosed stone corridor that seemed like an escape passage, I saw the light. Literally, I saw the light of the sun since the corridor led me to a backyard.*
>
> *As the old saying goes, "Don't judge a book by its cover," it goes perfectly with my first impression. I didn't think much could come from such a creepy place when in reality there was a warm embrace awaiting me. I was attacked by normalcy which in turn made me loosen up. I was prepared to be interrogated and dismissed by men in suits. I was astonished when I saw people in casual clothing (and not suits), and I indeed felt overdressed.*
>
> *The day itself was filled with fun and games which were designed to get us all to know one another. This was a shock seeing as it's not what I expected. I also was lucky enough to meet some new people and make friends that were just like me in some ways. I like surprises, and the surprises that I encountered on my first day at HarlemLIVE have motivated me to be myself and feel welcomed in a home-like facility. I can't wait to see what's in store next.*

* * *

Our small office took up just a fraction of the space of our old 125th Street loft, divided into a workspace and administrative area, with an adjacent video editing room, half bathroom, and a full kitchen with a tiny dining area. We transported vital items, including podium, computers, cameras, books, files, a few plants, cabinets, and the dining room table to our new location, leaving behind unused appliances and fixtures for our contractor, Arturo, to keep. Excess items went to storage.

Arturo was a dependable ally, invaluable during our move and the re-design of our new basement office. Its harsh lime green walls and blinding fluorescent lights were soon replaced by Google logo-inspired hues and softer track lighting everywhere but the kitchen and bathroom. We relocated our ficus tree and a vine plant, though the sun-starved basement would soon kill the ficus.

A silver lining was our new functional kitchen, which enabled prepara-tion of fresh meals by both students and adults, launching a healthy eating initiative years before Michelle Obama's efforts.

Healthy Eating with Chef Cocoa

Kareem Smith, now an ordained priest, had been with the program a couple of years, serving as a reporter and PR person. Kareem had learned to cook from his catering mom, so we hired him to enhance the healthy eating and cooking aspect of the Summer Media Challenge.

We nicknamed Kareem "Chef Cocoa." As part of the summer chal-lenge, each week teams would assign one or more different team members to help Kareem in the kitchen. They provided healthy snacks and meals for the youth and staff. Sodas weren't allowed on the premises. We made fresh lemonade and had a filtered water dispenser.

Incorporating meal preparation and the promotion of healthy eating habits should be fundamental to all educational experiences involving young people. Health forms the bedrock of every other aspect of life, and indi-viduals are often swayed by marketing strategies that promote unhealthy choices.

* * *

For the majority of 2007, as I pursued tech classes and side work, HarlemLIVE found its natural leaders in Gisely and Melvin. They efficiently managed the relationship with our space provider, Urban Homes, bringing a much-needed organizational harmony. Their years of dedication and unwavering commitment toward HarlemLIVE made them the de facto parental figures of the organization.

Melvin, with his innate advocacy skills and charismatic persona, was exceptional in interfacing with anyone who showed interest in supporting or funding HarlemLIVE. Not only was he a remarkable ambassador for the program, but his magnetic character also drew new recruits to HarlemLIVE, enhancing our dynamic team. His legacy, though cut short, remains an integral part of our collective identity, a testament to the impact of passionate dedication and resilience of spirit. His story of transformation, from participant to the organization's most fervent advocate, continues to inspire and guide our endeavors.

Gisely was an exceptional administrator who managed the relationships with the numerous schools that offered internships to HarlemLIVE participants. In addition to securing our train passes, she also connected us with a program that provided funds to buy food for our healthy eating. She was also able to get us a Department of Education vendor number in case we ever wanted to provide professional development. She did it all.

Shifting Dynamics: The New Wave of HarlemLIVE Participants

By this time, a majority of the youth were coming to us through internships for school credit and, in the summer, through the youth employment program for pay.

Students who came of their own volition were mostly holdovers from 125th Street, like Matthew Sneh, 2007 Editor in Chief Shelise Roberts, and longtime techie Brad Harbans. Alums Chris Frierson, Torin Amar, and Aisha Al-Muslim continued mentoring new students.

There were some notable exceptions, like Dushawn Bryan. He started coming for credit but then stayed beyond his required hours. His enthusiasm and work ethic were contagious. He made sure laptops and cameras were charged and set up every morning during the hectic summer sessions. He made all the press badges and went out to get them laminated. He went on our trips to Scranton, to cover the 2008 election, and to DC for Obama's inauguration.

Nyiesha Showers and Stanley Antoine were two other individuals who went above and beyond their internship hours at HarlemLIVE. Stanley, who joined the program at the age of eighteen, soon purchased his own MacBook Pro, igniting a passion for video production and dreams of carving out a path in the movie industry. Stanley's radiant spirit and endless potential were cut short by a drunk driver, leaving an immense void, given the deep enduring bonds he had formed with so many.

Nyiesha, who publishes under the pen name Penny Blacwrite, is an accomplished author with multiple books to her credit and a graduate of Howard University. She currently resides in Atlanta.

Adapting and Evolving

To handle the increase in participants for the summer media challenges in the smaller space, we had to find a way to accommodate them.

We decided to put up large picnic tents in the unused area behind the residential building. The tents provided some shade and coverage for tables and chairs, essentially doubling our overall space. It wasn't enough protection from the elements during strong summer thunderstorms, but it was sufficient for the first year in the new location.

As usual, our first attempt at anything was a poor representation of what would follow. For instance, our first annual award ceremony was held in Central Park. But we eventually moved on to bigger and better venues such as Bloomberg, Thompson Reuters, Time/Warner, and ABC TV.

When Melvin passed away at the start of the COVID-19 pandemic, in early 2020, our alumni quickly put together an online memorial—one of the first of its kind during a time when everyone was practicing social distancing. We put in intense work over three days in early April, aiming to hold a memorial by the weekend following Mel's passing. It was heartfelt and sincere, but naturally there were hiccups and miscues—it was, after all, our first attempt, designed just for the alumni as a trial run.

Then, having learned from that experience, we invested several weeks into a much more refined production. We kicked off with the familiar count-down clock, supplemented with prepared segments and heartfelt renditions of songs. The entire production was markedly improved, as we managed to incorporate poignant testimonies such as Clifton Taylor's, blending them with relevant images and videos, ultimately creating a more immersive and touching homage to a dearly missed figure.

* * *

Our organization believes in the philosophy of 'starting somewhere,' under-standing that perfection comes with iteration. Just like our initial ventures into award ceremonies or Melvin's online memorial, we recognize that there will be challenges and imperfections in our first attempts. But these early ex-periences are invaluable; they provide us with insights and lessons that guide our future endeavors. We have often launched initiatives with the intent of learning and refining, rather than delaying for a perfect outset.

In that vein, the following the following summer, in 2008, we decided to paint the gray alleyway walls white, brought in dozens of plants and flowers, and built a sturdy structure with a pitched corrugated metal roof to withstand the heavy summer thundershowers. We snaked extension cords through the office windows to run several fans and strung Christmas lights along the top perimeter of the structure to add some pizzazz.

We now had a durable, versatile space that could be used for mul-tiple purposes: to teach larger classes, for the teens to work and escape the cramped offices, or for quick getaways (sometimes necessary when the kitch-en experiments went awry). We also served hot meals prepared by Chef Cocoa (Kareem Smith) and his rotating sous-chefs.

On Fridays, we turned the "backyard" into a small theater with our po-dium, projector, screen, and wireless mics for team presentations. We cleared out the tables and set up rows of folding chairs facing the "stage."

Each week, we invited guest judges such as advisors, alumni, and com-munity leaders to critique and award the best team presentation.

One week, Gisely managed to get *Today Show* host Hoda Kotb to be a judge. She was impressed by the teens' work and commitment, and invited over a dozen of them to visit her at the *Today Show* studios in Rockefeller Center a few weeks later.

* * *

With the additional resources from the Ford Foundation, we were able to hire some alumni, including Shem, Kareem, and Aleah McGaney, to provide more support. Shem, who had become an accomplished graphic designer, also took on the task of redesigning our website.

Aleah was responsible for tracking each team's progress using an elaborate point system to reward individuals and teams for their accomplishments. Her sharp wit, unflappable demeanor, and intelligence made her a standout member of HarlemLIVE. Tragically, she passed away while giving birth to her son in the summer of 2009.

From Desk to Newsroom: Volunteering Unplugged

We continued to have many adult professionals volunteer their time and expertise. John McKay, a lawyer and legal adviser, taught the youth about public speaking, while Carter Evans, a national reporter for CBS News, provided valuable instruction to our video team on camera angles and interviewing techniques for reporters.

Kathryn O'Dell, a freelance writer, recalls her first time volunteering with HarlemLIVE's youth:

> *I was desperate to get away from my work-at-home desk, and I thought volunteering was a good way to do it. I missed teaching, even though I didn't want to go back to it full-time.*
>
> *After a few weeks of internet research, I found HarlemLIVE. I was excited to start volunteering at the online news magazine for teens.*
>
> *Excited, but not prepared.*
>
> *Being a writer and editor of educational materials, I showed up expecting to work with teens editing their writing. When I walked into the*

building, it was a buzzing newsroom with students working on stories at all stages of publication. Quick introductions were made, and then I was asked to go out in Harlem with a group of students to look for story ideas.

I didn't have time to explain: I'm not reporter. I don't have any training in journalism. I'm not comfortable talking to strangers. I have no idea how to do this! This is what I was thinking as I set out on 125th Street with a group of six teenage reporters-in-training. They were all looking to me for direction.

We started walking down the street, and I wasn't sure what to do. Nyiesha, the youngest student in the group (she wasn't quite thirteen), sensed my nervousness and perhaps my inexperience. She took charge. She pointed out new businesses that her peers could go into, suggested that others go to the Apollo Theater to see what was happening there, and asked individuals in the group who knew more about the neighborhood what they were interested in. Before long, the entire group was exploring the area and scoping out story ideas.

HarlemLIVE welcomed me even though I was not a seasoned reporter like some of the other volunteers. I edited stories, taught a memoir-writing workshop, and continued to go out on beats. I accompanied Nyiesha when she was gathering information for several of her stories. She was never afraid to step out of her comfort zone, for example, when interviewing spiritual leaders at a local mosque. I got a crash course in journalism and loved being in the vibrant, fast-paced newsroom—a much-needed change from only interacting with my computer all day. I also made a lifelong friend in Nyiesha.

I'm still writing in the comfort of my home, but I step away from my desk and out of my comfort zone a bit more often, thanks to HarlemLIVE. —Kathryn O'Dell, adult mentor, 2008–2010

Capturing a Superlative Summer

For that superlative summer, we asked Louisa, the main video editor for over a year, to document everything, thinking we could create a reality-TV type of show using all the footage and interviews of various team members with their testimonials, backstories, and plotting. We collected well over one hundred hours of activities during that summer.

It was one of our best summers. We had more equipment, more room with the structure in the back, more staff... but the sense of accomplishment was short-lived.

After the Summer Media Challenge concluded (thankfully AFTER), building management said we had to take down the structure and remove everything else. A new condo had been constructed on the next block, and the tenants in the back units complained about the noise. We could only utilize the back area for what it was—a bare, unsheltered concrete desert.

Furthermore, the board chair saw we had spent two-thirds of the two-year Ford Foundation grant in only a few months, and he wasn't happy.

Cynthia Simmons reflects on that summer's expenses:

I was no longer living in New York when the capacity building grant that Michelle and I had labored over was funded. Paid staff—that's what we'd been working toward. I wanted to know how this would affect the program and was in touch with Gisely. I didn't know that Ford had given HL the money for two years up front. But even if they'd received half of the two-year grant, I thought we were spending too much money.

I knew Rich's thoughts on youth empowerment. But HL had never had to oversee this much money. I assumed that there was a budget, assumed some adult was overseeing the purse strings. No one was.

This mess was really my fault. I abdicated much responsibility to the youth, but with something this serious, it should have been up to me to be paying closer attention to make sure we were following a budget.

The board chair brought in an administrative assistant to oversee the finances and conduct other admin duties. Then the economy collapsed. The global financial crisis made fundraising harder and caused additional stress.

The constant struggle after struggle pointed me toward burnout.

Witnessing Change: The 2008 Election

The state of New York was a relatively safe bet for the Democratic Party during the 2008 election, with no visible signs of electioneering for our youth to observe. However, John McCain, a war veteran and senator from Arizona, was gaining popularity in the neighboring swing state of Pennsylvania.

In October, we decided to take our group of young journalists to Scranton, Pennsylvania, a town famously associated with the hit TV show *The Office* and former home of then vice-presidential candidate Joe Biden, to witness the intense campaigning and competitiveness happening there. The teens were fascinated by what they saw, particularly because it was a stark contrast to the relatively calm election atmosphere in solidly Democratic New York.

On the night of the election, we covered the lively, celebratory streets of Harlem after Barack Obama was announced as the winner. Our teen reporters had the chance to meet with Chris Glorioso, a longtime mentor at HL and a local broadcast reporter, who gave them an inside look at the workings of a live broadcast from one of the TV satellite trucks.

Once again, exposure.

* * *

On the eve of the inauguration, which also happened to be Martin Luther King Jr. Day, I made my way to JFK airport around 10 p.m. via public transportation to pick up the rental van that would take us to Washington, DC. After securing the van, I began the drive through Queens. The plan was to first pick up Gisely and Nyiesha in Brooklyn before heading to our Harlem office to meet up with Mel and the rest of the team.

As I approached a red light in the rental van, I noticed single cars in both lanes waiting for the light to change. I pressed on the brakes, but they barely engaged. To make matters worse, the roads were covered in ice.

"Bam!" I rear-ended a red car waiting at the light. Though I wasn't driving fast, I left a big dent in the trunk and bumper of the other vehicle.

Fortunately, the driver was calm and even joined me in the passenger seat of my heated van as we waited for help and I called 911. I anxiously showed him HarlemLIVE flyers with pictures of our young media producers as I prayed he wouldn't sue us. Was HL's perfect record of no lawsuits or mishaps over? I was relieved when he said he preferred to get it fixed himself to avoid increased insurance premiums.

But just as I began to relax…

"Bam!"

Another car slammed into the rear of our van while we were waiting. My back and neck felt "off" for several days afterward. A few minutes later, another car hit the car that had hit us, followed by yet another collision. The icy roads made driving treacherous and caused a multicar pileup.

As it turned out, there was little to no brake fluid in our rental van, which explained why the brakes weren't working properly. After picking up Gisely, we drove a short distance before realizing the problem. We decided to head back to JFK to exchange the van. This ate into the short break we had planned to take at HL before heading to DC.

Gisely ended up driving for the rest of the trip to and from DC, and we narrowly avoided a potential disaster on our way to Obama's inauguration.

* * *

Temperatures were in the teens, and the crowds and crowd control were expected to be challenging. We had to park outside the city limits and take the Metro to the capital. But no matter what obstacles we had to overcome, we knew HarlemLIVE had to be there to cover this historic inauguration.

Luckily, Gisely had arranged for us to be hosted by the newly opened Newseum (now defunct), which was on Pennsylvania Avenue midway between the White House and the Capitol Building. We were able to set up camp in one of their spacious auditoriums, complete with a large screen broadcasting the day's events. For our teen members—Kendra Phillips, Nyiesha Showers, and Dushawn Bryan—and our alumni members—Kamal, Gisely, and Melvin—it was a relief to have a warm, comfortable place to gather.

As for me, I was mostly useless, still feeling the effects of the long night and multiple fender benders.

Kendra Phillips (now Crosdale) recounts her experience during the inauguration:

Going to DC, I was tired but also excited to report on the inauguration of the first president who looked like my cousins. On the way, I remember smelly feet and good music.

We arrived at a parking lot outside of a DC metro station. We began handing out HL flyers to the passengers on their morning commute and asking questions about their thoughts on the inauguration. Some smiled, while others showed they did not want to be disturbed. I had already gotten used to the "do not disturb" looks after spending a few months interviewing people on the streets of Harlem about various topics.

When we got to the Newseum, we decided to split up. I was with Melvin, who was doing the videographing and being the unofficial coach/motivator when I needed it. I was standing near a manicured bush that was enclosed by what seemed like a four-foot-tall brick wall.

Out of nowhere, Melvin told me to climb the wall so that he could shoot from a low angle. He said it would be a dope shot. I was not interested in climbing a four-foot wall, mostly because I'm 5"2' but also because I was a little timid, plus there were police officers all around us, and I assumed I would get in trouble, but Melvin encouraged me, so I did it. When I got up there, he began recording, and I began talking about where we were and why.

Later, we met up with the rest of the inaugural crew. We had special reserved tickets that allowed us to withstand the unbearable weather that day by watching Obama's inaugural speech in the Newseum's 4D Theatre.

When we entered the Newseum, we walked around the different exhibits. I learned the rich history of journalism and how it impacts the world. Their exhibits included The Great Hall of News, News Corporation News History Gallery, NBC News Interactive Newsroom, ABC News Changing Exhibits Gallery, and many more.

The NBC News Interactive Newsroom was by far the most entertaining. You could experience what it is like to be a reporter: reporting what you see on the teleprompter in front of a green screen and, once you've completed your segment, you get to see yourself reporting with a background of the White House, Capitol Hill, or a newsroom.

We visited the gift shop, and I bought a key chain, which I still carry over ten years later. One memorable moment was seeing ABC-7 news anchors Sade Baderinwa and Dianna Williams enter the building. I watched their news programs every day after school.

That was the cool thing about the museum—it was a space to learn about the significance of journalism in our world and connect with other reporters and professionals in the field.

It was time to take our seats in the theater. We were all about to witness the inauguration that was happening scarcely a mile away from us. Aretha Franklin performed. As I continued to sit with my eyes glued to the screen, I had an immense feeling of gratitude for being invited to be so close to a moment in history. —Kendra Phillips, 2008–2009

Basement Burnout

The election of Barack Obama was a momentous occasion and a turning point in the history of our country. It felt as if a significant milestone had been reached. The people's struggle had been won.

As if!

Nevertheless, I was exhausted—worn out from years of teaching the same lessons over and over again. How to download photos, complete a profile, conduct a person-on-the-street interview. The program also had a different dynamic now that most participants joined via school internships for credit or pay.

With the introduction of the iPhone in 2007, technology rapidly advanced, enabling anyone to become a media producer, reporter, or influencer.

While our space on 125th Street was big draw, the basement lacked the same appeal. Unlike in our loft, we no longer had throngs of people eager to spend time with us around the clock. To reach our office, people had to navigate through the walkway, which was frequently littered with large bags of garbage and the occasional scurrying rat. To make matters worse, we would now have to endure hot New York City summers in our cramped offices with no outdoor space to escape to.

In many ways, I was ill-prepared and unskilled to run an organization. Much of our success was thanks to the youth, the countless adult volunteers, and the resources that the students had attracted. Longtime advisor Pat Nicholson confided that, in her discussions with the board's leadership, they didn't seem to give much thought to me in their future plans.

* * *

In early June 2009, as I arrived to open our basement offices, I was greeted with the usual sight of candy and potato chip wrappers, cigar innards, used tissue, and even a used condom in the outside walkway leading to our office. The tenants of the apartments above routinely used their windows as a trash chute, resulting in a sometimes disgusting cleanup each day. One day, a gun even came flying out the window and went off when it hit the ground while Melvin was teaching a class inside.

I was done putting up with it.

I swept up the garbage from the alley into a dustpan, took the elevator to the third and fourth floors of the suspected culprits, and deposited the garbage at the doors of their apartments.

I went back to the office, locked up, and went to run some errands. When I returned, the tenants I'd targeted were loudly and angrily arguing with Gisely. I exchanged words with them but decided it was best to remove myself from the heated conflict and rode my bike home, twelve blocks away.

After some reflection, I called Gisely and asked her to meet me on a nearby corner.

"That's it," I said. "I've had enough. The neighbors are upset with me, and their negative energy will only harm our space where our kids are working. I can't have that. I'm out."

The News That Broke the Internet

Two weeks later, an earth-shattering event occurred. The news of it remains vividly etched in Olivia Johnson's mind:

I was conducting a person-on-the-street (POS) interview about President Obama with a notetaker and cameraman when a man ran down the middle of 125th Street screaming.

"Michael Jackson is dead!"

No one believed him, and we dismissed it, continuing the interview.

But then, the energy on the street changed, and we decided to go back to the office. Everyone in my group and the advisor began googling if MJ was actually deceased or if this was a hoax. We each searched different news sites, and one by one, all the web pages crashed.

When one page finally loaded, it said MJ had died due to cardiac arrest. We were all shocked and devastated.

By this time, Harlem was inconsolable, and people were literally collapsing on the street. At the Apollo Theater, Al Sharpton, other dignitaries, and Michael Jackson fans were gathered at the historical venue to mourn and commemorate his life.

I was too distraught to attend, so I went home.

* * *

As the world grappled with this monumental loss, internally, HarlemLIVE was undergoing its own set of changes.

After my abrupt departure, internal conflicts, and the impact of the Great Recession, HarlemLIVE experienced a decline. Although I wasn't physically present during these challenges, it is important to acknowledge that there are multiple perspectives on what transpired. Ultimately, the board made the decision to officially close the organization in early 2011.

Perhaps the closure of HarlemLIVE was as organic as its evolution. As noted earlier, the landscape of journalism underwent dramatic shifts with the advent of social media and mobile devices. In today's context, HarlemLIVE might assist teens in building their own individual or team platforms and channels through experiential learning and journalism, empowering them to take control of their narratives. It's conceivable that programs like HarlemLIVE have a natural life span; they don't necessarily need to be sustainable or scalable indefinitely. What truly holds value is the lasting impact they impart to participants and communities, as well as their organic evolution in response to changing times.

Such is the legacy of HarlemLIVE—a legacy that, as you'll discover in Part 4, continues to resonate within those who were involved. Even in its absence, the echoes of the program's enduring impact are still perceptible.

HarlemLIVE's Reverie: Nana Poku's Endnote

HarlemLIVE was granted access to the basement space by Urban Homes with the purpose of catering to the youth residing there. While there were no kids of the typical age for HarlemLIVE in the building, Nana Poku, who was only eleven and had recently immigrated from Ghana, joined HL. Though younger than our usual members, we made an exception for him, just as we had for Shem years before.

Nana was extremely bright and became committed to all aspects of the program, from covering stories and grocery shopping to meal preparation and cleaning up. He had an engaging smile and piercing eyes. You couldn't be at HarlemLIVE and not know who Nana was.

His experience at school was a different matter. We did help him enroll in a better school, Frederick Douglass Academy. However, he still faced challenges, such as kids making fun of his West African name.

One time, when he was on suspension from school, he and I biked all over the city. We pedaled all the way to Brooklyn and back, stopping at one point to have lunch near New York University.

While we ate, and unbeknownst to me because I was facing the opposite direction, a man was eating at the bar. Later, Nana told me the man had been glaring at us until he decided to approach our table.

"What's going on here?" he asked in a paternal voice.

"We're eating lunch," I said.

"It's a school day..."

I could see where this was going, so I pulled out my iPhone and called Nana's mother, who could be known to talk the ear off a donkey. After greeting Ms. Poku, I handed the phone to the man who was standing over our table disapprovingly.

For a minute, there was silence as he listened to Nana's mother on the other end of the line. Then, abruptly, "Okay. Okay," he said into the phone before throwing it back at me and running out of the restaurant.

* * *

On another biking trip, Nana and I rode up to upper Manhattan, near the Cloisters, a museum resembling a medieval European monastery, surrounded by the lush, hilly terrain of Fort Tryon Park. After going up and down some of the hills, Nana called out to me.

"Rich! I'm having trouble pedaling this bike," he said.

"Let me try," I said. Mounting the bike, I immediately struggled with the resistance. Taking a closer look, I noticed the rubber brakes pressing against the wheel rim.

"Nana," I exclaimed, "how did you ride with it like this?"

This just spoke to Nana's sheer determination and inspiring spirit.

* * *

Nana faced many challenges beyond just school issues. His father passed away when he was nine, before they moved to America. Later on, after our time at Urban Homes, Nana's older brother, who frequently used our computers for resume building and academic projects, was tragically shot and killed outside his building. Sadly, a few years afterward, Nana's mother suffered a heart attack and died. There was a time when Nana was sent to a detention home in upstate New York, prompting me to visit Poughkeepsie to vouch for him as a character witness.

Time has a way of changing our paths, and as the years rolled by I lost touch with Nana. I often reflected on our group's potential shortfalls—could we have offered him more support?

However, life has its surprises. After leaving the Whole Foods on 125th Street and as I was engrossed in unlocking my bike, Nana unexpectedly approached. It was as if the universe had conspired to reconnect us during the final phases of writing this book.

Nana's smile, reminiscent of our HarlemLIVE days, carried traces of a past shadowed by adversity. Yet despite all the hardships, Nana's spirit remained undiminished. We exchanged contact details, and he later sent me a message: live as if there's no tomorrow.

Two weeks later, in the same Harlem cafe located within my apartment building—a place where I had composed most of this book—I was selecting photos for its final pages when I stumbled upon photos of Nana from his time at HarlemLIVE. I texted him the photos, and to my amazement, he was nearby and decided to drop in. The joy of reminiscing about our days at HarlemLIVE, catching up on life, and realizing the resilient spirit within him was a testament to his talents, which many admired.

This serendipitous reconnection with Nana, especially at the concluding phase of this book, was profound. It prompted a deeper reflection on the trajectories of many HarlemLIVE participants once the program ended abruptly.

Their stories emphasize the pivotal role of continuous support for the youth and how community projects can shape destinies. Every person, regardless of the obstacles they've encountered, can thrive when provided with the appropriate support and nurturing surroundings.

While we proudly acknowledge the achievements of several HarlemLIVE alumni, we must remember our mission is far from accomplished. Many others like Nana, Miriam, Melvin, Kelvin, and Nyiesha await the benefits of projects like HarlemLIVE.

Second generation HarlemLIVE students, Ohjani and Taylor reporting

Epilogue

THE HARLEMLIVE EFFECT: EMPOWERMENT THROUGH ENGAGEMENT

After the tragic and sudden death of HarlemLIVE alum Stanley Antoine in September 2014, my passion for education was rekindled. It drove me to seriously consider writing this book and reengaging with HL alumni. We began hosting annual reunion picnics in Central Park and embarked on domestic and international trips. I also started working with children in my building, including Muhammad and Abdoulaye Diop, and the children of HarlemLIVE alumni Melvin, Ena, Shaunetta, and Ife. Together, we explored the city and beyond, cooked meals in my apartment, and even created homemade press badges to cover events.

Eventually, we published a few newsletters for the residents in my apartment building to demonstrate how journalism could be used in a hyper-localized context with younger kids. These newsletters, which were a double-sided single sheet, included stories about the communal pet cat in the basement, a broken elevator, new tenants, building information, and the filming of *West Side Story* just down the block. They showed that a localized version of HarlemLIVE could build skills, create a portfolio, and foster community.

* * *

As an educator and mentor with three decades of experience, I passionately advocate for incorporating journalism into school curricula, particularly during the freshman and/or sophomore years. Journalism offers an engaging alternative to traditional grammar classes, instilling critical skills through a dynamic learning process. In the first semester, students can learn research, reporting, and writing techniques by contributing to a school publication.

Equally pressing, in my view, is the reintroduction of civics in schools. As someone who was fortunate to have a semester of civics in high school, I can attest to its profound impact on understanding the workings of our government. A startling number of citizens today seem disconnected from the intricacies of governance, and a strong civics foundation can bridge this knowledge gap. It's not just about knowing the three branches of government, but about fostering a deep understanding and appreciation for the democratic processes that shape our nation.

When paired with journalism, these two disciplines can create a potent combination to ensure students are not only well-informed but also active participants in their democracy.

In an optional second semester, students can delve deeper, exploring stories that align with their career interests. Those who continue to show interest in journalism can take on leadership roles in school publications and possibly even consider a career in this field.

These high school journalism classes could play a crucial role in teaching media literacy skills, enabling students to evaluate the validity of news sources and understand the impact of technology platforms on society.

* * *

I am a staunch supporter of taking one or more gap years after high school and before college. In this context, it's worth noting that a first-in-nation paid service law was signed by Maryland's governor, Wes Moore, in 2023.[1] These gap years allow young people to explore apprenticeships and other hands-on learning experiences in conservation, health care, and other fields. Governments could further incentivize this by offering higher education tuition vouchers, as they do for military entrants.

---

1. Jack Hogan, "Moore signs service year option for recent high school graduates into law," *The Daily Record*, April 24, 2023.

Programs like these not only build civic engagement but can also augment local issue coverage, particularly if service is provided through journalism. Many local news operations are now controlled by investors and hedge funds with scant concern for community well-being. Colleges and universities could step into this breach, offering news coverage in areas where local journalism has been gutted. This not only benefits local communities but also equips students with essential skills and nurtures a sense of civic responsibility.

* * *

Our founding fathers viewed a free press as a vital component of a thriving republic. Today, the explosion of news sources and proliferation of disinformation threaten to undermine public trust and faith in reporting. Given these circumstances, I believe it is crucial to increase the accessibility of journalism programs in schools and communities.

Over the years, HarlemLIVE has provided ample proof that journalism skills lay a solid foundation for students, enabling them to become productive, resourceful, and creative in their future endeavors.

The impact of HarlemLIVE reaches far beyond its founding in Harlem. Alumnus Shem Rajoon and his wife, Jean Chung, have used drafts of this book to launch a youth community journalism newsletter[1] in Newburgh, New York, showcasing the enduring influence of HarlemLIVE's mission. As the ripple effect spreads, it exemplifies the transformative power of youth journalism programs, empowering proactive individuals ready to take on challenges and discover the power of self-expression and finding their voice.

* * *

Reflecting on HarlemLIVE's journey, adaptation has been crucial. Now, as artificial intelligence (AI) emerges, it presents both opportunities and

---

1. https://thepeopleofnewburgh.com

challenges for youth media. While AI can refine and amplify young voices, its role should be supportive, not dominant. It's vital that we teach the next generation to harness AI to ensure that their narratives stay authentically theirs in this evolving technological landscape.

PART 2

Building on Legacy: Strategies, Success Stories, and Resources

Section C

TENETS OF A SUCCESSFUL YOUTH PROGRAM

Eddie Aung, Shem Rajoon, Katrina Shakarian

Chapter 17

UNIVERSAL COMPONENTS

To gain insight into the elements that contributed to HarlemLIVE's success, one can reflect on valuable lessons that can be applied to other youth enrichment programs seeking to make a meaningful impact on the lives of young people.

At the core of HL's success was our commitment to universal tenets and values that created a strong foundation for our achievements. We believed in the power of experiential learning and providing a setting in which students were encouraged to learn by doing. Through this approach, we provided them with opportunities to engage intellectually, creatively, emotionally, socially, and physically.

We also recognized the importance of trust in building strong relationships with our students. By giving them responsibilities and agency, we allowed them to develop leadership skills that would serve them throughout their lives. We fostered an environment where young people were encouraged to take risks, make decisions, and be accountable for the results, including the mistakes they made along the way.

Finally, we believed in the importance of community and building strong networks of support for our students. We recognized that the success of our program was not just about what we did within our walls but also about the connections we built outside of them. We invited professionals to come in and share their experiences, and we encouraged our students to connect with their communities to make a positive impact. We hope these insights can serve as a guide for other programs seeking to make a difference in the lives of young people.

Trust

At HarlemLIVE, we believed that young people were capable of achieving greatness if given the opportunity to prove themselves.

In a world that often stifles creativity and exploration, we created an environment that encouraged risk-taking and personal growth. Our students were given responsibilities and the support they needed to succeed. They were trusted to take on challenging tasks and make a difference in their communities.

From the moment they walked through our doors, our students were thrown into the thick of things. They filled out applications, were interviewed, and hit the streets to conduct interviews with the guidance of experienced HL veterans. It was sink or swim, and those who demonstrated initiative and responsibility were able to earn our trust and take on even greater responsibilities.

Of course, not every student was cut out for this type of environment. But by setting high standards and providing the necessary support and guidance, we were able to create an environment where young people could thrive and achieve their full potential.

At HarlemLIVE, we knew that the next generation had the power to change the world. And by giving them the tools and opportunities they needed to succeed, we were able to help them achieve greatness.

But trust is a two-way street. The program manager also needed to gain the students' trust. HarlemLIVE's first editor in chief, Tameeka Mitchem, explains:

What I would say to anybody looking to start that type of program is that you really have to believe in it, have a love for youth, and really want them to succeed. That's what made HarlemLIVE the best and biggest success. Rich was this white guy in a mostly Black and Latino community, and he could definitely be seen as weird and awkward, but he earned our trust and our parents' trust. He cared about our safety. He cared about our well-being. But he also trusted us, and that mutual respect alone allowed for the program to run really well.

If there was a violation or somebody didn't do whatever they were supposed to do, Rich was going to lean back on the rules, but there wasn't a situation where he felt he couldn't trust you. Because of that, you didn't want to let the organization down.

Building trust is very important for anybody who tries to run these programs, because nobody wants to go to school after school. And if there's going to be a safe space for youth to spread their wings, you got to trust them.
—*Tameeka Mitchem*

Experiential Learning and Exposure

The philosophy of experiential project-based learning was ingrained in HarlemLIVE, a program that manifested it to the core. By doing, the scores of alumni who now hold leadership positions around the world stand as a testament to its effectiveness. While HL employed journalism and technology to teach in the present, the methods that contributed to its triumph can be applied to any program, allowing youth to engage in their passions, whether in law, engineering, finance, religion, media, government, entertainment, or other ventures.

Experiential learning demands reflection, critical analysis, and synthesis as well as a platform for students to take charge, make choices, and own the outcomes. It presents opportunities for students to engage intellectually, creatively, emotionally, socially, and physically.

In these unprecedented times when the pandemic has shattered the institutional settings of education, experiential learning may provide an avenue as we discover better ways to teach. And if youth can't go out into the field, bring professionals in to share their experiences and insights.

Ownership

In order to mold young people into leaders, we must first give them the chance to lead. When we offer children responsibilities and agency, we give them the freedom to grow and develop critical leadership skills necessary for success. But true leadership isn't just about taking charge—it also involves embracing the possibility of failure and recognizing the value in the process, not just the outcome. In short, great leaders take risks and aren't afraid to learn from their mistakes. Here are some alumni reflections on leadership:

Leadership Skills

There are tons of programs that impact people's lives, but what made HarlemLIVE special was that Rich focused on making sure that we told stories in our own voices. He was adamant about us controlling the dynamic. Oftentimes when you go into these programs, they're child-centered but the adults run everything.

It's a common misconception that when young people are in charge, they're going to run wild and not be organized. In fact, it's really the opposite. By believing in us and saying, "Hey, this is your thing. How do you want to cover it? How do you want this to go? What do you want to talk about? How is this your way?" and not micromanaging us, it allowed us to feel ownership and in charge.

You don't often get that in the traditional newsroom. You have some leeway, but you're pretty much doing what the publication asks. In HarlemLIVE, we WERE the publication, and that never changed. As a result of having somebody who believed in you and who genuinely wanted to see you be great, you soared. —Tameeka Mitchem

Get Real!

Rich explicitly invited the students to be leaders. There were students in leadership roles who were tasked with making important decisions that impacted the program. More and more as it progressed, they were driving things. Rich was very comfortable surrendering power in service to learning.

Teens are given a bad rap in our society, but they are incredibly competent and capable humans when given the space to mess up and to demonstrate what they care about and what they are capable of. The authenticity of that experience is really powerful because they are not doing the job just to get a grade to get into the college of their choice. You are actually inviting them to be agents of change and asking them: What do you care about? What do you want to write about? Where are your gifts? What skills do you have? What skills do you want to build? And add to that the fact that you're building skills in service of something that's a community effort.

All of this stuff creates a more authentic opportunity for learning than is often found in a traditional school. Built into HarlemLIVE was the idea of grounding education into the real world instead of making it all hypothetical and learning lots of facts and figures. This approach inspires people to be lifelong learners. The students had a sense of belonging, community, and purpose. —Mara Rose

Succeed or Fail

I loved Richard's philosophy. On some level, he didn't care whether the kids succeeded or failed when they did projects for HarlemLIVE because he said that you learn as much from a failure as you do from success. That's wonderful when you're working with kids because there isn't so much pressure for them to succeed all the time. —Cynthia Simmons

Adult Mentoring and Peer Teaching

The success of HarlemLIVE hinged upon the support of a dedicated group of adult volunteers who went above and beyond to help the organization thrive. They taught classes on everything from technology to social etiquette, edited stories, and accompanied the kids on trips, providing invaluable guidance and support.

But perhaps just as important was the peer teaching that took place within the organization. Without the funds to hire a full staff, HarlemLIVE relied heavily on peer mentoring to keep the program running smoothly. The benefits of this approach went beyond simple economics; it fostered a strong sense of camaraderie and teamwork among the students, creating a tight-knit community of young people who supported and encouraged one another.

In fact, many alumni continued to give back to HarlemLIVE even after leaving the program. They returned during summer breaks or after finishing their studies to continue mentoring the next generation of youth, often as volunteers or later as paid staff. This legacy of support and generosity helped ensure that HarlemLIVE continued to thrive.

This team spirit made HL feeling like a family to much of the youth. Some alumni and mentors explain:

After I went to college, I started helping at HarlemLIVE as a volunteer, mentoring youth. At one point, Rich gave me a stipend for a few months as video coordinator and I helped the students put together a TV show that aired on the Manhattan Neighborhood Network. I liked the feeling of giving back and giving someone else an opportunity that others gave me. —Aisha Al-Muslim

* * *

Rich paired me up with Khalid, and he explained to me what they did. I felt at home. I always felt welcomed there, even if I missed two or three days. I became really close with the other students. I was there all the time. I often got home at 11 or 12 at night. We had a good group of kids that I felt safe around and an adult mentor, Elaine, who used to take me home. It's not that Rich said we had to stay until late; you stayed because you wanted to get the story done. —Ebony Myers

* * *

HarlemLIVE was really the first place where I experienced what it meant to use my writing talent in combination with other talents. Going on a story with another reporter, a photographer, and a videographer meant working with people who wanted to capture vantage points that maybe I wouldn't catch. Having an adult mentor on hand meant having someone there to answer questions and to steer you back to the task at hand lest you forget why you came out in the first place. The team setting of

HarlemLIVE was always a fun part of the experience. —Guyan Wilks

* * *

Right before I went to college, the New York Times *came to HarlemLIVE and covered me in a feature because I was the editor in chief. When I went to college, I chose to major in journalism, and that freshman year, I was already on the school paper as news editor. Eventually I became editor in chief of my university paper. I remember talking to Rich then, and of course he said, "Hey, you need to come back. I would love to have you work for the program in the summer. You'll be a mentor." I was like, "Sure. I could use the money." It was a great opportunity to connect with the new students and see who was passionate about it. I ended up focusing more on administrative things, and I learned to write grant proposals.* —Tameeka Mitchem

* * *

I had several significant mentors in HarlemLIVE. One of them was Brad. He started me on the path of comprehensive and critical thinking around computers: if I do something, I need to think beforehand, because there will be an effect; if you install this program, this other program will be affected; that reasoning was vital for me. Thanks to my experience in computers at HarlemLIVE, I was able to get a job at Queens College. They were impressed with my skills, and they hired me right away. — Johnny Alarcón

* * *

I worked with the kids on empowering them to get interviews and to speak up in a world that thinks kids have nothing to say. I told them that celebrities—well, everyone—likes to talk about themselves and how to turn the conversation around to get back to the question they asked.

We did mock interviews as well as mock social events, something they

really needed help on. They had to learn not to remain in a pack when they went to an event and to circulate alone. They also had to learn that the free food was not dinner. So when we had our mock social events, they were not allowed to have any of the food or drink until they had introduced themselves to at least five people. —Minette Coleman

Public Speaking and Networking

At HarlemLIVE, we knew that the only way to truly prepare our young writers and reporters for the real world was to throw them into the fire. We were one of the first programs to produce a fully youth-run online publication, which meant that we were constantly called upon to showcase our work and share our stories with others.

It wasn't long before our students were taking the stage at schools and conferences, sitting on panels, and appearing on radio and television programs. We wanted them to gain experience in public speaking, to feel comfortable and confident in front of any audience, and to have the skills necessary to share their ideas and opinions with the world.

And it paid off. Even years later, we still hear stories about our alumni who have gone on to hold leadership roles and positions of influence, thanks in large part to the communication skills they developed at HarlemLIVE.

We saw several examples throughout the book, but here are a couple of takes on this topic:

I covered speaking engagements several times with Rich because I was editor in chief, so I would talk to different people about the program. I was interviewed with the organization, I was on camera with CNN, the New York Times *covered me... Those things force you to open up to new experiences, they force you to come to a sense of leadership and responsibility, so when I got to college, it wasn't a new experience. I wasn't afraid to apply for a position I wanted.*

I also have no fear of competing with men because HarlemLIVE was mostly boys, and even though it wasn't a competition, I learned to speak up for myself. Guys often volunteer for anything, even if they are underqualified, and girls sometimes shrink in the face of opportunities like a promotion. But seeing guys volunteer and say, "Hey, I'll try it out" even if they weren't sure, I learned to also raise my hand. —Tameeka Mitchem

* * *

Being able to put on my college application that I was the editor in chief of an online internet publication and having the experience of speaking publicly as a high school student and being confident enough to raise my hand during college prep all helped. I was invited to an event for Cornell. There were fourteen students in the room. They gave you a mock scenario, and you had to write how you would handle it. I wrote down my examples, and afterward they said, "Who wants to present?" I was the first person to raise my hand and the only person to share. After that, the head of admissions at Cornell said, "That was super impressive." He was very interested in my time at HarlemLIVE, so I spoke to him for a long time about what I had done and what the program had done for me.

For me, HarlemLIVE was a life-changing opportunity, and I'm really grateful for it. —Nicole Schneider

Critical Reflection

The process of producing a story for HarlemLIVE's online newsletter demanded both action and reflection. The youth had to thoughtfully consider what topic they wanted to pursue and then strategize how to obtain the story. They had to venture out into the community, conduct interviews, and collect information. Finally, they had to return to the office, write the story, and publish it. It was a rigorous process, but one that helped the students develop valuable skills in research, critical thinking, and writing.

Shem Rajoon explains how this impacted him:

The authors and thinkers that I relate to in my life articulate a lot of what I was experiencing in HarlemLIVE. I always think of bell hooks;

she said that help in community is really reciprocal, and it made me think about the relationship between action and critical reflection.

HarlemLIVE was an action, it was a newspaper, you became a journalist when you went through that door, but you also had to critically reflect: "What am I trying to say? Why am I doing this story?" We had to balance both aspects, because if we only acted, where would we be going? And if we only critically reflected, what would we be doing? HarlemLIVE really hit that balance for me. —Shem Rajoon

Heart and Soul

An enrichment program can only thrive when its curriculum and activities are both stimulating and engaging. But beyond that, there must be a sense of safety, warmth, and connection that allows the participants to truly feel a sense of belonging. When these elements are present, youth can flourish and develop skills that will last a lifetime.

In the words of several HL members:

If you walked into HarlemLIVE, you would find pockets of energy and excitement. You'd find Khalid and Clifton talking about the camera and going over pictures. You might see Shem and Oscar going over a web page. You might see me sitting with Jerlena talking about a story we just covered and what parts we're going to type up. It was always abuzz with activity. You would hear music. You'd see Melvin dancing. You'd hear Rich yelling about who wants pizza... There never was a boring day. Having had some jobs in journalism, I can honestly say that you would see an active newsroom. Younger kids, browner kids, but an active newsroom.

It was more than an after-school program; it became like a family. We spent time there because we wanted to be there and not because we had to be there. It became a safe space. Rich always provided that. It was a magical experience. —Tameeka Mitchem

* * *

Rich's style of leadership was all heart. He definitely spoiled us because it's really difficult to find a person who is so committed, even beyond his own self-interest. Seeing someone so truly selfless, willing to contribute all their time and their energy, was one of the biggest benefits of HarlemLIVE. There was nothing that Richard had a boundary around. He literally opened himself up to people and allowed everyone to come through this program and become a better person. —Treniese Ladson

* * *

Rich accepted people for who they were. He knew when the right moment was to hold someone accountable and when was the right moment to let them be. And in that way he was able to foster very unique, personal, and genuine relationships. That's something I learned from him over the years—what it means to see the humanity in people and to accept people. —Reuben Quansah

Collaboration

At HarlemLIVE, we recognized the importance of interconnectivity in every aspect of our program. From working on stories in teams to competing in the Summer Youth Challenge and traveling to conferences together, our youth were encouraged to collaborate and learn from one another.

Even in mentor-mentee pairings, the emphasis was on mutual learning and support. This sense of community and shared purpose was a driving force behind our success, and it's a lesson that has stayed with our alumni long after their time with HL came to an end.

Reuben Quansah explains:

At HarlemLIVE I learned many skills that served me in my career, like public speaking and writing, as well as leadership skills because I was editor in chief and I got to work with other people. I had to think about operations in a very broad and detailed way. How do I get my team members to complete certain tasks? How do I build camaraderie with the people I'm working with? That was the first time I was responsible for the mission of an organization, without the pressure, which I appreciated.

After I was named editor in chief, I wrote out detailed outlines about how I was going to organize a team and who was going to do what. I was only 17, and I was nervous because I felt like I had to bring my best. I realized that I couldn't focus on little details—I had to find out who had certain skills and what they were passionate about and leverage that to build our collective spirit.

It was the first time that I got to learn that teamwork makes the dream work: working collaboratively, not being the person who's on top of the throne. I really appreciated having that experience.

I come from an African family, and there's a push in that African diaspora culture to achieve in a particular way. At the same time there is your journey of self-discovery and figuring out for you what that path looks like. I pushed back in my college years in terms of what was expected from me in comparison with what I felt passionate about doing.

The work I was doing in HarlemLIVE showed me what my skills were, how to leverage them in the college space, how to leverage them in academia. In working with students later as an educator, I brought the same kind of energy, getting to know them, getting to see where their strengths and weaknesses were and leveraging them for their own success, learning how to go to your community and build a team that can help you with your challenges.

I'm glad I had the conceptual tools at that early age to begin at least mimicking what it means to be a leader and to work in communities, to leverage the talent of others, and to meet people where they are. HarlemLIVE introduced me to those skills. —Reuben Quansah

Space

The lack of safe and welcoming spaces for youth programs is a widespread issue in many cities and communities. However, with the right approach, unused spaces can be transformed into havens for young people, fostering a sense of belonging and community.

HarlemLIVE, an organization dedicated to providing media education and training to young people, found success in transforming a 2,400-square-foot third-floor walk-up loft on 125th Street. The space featured fourteen-foot ceilings, tropical plants, wood floors, and warm lighting, which created an inviting and creative environment for both youth and adults.

It's essential for private enterprise and government to prioritize the creation of noninstitutional and interesting spaces for young people. By offering vouchers to deserving programs to help with rent, more organizations could have access to the resources needed to transform unused spaces into safe and welcoming havens for youth.

Investing in the transformation of spaces for youth programs is an investment in our future. By providing young people with safe and supportive environments, we can help them develop the skills and confidence they need to succeed. This investment could pay dividends for generations to come, ensuring a brighter and more prosperous future for all.

Healthy Eating

In our last office space in the basement, we finally had a kitchen. It was a simple setup, but it held incredible potential. We quickly seized the opportunity to introduce cooking and healthy eating as another aspect of the program.

The United States is in the throes of a public health crisis caused by the toxic chemicals that the food industry disguises as nourishment. The result is a sharp rise in diabetes, heart disease, and obesity, among other illnesses. It was imperative for us to address this issue and make healthy eating a core component of our program.

We started by banning soft drinks and juices, instead stocking an ample supply of filtered water. The kitchen allowed us to promote healthy eating using fresh, wholesome ingredients. It was a small step, but it felt like a significant victory against a harmful industry.

Adaptability, New Technologies, and Artificial Intelligence

Throughout the narrative of this book, one of the enduring themes is the incredible adaptability of HarlemLIVE. Time and again, especially in the later chapters, readers witness the resilience of this youth program as it navigated myriad challenges and ever-changing circumstances. From dealing with resource constraints to adjusting to shifting societal dynamics, HarlemLIVE's ability to pivot, adapt, and evolve stands as a testament to its longevity and relevance.

Just as HarlemLIVE demonstrated adaptability in its formative years, the next generation of youth programs will need to showcase similar resilience, particularly in the face of rapid technological advancements.

As the digital landscape perpetually evolves, youth programs must remain agile, integrating emerging tools that can enhance their core objectives. One such transformative tool is artificial intelligence (AI). AI offers potential avenues to streamline content creation, optimize audience reach, and even provide real-time feedback. However, it's essential to integrate AI with caution.

The true value of youth media programs lies in capturing the authentic voices of young participants. AI can be a powerful ally in suggesting edits or optimizing content. Still, it should never eclipse the raw, genuine voices of the youth. When integrating AI, the emphasis should always be on empowerment and education. Participants should be trained to use AI as a tool that shapes and refines, while always ensuring that the outputs resonate with their true sentiments.

In an age dominated by algorithms, the next generation must be equipped not only to use AI tools but also to understand their underlying mechanics in order to ensure that the youth remain masters of the narrative. By doing so, youth programs can ensure that while technology might change, the authenticity, passion, and creativity of young voices remain unaltered.

Jianna Caines interviews Jermaine Dupri

Chapter 18

CREATING YOUTH JOURNALISTS

This section underscores the simplicity of tools required to initiate a journalism program and accentuates the significance of press badges for young journalists. It also provides tips for conducting person-on-the-street (POS) interviews, emphasizing the need to be comfortable with the topic, pick the right interview subjects, and learn how to engage and follow up with interviewees.

* * *

Children are natural-born journalists, at least when it comes to questioning: What? Why? How? An enrichment program based on teaching journalism skills to youth can help them rekindle their natural curiosity, expose them to different topics so they can find their passion, and give them the confidence to go out into the world to pursue their goals.

Equipping them doesn't have to be complex or costly. A pen, a notebook, a camera, and a venue to publish the story are the only real tools needed to begin a journalism program. The web provides a free or inexpensive venue via a blog, a website, or any number of internet platforms. Pen and paper are negligible expenses, and most youth now have a camera and computer in their pocket through their smartphone. Yes, you can get more elaborate, but that's a start.

The press badge serves multiple purposes. It bestows a sense of authority upon the students. It also communicates a clear intention to interview subjects: that their words may be published or broadcasted. In the U.S., such an intention garners protection under the First Amendment. This amendment safeguards the freedoms of expression and the press. As a result, journalists have a legal shield to publish their content without facing undue interference from the government.

POS interviews are the easiest stories to publish. They can often be the first assignment on which a young reporter is sent. Generally, reporters choose a topic from the day's headlines on which to query folks on the street. The team that goes out includes a reporter, a photographer or videographer, and, initially, a veteran reporter or adult mentor.

Easy Targets

One of the primary tasks of a youth journalist is finding interview subjects. POS stories generally consist of a brief lead-in (an intro on video or a brief paragraph in writing) followed by questions and answers. However, they can be some of the trickiest stories to report, as they aren't prearranged interviews; the reporter has to find interview subjects on the spot. Selecting the right interviewees is an art. Folks on their way from point A to point B at a brisk pace are not likely to have time to talk. Easy "targets" include folks sitting in a park, waiting for a bus, or hanging outside a movie theater, perhaps waiting on friends. Tell your students to pick those people who look as though they have a bit of time.

Before hitting the streets, youth veterans of the program or adults should role-play with new students, teaching them how to conduct themselves. The team needs to learn how to greet and engage their subjects by introducing themselves and their organization. During the role-play, work with various potential scenarios: the difficult or rude pedestrian, the crazy talker, and so on. Let the newbie know that not every interviewee is worth pursuing or maintaining.

Working Knowledge

Make sure the reporter is comfortable with the topic and not just reading off questions. Discuss the topic beforehand among students and adult members of the organization so the reporter has a working knowledge and can engage the person with follow-up questions. Encourage the reporter to actively listen and occasionally paraphrase the interviewee's statements, which ensures clarity and allows for possible corrections.

At the start of the interview, the reporter needs to get at least a first name, occupation, and neighborhood of residence (not address). You may want to include age, but the photo can make the age relatively evident, and some interviewees do not wish to answer this question, so it may be best not to ask it.

In the case of the photographer, make sure they know how to work the equipment. It's important in training the photographer to show them how to position themselves, not just point and shoot. Move around. Try different angles. Try standing on a bench or shooting up from a crouched position. Include shots with both the reporter and interviewee, and get their full stance or body in the frame as well as close-up shots. Move around in 360-degree fashion to see what backdrop and lighting make for the best photo. You may have to position the subjects differently if the lighting isn't optimal.

If using video, a common error is not checking the sound input beforehand.

Immersion

Having equipped budding journalists with the foundational skills, it's equally important to give them real-world exposure. Immersion in actual scenarios can provide invaluable experience beyond any classroom setting. At HarlemLIVE, it was common for new trainees to transition from instruction to on-the-ground experience on their very first day. This approach wasn't just about thrusting them into the thick of things but also aimed to nurture resilience, instill confidence, and facilitate hands-on learning.

Guided by veteran HarlemLIVE youth reporters or adult volunteers, our young members ventured onto the vibrant streets of New York City using journalism not merely as a profession to master, but as a catalyst to help them discover their interests, develop their individual voices, and enhance their transferable skills for future endeavors.

* * *

For those looking to delve deeper into the world of youth journalism and its many nuances, there are two particularly insightful books. Katina Paron and Javier Guelfi's *A Newshound's Guide to Student Journalism* (McFarland & Company, 2018) offers a vibrant exploration of the craft. The book is filled with reporting exercises and the essential principles of journalism creatively integrated into engaging narratives. Readers are also provided glimpses into the real-life events that inspired each tale.

Another invaluable resource is Jim Streisel's *High School Journalism: A Practical Guide* (McFarland & Company, 2007). This book provides a wealth of information on various aspects of journalism, from identifying news and refining interviewing techniques to mastering the art of narrative writing and understanding the rights of student journalists. Streisel's guide offers a comprehensive look into the world of high school journalism.

Both of these resources augment the foundational knowledge shared in this chapter and can serve as stepping stones for those keen to gain a deeper understanding of youth journalism.

* * *

While the basics are essential, the success of any youth journalism program hinges on the deeper intricacies of the craft. A thorough exploration of the following key topics is vital for the success of a youth journalism program.

- Technical Details: Learning about camera settings, doing thorough sound checks, and grasping light exposure adjustments. Also, improving badge designs, navigating multimedia platforms, and becoming skilled in different editing software can greatly boost the program.
- Safety Considerations: Ensuring the well-being of young journalists during their fieldwork.
- Ethical Considerations: Forming the backbone of responsible journalism, guiding how reporters approach their work.

- Content Creation Process: Encompassing tasks like transcribing interviews, crafting engaging stories, and editing.

* * *

For a firsthand account of how we tackled these challenges, delve into Chapter 8, Building Blocks and Empowerment: How-to for HarlemLIVE. This chapter offers a narrative-style exploration of HarlemLIVE's distinct methods.

The internet is a vast treasure trove of resources, with platforms like YouTube and countless others offering comprehensive information on almost every topic discussed in this book. While this broad digital landscape is invaluable for budding youth journalists, our dedicated website, harlemlive.net, provides supplementary multimedia content that aligns with our HarlemLIVE narrative. However, the wider Web remains an indispensable resource, providing depth and breadth that cater to the ever-evolving needs of today's young reporters.

With the proper tools, guidance, and plenty of online resources, creating a journalism program with youth can be a rich and rewarding experience for all.

Section D

FROM HARLEMLIVE TO THE WORLD: ALUMNI UPDATES

For over a decade, HarlemLIVE gave young people a chance to shine and an opportunity to succeed, offering them the tools and resources they needed to tell their stories and make their voices heard. Through HarlemLIVE, these young people developed skills and gained the confidence they needed to navigate the world.

Please note: As of the time of this book's publication, many alumni's professional situations are fluid, with some having experienced promotions or career shifts. For the most recent updates, visit our website.

This section offers glimpses of those who have participated in HarlemLIVE who have gone on to make a difference in fields ranging from the arts to education, from government to journalism. While this section of the book provides a brief overview of their achievements and paths, you are invited to visit **https://www.harlemlive.net/alumni-updates** for more in-depth information and updates.

Career Paths

The paths our alumni have taken are varied and impressive, as they've ventured into multiple sectors and professions. The data compiled show that HarlemLIVE alumni have made a significant impact in various fields. While technology (14.5%) and education (14%) were the most popular career paths among the sampled alumni, creative arts/entertainment (12%) and government/politics/law (9%) were also well represented. Moreover, many alumni have pursued diverse career paths that cross over into multiple categories, demonstrating the breadth and depth of their talents.

In addition, a significant number of alumni have secondary or side gigs, with education (16%) and technology (14.3%) being the most common. On top of that, many alumni independently embark on entrepreneurial ventures not necessarily tied to their primary careers or side gigs. Concurrently, a notable portion of these alumni are also parents, an aspect not explicitly captured in the data.

Geography

HarlemLIVE alumni have gone on to work in various locations around the world. A significant number have stayed in the New York City area (58%). Other alumni have moved to different parts of the United States, including California and Washington, DC, as well as abroad, including Australia, Armenia, Ethiopia, Germany, and Japan.

It's not just about career success for HarlemLIVE alumni; many have also caught the travel bug and taken their talents across the globe. HL alumni don't just think outside the box—they live outside the borders. Dion Yang has been sharing his jet-setting adventures on his YouTube channel, while Aisha Al-Muslim is probably racking up frequent flyer miles as we speak. Danya Steele lived in Bali, empowering and teaching locals by accessing resources on the web. Eddie Aung created startups in Myanmar. Ena Johnson and several alums traveled to Cuba in early 2017. Suffice it to say that the wanderlust bug has bitten many HL alumni, inspiring them to explore new horizons and broaden their cultural perspectives.

HIGHLIGHTS

Technology / IT

It's no surprise that technology takes the top spot among HarlemLIVE alumni career paths. The earliest HL members were pioneers on the web.

Even those who didn't pursue tech as a profession became the go-to tech people for family and friends. It was also a popular secondary profession and a source of income for side gigs. And with HarlemLIVE being an Apple house from the start, many alumni had a head start when it came to their tech skills.

Treniese Ladson, inspired by Editor in Chief Tameeka Mitchem's She Thang section, got involved in HarlemLIVE through Melvin Johnson, a high school friend. Now she's a successful software programmer.

In Treniese's words, "As a software engineer, my time with HarlemLIVE was truly transformative for both my career and personal life. My passion for technology was ignited at HarlemLIVE, where I gained technical and soft skills as well as problem-solving capabilities."

Brad Harbans and Jonny Alarcón head the tech teams at CUNY campuses, City College and Baruch, respectively. Other alums who went into tech include Eddie Aung, Michael Blanco, Tyrell Carlton, Edward Diego, Michael Flowers (RIP), Melvin Johnson (RIP), Elliot Frantz, Iyana Garry, Giancarlo Morillo, Enita Okodiko, Tanisha Robinson, Jaime Robredo, Oscar Santana, Lamont Sparrow, Bernard Befoe, and Justin Young. Also involved in tech are Frankie Brannon, Charles Chavis, Michael Popo, Shem Rajoon, Danielle Kavanagh-Smith, and Clifton Taylor.

Education

HarlemLIVE alumni are making a significant impact in education, with many pursuing careers in teaching and crossing over into other fields. Lamont Sparrow, for example, honed his tech skills at HarlemLIVE before becoming the head tech person at CPESS High School in Harlem. Twin sisters Dejinay and Denaira followed their passion for education and became teachers, while Torin Amar now teaches English in Japan.

Ebony Myers won an education Fulbright Scholarship and spent a year in Finland learning about their education system. Odie Santiago earned her doctorate in 2000 and is now a professor at the University of San Diego. Gisely Colón López, who is working on her doctorate and teaches at colleges and high schools, says, "I've always wanted to be a teacher. HarlemLIVE

supported my development in understanding that teaching can occur beyond schooling."

From teachers to professors, HarlemLIVE alumni are passionate
about education and making a difference in the lives of the next gen-
eration. Other alumni who pursued work in education include Kevin
Benoit, Charles Chavis, Richard Echevaria, Ryan-O'Neil Edwards, Chris
Frierson, Damian Gaillard, Samantha Gonzalez, Adam Hassan, Janelle
Jemmott, Shem Rajoon, Anthony Rhodes, and Dyeemah Simmons.
Additionally, Kelvin Christie, Alicia Crosby, Qasim Davis, Ky'esha
Edwards, Reuben Quansah, Katrina Shakarian, and Justin Young are
involved in this field.

Creative Arts and Entertainment

This category is home to a diverse group of talented HarlemLIVE alumni,
including painters such as Anzania Barnes and Aboulaye Ballo; musicians
like Shomari Chinnery, Ryan-O'Neil Edwards, Matthew Sneh, and Bernard
Befoe; and stand-up comedians Isabelle Pierre and Neruda Williams.
Isabelle is also an accomplished actress with her own IMDB page.

A number of alumni have found success in film and entertainment, with
Sienna Pinderhughes making waves as a filmmaker in New Orleans and
Ranale Toddman producing videos for the NBA.

Some alumni have even made a name for themselves as writers, including screenwriter Kuamel Winston Stewart and published novelist Nyiesha
Showers, who goes by the pen name Penny Blacwrite. Jordan Cook, a talented cartoonist, also sharpened his skills at HarlemLIVE.

Other notable alumni in the creative arts include Louisa Jaramillo,
who's learning the ropes of production, first at ABC and now on major
television productions. In her words: "HarlemLIVE helped me work with
different people, think on my feet, follow my gut, and not be afraid of
pursuing an idea."

Oscar Brown IV, Shelise Roberts, Sunny Roberts, and Oscar Peralta are
also using their expertise in video and camera work, following in the footsteps of the beloved Melvin Johnson (RIP).

Cameron Cook is now a music critic in Berlin, Germany, while Shagari Guity is a successful graphic artist based in Brooklyn, and Antoinette Mullins has become a creative director at Urban Stages. Additional impressive alumni in the creative arts and entertainment industry can be found at www.harlemlive.net/alumni-updates.

As Sienna Pinderhughes put it, "Having the audacity to say, 'I can do this' despite being one of few women and people of color in my industry is a skill that I believe was fostered as a youth journalist at HarlemLIVE. I think that HarlemLIVE attracted a certain kind of young person—one who had the audacity to dream big."

Journalism / Media

HarlemLIVE was not just about producing an online publication; it was also about imparting journalism skills to youth in order to empower them to navigate the world with confidence and preparedness. While producing journalists was not the primary objective, many alumni have gone on to pursue careers in journalism and media, including Aisha Al-Muslim, who worked at *Newsday* before joining the *Wall Street Journal,* where she now produces podcasts.

Keisean Marshall is a producer at the daytime talk show Sherri, after working many years on the top-rated show Dr. Phil and a stint at ABC's Tamron Hall. Freddie Joyner is a video producer for Reuters in New York. Joyner wrote in a recent survey, "I had no clue what my career path would look like when I first joined HL. I thought I would possibly be a business/Wall Street dude... but to think that HL was essentially a training ground for the stuff I do now every single day for a widely respected news agency like Reuters is mind-boggling to me."

Khadijah Abdurahman has continued to pursue her passion for creating publications, even after moving to Ethiopia with her children. She credits HarlemLIVE with introducing her to a network of dynamic teenagers who shared her interest in journalism and computer science. As she says, "I have been an editor or starter for so many publications, which is a testament to how much HL influenced me."

Rhonesha Byng and many other HL alumni could be a category unto themselves. Rhonesha is the founder and CEO of Her Agenda, "a digital media platform that bridges the gap between ambition and achievement for millennial women." Rhonesha, along with HL alumna Raven Robinson, sits on the advisory council of ForbesBLK, a community for Black professionals, leaders, and creators. Additionally, Rhonesha cofounded the nonprofit organization The Black Owned Media Equity and Sustainability Institute and has been honored by *Essence, Forbes*, and BET as someone to watch.

Kevin Benoit has been a dedicated educator for many years, working to empower youth in various capacities. However, we can't overlook his impressive achievements as the publisher of *Parlé*. He founded the publication around the same time he joined HarlemLIVE, and it thrives to this day.

Other notable alumni in the field of journalism include Al-Amir at the *New York Times* and multimedia journalist Andrew J. Jones, among others. More HarlemLIVE alumni in the field of journalism and media are listed on our website at www.harlemlive.net/alumni-updates.

Business / Real Estate / Fashion and Apparel

This category boasts a wide array of entrepreneurial HarlemLIVE alumni. While not all of them work exclusively in these fields, many have pursued business ventures and found success.

For example, Jonny Alarcón is mainly involved in tech, as one of the lead techies at Baruch College, but has also cofounded his own real estate firm. And Michael Wills Jr. heads one of the largest cleaners in New York City. In Mike's words: "One of the most important lessons I learned from HarlemLIVE is that it's not that hard to learn anything you need to learn. For example, the first version of Maid Marines was a website that I built using the skills I learned at HarlemLIVE. Although it wasn't perfect, it was better than waiting around for someone else to do it. Learning how to write articles there also helped me when I created the Maid Marines blog, which helped tremendously with the SEO and propelled us to the #1 spot in the city for the biggest house cleaning service."

Danya Steele recently started her own PR and communications business, Shiva Group, in Washington, DC. Frankie Brannon has his own startup, Measured, in Los Angeles. Also in Los Angeles is Kat Dey, president of ettitude, a company that produces bedding products from bamboo.

Tamara Leacock has a successful clothing line, R E M U S E, based in Melbourne, Australia. Eddie Aung was involved in start-ups in Myanmar until the country's political climate became turbulent. Anthony Henry designs and produces high-end outdoor furniture and is looking to expand his business nationwide. Elliot Price describes himself as a serial entrepreneur, walking in his purpose while helping those around him.

Many other alums have pursued construction, T-shirt businesses, sneaker sales, and a plethora of other creative avenues to produce and create.

Service

(This section includes community outreach, social support, health care, wellness, religion, law enforcement, the military, politics, and law.)

One of the standout impacts of HarlemLIVE is evident in the choices of its alumni. An astounding 30% have dedicated themselves to various service fields, a testament to the program's emphasis on community and positive change. This includes roles in healthcare, law, military, and more.

Medical doctors like Seshat Mack are at the forefront of healthcare, while lawyers such as Toochi Ngwangwa and Aboulaye Ballo are championing justice in their communities. Anthony Henry, Jerlena Rhodes, Angel Colon, and Tanisha Robinson, as well as others still on active duty, exemplify commitment and courage in the military. Jahad Bilal, a former New York City police officer, has made a significant shift to community outreach with youth.

In Oklahoma City, Clifton Taylor is making strides in law enforcement while serving in the National Guard. Over at the US Coast Guard, Michael Popo has reached the prestigious position of a white-capped captain. In the realm of religion, we have Reverend Kareem Smith, an ordained priest leading a church in Westchester, as well as several other alumni who hold significant roles within their religious communities.

Chris Davis, HL's editor in chief in 2003, is now a VP, Client Partner in healthcare marketing, specializing in pharmaceutical and biotech clients.

Beyond these examples, many other alumni are serving in the fields of politics, social support, and wellness, continuously striving to give back to their communities and make a difference in the lives of others.

* * *

To learn more about the inspiring achievements of these and many other HarlemLIVE alumni, visit www.harlemlive.net/alumni-updates. There you'll find additional information, as well as images, highlighting their impactful contributions.

* * *

In Memoriam: Remembering Our Beloved HarlemLIVE Alumni

Finally, we pay tribute to the following HarlemLIVE alumni who have passed away. Each of them brought their unique talents and contributions to the program, and we will always remember their spirit and energy: Dupree Phillips, Kevin Bell, Aleah McGaney, Jabari Blackmon, Stanley Antoine, Melvin Johnson, Michael Flowers, and Oyewole Odutola. Their legacy lives on in the countless lives they touched, and they will always be missed.

* * *

Final Thoughts

This section concludes with the words of some HarlemLIVE alumni. These inspiring quotes are a testament to the impact this program had on the lives of so many young people.

- *"I find myself as the person who is always willing to ask the hard questions, and it has benefited me greatly." —Edward Diego*
- *"I can literally walk into any environment and talk with anyone no*

matter their background. HL gave me that confidence to not be afraid to put myself out there." —Catalino Rodriguez

- *"HarlemLIVE taught me about community and being able to give back to impoverished communities by providing them skills that they normally would not have access to. As a business owner, I always reach out in my local communities to find workers and train them in the manufacturing field for free."* —Anthony Henry Jr.

- *"HL taught me three principles that helped me define certain milestones in my life. Those three things are to keep on learning, keep on trying, and learn to take risks."* —Eddie Aung

- *"HarlemLIVE had the biggest impact on my life by exposing me to the field of philanthropic and nonprofit work. Years later, after my tenure at HL, I helped formalize a nonprofit organization, and my experience with HL gave me the institutional understanding of the logistics for nonprofit governance and operations and an understanding of the expectations of nonprofits."* —Gisely Colón López

- *"HL supported my desires for being a part of a larger community and bringing light to social justice and human rights."* —Kelly Koblaki

- *"HL presented me with many opportunities to interact with politicians when reporting at events. As an advocate for education reform, I am often meeting and presenting ideas to politicians, and I feel more prepared and at ease to do so."* —Janelle Jemmott

- *"HarlemLIVE empowered me to take control of my reality and to create opportunities rather than wait for them to happen."* —Rhonesha Byng

- *"HL trusted me, gave me autonomy and a safe space to rehearse for life. Throughout my career as a young designer into a leader, I chose who I wanted to work for because I knew my value."* —Shem Rajoon

Section E

RESOURCES

Youth and Media

Student Press Law Center and their New Voices initiative

https://splc.org/

https://splc.org/new-voices

New Voices is a student-powered nonpartisan grassroots movement of state-based activists who seek to protect student press freedom with state laws. These laws counteract the impact of the 1988 *Hazelwood v. Kuhlmeier* Supreme Court decision, which dramatically changed the balance of student press rights.

(Source: https://splc.org/new-voices)

Hard News. Angry Administration. "Teenage Journalists Know What It's Like"

By Jaclyn Peiser, *The New York Times*, July 1, 2018

High school educators across the country have been clamping down on students who publish articles on protests, sexuality, and other hot-button issues.

(Source: https://www.nytimes.com/2018/07/01/business/media/student-journalism-school-newspaper.html)

"When the Student Newspaper Is the Only Daily Paper in Town"

By Dan Levin, *The New York Times*, October 19, 2019
As more than 2,000 newspapers across the country have closed or merged, student journalists from Michigan to Arizona have stepped in to fill the void.
(Source: https://www.nytimes.com/2019/10/19/us/news-desert-ann-arbor-michigan.html?action=click&module=News&pgtype =Homepage)

"To Anyone Who Thinks Journalists Can't Change the World"

By Marie Tae McDermott, *The New York Times*, September 5, 2018
Over the course of one month, three separate stories from our International desk—reported on the ground in Iraq, Thailand, and South Africa—helped lead to immediate reforms.
(Source: https://www.nytimes.com/2018/09/05/insider/isis-thailand-south-africa-reforms.html)

"Baltimore's Wide Angle Youth Media Matches Students' 'Hustle' with Real World Experience"

By Yvonne Wenger, *The Baltimore Sun*, November 10, 2020)Wide Angle Youth Media, a Baltimore-based organization, empowers young people by providing them with opportunities to gain re-al-world experience in media production and journalism.
(Source: https://www.baltimoresun.com/entertainment/arts/bs-fe-wide-angle-youth-media-20201110-mgjkogvtvzaijipg2f6thn7 fxm-story.html)

Wide Angle Media

A Baltimore-based youth media program that provides students with opportunities to develop practical skills in media production and jour-nalism. The organization empowers young people by teaching them how to create and share their stories using various forms of media.
(Source: https://www.wideanglemedia.org/)

The Boyle Heights Beat

Youth-produced local newspaper based in Los Angeles, California. The publication is written, edited, and produced by young people who live in Boyle Heights, and covers issues that are important to the community, such as immigration, housing, and education. The website provides access to the latest issue of the newspaper as well as an archive of past issues.
(Source: https://boyleheightsbeat.com)

Student Reporting Labs

Student Reporting Labs (SRL) is a national youth journalism program and public media initiative that trains teenagers across the country to produce stories that highlight the achievements, challenges, and reality of today's youth. The program is now in over 180 middle and high schools and offers young people the opportunity to develop their skills in journalism, digital media production, and storytelling while creating stories that reflect their unique experiences and perspectives.
(Source: https://studentreportinglabs.org/)

"Black And White And Forgotten All Over?"

By Anna Phillips, *City Limits*, September 10, 2007
This *City Limits* article, written by Anna Phillips in September 2007, explores the disappearance of public high school newspapers in New York City. The piece highlights the lack of resources and support for student journalism programs and the impact of this on young people's access to important information and opportunities for civic engagement.
https://citylimits.org/2007/09/10/black-and-white-and-forgotten-all-over/

A NewsHound's Guide to Student Journalism

By Katina Paron and Javier Guelfi, 2018, McFarland & Company
Packed with reporting exercises and fundamentals of the craft woven into engaging narratives, each comic also gives readers a look at the real-life event that inspired the tale.

High School Journalism: A Practical Guide

By Jim Streisel, 2007, McFarland & Company

Students will find valuable information about identifying news, interviewing, research, narrative writing style, editing, visual presentation, and layout. The book also covers the legal rights of student journalists, objective versus opinion writing, staff planning and organization, and Web-based journalism.

Organizations Supporting Journalism

American Journalism Project

Empowering communities, preserving democracy, and rebuilding local news, this organization focuses on revitalizing local journalism to support informed communities and a healthy democracy.

(Source: https://www.theajp.org/)

"Save Local Journalism! A New Project is Trying"

By David Leonhardt, *The New York Times*, December 10, 2019

This article discusses the efforts of the American Journalism Project to support and revitalize local journalism across the United States.

https://www.nytimes.com/2019/12/10/opinion/local-news.html

Tiny News Collective

The Tiny News Collective is an organization that supports the creation and sustainability of local newsrooms across the United States. Their goal is to help communities build and maintain independent, community-centered news sources that are accountable to the people they serve. The organization offers training, mentorship, and support to help local journalists and publishers succeed in their work.

(Source: https://tinynewsco/about/)

Institute for Nonprofit News

The Institute for Nonprofit News is a network of over 300 independent news organizations across the United States. Their mission is to

strengthen and support nonprofit newsrooms by providing resources, training, and collaboration opportunities. The organization also advocates for the value of nonprofit journalism and the critical role it plays in promoting a healthy democracy.
(Source: https://inn.org)

Propublica Local Reporting Network

ProPublica supports local and regional newsrooms as they work on essential investigative projects impacting their communities, fostering collaboration and sharing resources to strengthen local journalism.
(Source: https://www.propublica.org/local-reporting-network/)

National/International Media Literacy Organizations

This comprehensive list of media literacy organizations, compiled by the Northwest Alliance for Responsible Media, provides a valuable resource for those interested in media education, research, and advocacy.
(Source: https://nwamedialiteracy.org/resources-2/
national-and-international-media-literacy-organizations/)

"How New York City Is Saving Its Local News Outlets"

By Sarah Bartlett and Julie Sandorf, *The New York Times*, May 20, 2021
This opinion piece explores the measures being taken by New York City to support and preserve its local news outlets amid the challenges faced by the industry.
https://www.nytimes.com/2021/05/20/opinion/newspapers-New-York-City.html

High Five

Our mission is to empower the local community, through media education and technology, to become civically engaged, express ideas, and advocate for causes.
(Source: https://www.highfivemedia.org/mission)

"Meet the Unlikely Hero Saving California's Oldest Weekly"
By Tim Arango, *The New York Times*, February 20, 2020
This *New York Times* article highlights the efforts of an individual working to save the *Sierra Messenger*, California's oldest weekly newspaper, and preserve local journalism in the community.
https://www.nytimes.com/2020/02/10/us/california-newspaper-sierra-messenger.html

International Women's Media Foundation
The IWMF provides safety training, reporting trips, and byline opportunities specifically tailored to support and empower women journalists in their careers.
https://www.iwmf.org

Journalism / Local News

NW Alliance for Responsible Media. (n.d.).
National/International Media Literacy Organizations.
A curated list of organizations committed to social, political, and cultural education in the realm of media literacy, provided by the NW Alliance for Responsible Media.
https://nwamedialiteracy.org

National/International Media Literacy Organizations
A curated list of organizations committed to social, political, and cultural education in the realm of media literacy, provided by the NW Alliance for Responsible Media. Published by NW Alliance for Responsible Media
https://nwaresponsiblemedia.org/resources-2/national-and-international-media-literacy-organizations/

"What Happens to Democracy When Local Journalism Dries Up? Every week, two more newspapers close—and 'news deserts' grow larger"

By Margaret Sullivan, *The Washington Post*, June 29, 2022

This article discusses the increasing number of "news deserts" in the U.S. as local newspapers continue to close down, leaving communities without credible news sources and posing serious implications for democracy.

https://www.washingtonpost.com/media/2022/06/29/news-deserts-newspapers-democracy/

"Local news isn't dying out: It's being killed off by corporate greed"

While hedge funds raid and kill local newspapers, Sinclair tries to build an empire of low-grade local TV stations.

By Matthew Sheffield, *Salon*, March 23, 2018

https://www.salon.com/2018/03/23/local-news-isnt-dying-out-its-being-killed-off-by-corporate-greed/

"News Deserts Are a Civic Crisis"

By Katrina vanden Heuvel, *The Washington Post*, July 19, 2022

Katrina vanden Heuvel highlights the importance of addressing the issue of news deserts to preserve democracy and local communities.

https://www.washingtonpost.com/opinions/2022/07/19/save-local-news-democracy/

"There are flickers of hope for local journalism. So far, it's not nearly enough."

By Margaret Sullivan, *The Washington Post*, December 20, 2020

https://www.washingtonpost.com/lifestyle/media/there-are-flickers-of-hope-for-local-journalism-so-far-its-not-nearly-enough/2020/12/18/bb-dbd64c-4077-11eb-8bc0-ae155bee4aff_story.html

"The Local-News Crisis Is Weirdly Easy to Solve"
By Steven Waldman, *The Atlantic*, August 8, 2023
https://www.theatlantic.com/ideas/archive/2023/08/
local-news-investment-economic-value/674942/

"A Revolution for Journalism—or a Death Knell?"
Book review: *The Remaking of Journalism and Why It Matters Now*,
by Alan Rusbridger, Farrar, Straus & Giroux (2019)
By Ann Marie Lipinski, *The New York Times*, January 23, 2019
https://www.nytimes.com/2019/01/23/books/review/alan-rusbridg-
er-breaking-news.html

"Laurene Powell Jobs ready to invest more in journalism, says democracy at risk"
By Mikey Campbell, *Apple Insider*, March 2, 2019
https://appleinsider.com/articles/19/03/01/laurene-powell-jobs-ready-
to-invest-more-in-journalism-says-democracy-at-risk

"I worked for Sinclair. I had to quit. The must-run segments and 'one-sided news' promos were too much."
By Justin Simmons, *The Washington Post*, April 10, 2018
https://www.washingtonpost.com/news/posteverything/
wp/2018/04/10/i-worked-for-sinclair-i-had-to-quit/?hpid=hp_no-
name_opinion-card-a%3Ahomepage%2Fstory

"Supreme Court Rules for Cheerleader Punished for Vulgar Snapchat Message." The decision set new limits on disciplining students for off-campus speech but did not totally bar administrators from doing so.
By Adam Liptak, *The New York Times*, June 23, 2021
https://www.nytimes.com/2021/06/23/us/supreme-court-free-
speech-cheerleader.html?referringSource=articleShare

"Coronavirus-Driven Downturn Hits Newspapers Hard as TV News Thrives. The financial state of the U.S. news media in the second quarter of 2020"

By Michael Barthel, Katerina Eva Matsa, and Kirsten Worden, Pew Research Center, October 29, 2020

https://www.pewresearch.org/journalism/2020/10/29/coronavirus-driven-downturn-hits-newspapers-hard-as-tv-news-thrives/

"Is There a Market for Saving Local News?"

By Clare Malone, *The New Yorker*, February 3, 2022

https://www.newyorker.com/news/annals-of-communications/is-there-a-market-for-saving-local-news

"If local journalism manages to survive, give Evan Smith some credit for it"

The *Texas Tribune* founder has been a "true pioneer" in finding ways to cover local communities as a non-profit.

By Margaret Sullivan, *The Washington Post*, January 23, 2022

https://www.washingtonpost.com/media/2022/01/23/media-sullivan-evan-smith-texas-tribune/

"As local news dies, a pay for play network rises in its place"

A nationwide operation of 1,300 local sites publishes coverage that is ordered up by the Republican groups and corporate PR firms.

By Davey Alba and Jack Nicas, *The New York Times*, October 18, 2020

https://www.nytimes.com/2020/10/18/technology/timpone-local-news-metric-media.html

"The disinformation system that Trump unleashed will outlast him. Here's what reality-based journalists must do about it."

By Margaret Sullivan, *The Washington Post*, November 22, 2020

https://www.washingtonpost.com/lifestyle/media/trump-disinforma-tion-journalism-next-steps/2020/11/20/6a634378-2ac8-11eb-92b7-6ef17b3fe3b4_story.html

"These mass shooting survivors were called journalism heroes. Then the buyouts came."

By Emily Davies and Elahe Izadi, *The Washington Post*, January 14, 2022

https://www.washingtonpost.com/dc-md-va/2022/01/14/capital-gazette-survivors/

"A Secretive Hedge Fund Is Gutting Newsrooms: Inside Alden Global Capital"

By McKay Coppins, *The Atlantic*, October 14, 2021

https://www.theatlantic.com/magazine/archive/2021/11/alden-global-capital-killing-americas-newspapers/620171/

"This journalist was her paper's only full-time reporter—until they fired her. Her small town wonders: Now what?"

By Elahe Izadi, *The Washington Post*, October 23, 2020

https://www.washingtonpost.com/lifestyle/media/floyd-press-local-news-media-cuts/2020/10/22/9390eb98-1307-11eb-ba42-ec6a580836ed_story.html

"How small news outlets are pushing back against Big Tech"

By Gary Abernathy, *The Washington Post*, June 25, 2021

https://www.washingtonpost.com/opinions/2021/06/25/how-small-news-outlets-are-pushing-back-against-big-tech/

"Five Pieces of Good News about the News"

A look at some of the ventures that have sprung up, fueled by a new sense of mission in American journalism and by the sheer quantities of money available.

By Ben Smith, *The New York Times*, July 11, 2021

https://www.nytimes.com/2021/07/11/business/media/good-news-media-sites.html

"When the Local Paper Shrank, These Journalists Started an Alternative"

An ambitious news site, The New Bedford Light, has sprung up in an old New England whaling town to fill a void in coverage.
By Katharine Q. Seelye, *The New York Times*, June 20, 2021
https://www.nytimes.com/2021/06/20/business/media/when-the-local-paper-shrank-these-journalists-started-an-alternative.html

"Local News Coverage Is Declining—And That Could Be Bad For American Politics"

By Joshua Darr, *FiveThirtyEight*, June 2, 2021
https://fivethirtyeight.com/features/local-news-coverage-is-declining-and-that-could-be-bad-for-american-politics

"John Oliver places fake sponsored content on to local news: 'Far too easy'"

The *Last Week Tonight* host digs into local news stations' misleading sponsored content shows, successfully placing an absurd 'wellness' product on several stations.
By Adrian Horton, *The Guardian*, May 24, 2021
https://www.theguardian.com/tv-and-radio/2021/may/24/john-oliver-fake-sponsored-content-local-news

"Axios is the latest media company to try to make money from local news. History is not on its side."

By Paul Farhi, *The Washington Post*, May 19, 2021
https://www.washingtonpost.com/lifestyle/media/axios-local-news-newsletters/2021/05/19/4d1760f8-b824-11eb-a6b1-81296da0339b_story.html

"In this moment of multiple crises, we need strong local journalism"

By Frank Blethen, *The Washington Post*, May 18, 2020
https://www.washingtonpost.com/opinions/2020/05/18/this-moment-multiple-crises-we-need-strong-local-journalism

"As the Press Weakens, So Does Democracy"

By Charles Blow, *The New York Times*, July 18, 2021
https://www.nytimes.com/2021/07/18/opinion/media-news-papers-democracy.html

"Nextdoor Is Quietly Replacing the Small-Town Paper"

While Facebook and Twitter get the scrutiny, Nextdoor is reshaping politics one neighborhood at a time.
By Will Oremus, *Medium*, January 27, 2021
https://onezero.medium.com/
nextdoor-is-quietly-replacing-the-small-town-paper-ca583962c15a

ProPublica / Local Reporting Network

https://www.propublica.org/article/
propublica-is-seeking-new-applicants-for-its-local-reporting-network

Tulare County Teens Share Through Media Contest

https://thesungazette.com/article/education/2020/11/11/tulare-coun-ty-teens-share-hopes-through-media-contest-about-covid-19/

Endangered (2022)

This documentary chronicles a year in the life of four journalists working in countries where freedom of the press is under threat.
HBO documentary on perils facing journalists in various parts of the world
https://www.hbo.com/movies/endangered

Journalism and Communities of Color

The National Association of Black Journalists

https://nabjonline.org/

"A Reckoning Over Objectivity, Led by Black Journalists"

Wesley Lowery, *The New York Times*, June 23, 2020
https://www.nytimes.com/2020/06/23/opinion/objectiv-
ity-black-journalists-coronavirus.html

"Inside the Tornado"

The Swarthmorean, Writing About Race, and Me
By Rachel Pastan, June 13, 2021
https://rpastan.medium.com/inside-the-tornado-a66f73c60ef7

Teaching / Curricula

Teachers College Reading and Writing Project (TCRWP)

Once based at Columbia University's Teachers College, TCRWP provided extensive support for literacy education, including workshops,
phonics instruction, and initiatives for social justice and culturally
responsive teaching. While the project has concluded, its legacy continues to influence educators. TCRWP has become the Advancing
Literacy unit at Teachers College.

Big Picture Learning

Big Picture Learning was established in 1995 with the sole mission of
putting students directly at the center of their own learning.
https://www.bigpicture.org.
ImBlaze
Big Picture Learning developed a tool to help educators manage
internship programs.
https://www.imblaze.org
(Article about the above link)
KQED. "Want to Offer Internships At Your School? A Tool To Make
It Easier."
By Katrina Schwartz, *Mind/Shift*, October 22, 2018
https://www.kqed.org/mindshift/52325/want-to-offer-internships
-at-your-school-a-tool-to-make-it-easier.

EdSurge

EdSurge reports on changes in education shaped by technological advancements, scientific research, demographic shifts, business interests and other socioeconomic forces. https://www.edsurge.com/

Education-Reimagined

Across the country in rural, urban, and suburban spaces, tranformational leaders are innovating with new ways of learning that put the learner at the center. Unified by curiosity, creativity, and boldness, growing numbers of intrepid innovators are creating learning environments that adapt and adjust to meet the needs of each and every child. https://education-reimagined.org

XQ Institute

XQ Institute is the nation's leading organization dedicated to rethinking the high school experience so that every student graduates ready to succeed in life.
https://xqsuperschool.org
"Want to prepare youth for the workplace? Let them lead."
https://xqsuperschool.org/rethinktogether/want-to-prepare-students-for-the-workforce-let-them-lead/

"How Being Part of a 'House' Within a School Helps Students Gain A Sense of Belonging"

By Gail Cornwall, May 14, 2018
https://www.kqed.org/mindshift/50960/how-being-part-of-a-house-within-a-school-helps-students-gain-a-sense-of-belonging

"Learn Stuff Computers Can't Do"

Article in part about the book *Human Work In the Age of Smart Machines* by Jamie Merisotis
By Tom Vander Ark, *Forbes*, October 30, 2020
https://www.forbes.com/sites/tomvanderark/2020/10/30/human-work-learn-stuff-computers-cant-do/

"What Kids Wish Their Teacher Knew"

By Donna De La Cruz, *The New York Times*, August 31, 2016
https://www.nytimes.com/2016/08/31/well/family/what-kids-wish-
their-teachers-knew.html

"Amplify Storytelling in the Classroom with 3 Tech-Enabled Projects Using Blogging, Podcasts and Instructional Videos"

By Robert Sevilla, *Getting Smart*, Jul 23, 2019
https://www.gettingsmart.com/2019/07/23/amplify-
storytelling-in-the-classroom-with-3-tech-enabled-projects/

"Today's assignment for classroom design: flexibility"

By Kim Cook, AP News, July 9, 2019
https://apnews.com/article/charlottesville-lifestyle-educa-
tion-us-news-virginia-d97d3d0070ba4498af05afaadeceb80f

"Meditation and teaching: When Teachers Take A Breath, Students Can Bloom"

By Anya Kamenetz, *NPR*, August 19, 2016
https://www.npr.org/sections/ed/2016/08/19/488866975/
when-teachers-take-a-breath-students-can-bloom

"What Productive Talk Looks Like in the Elementary Grades"

Using sentence stems to scaffold classroom discussions guides students to speak, actively listen, and build on each other's ideas.
By Susan O'Brien, *Edutopia*, October 14, 2019
https://www.edutopia.org/article/
what-productive-talk-looks-elementary-grades

"8 Inspiring Student Projects to Jumpstart Your School Year"

By Carri Schneider, XQ Institute, August 13, 2019
https://xqsuperschool.org/rethinktogether/8-inspiring-student-pro-
jects-to-jumpstart-your-school-year/

"How To Develop Poised, Thoughtful, Articulate Teenagers"
By Tom Vander, *Forbes*, November 20, 2018
https://www.forbes.com/sites/tomvanderark/2018/11/20/
how-to-develop-poised-thoughtful-articulate-teenagers/

"Digital Tool Box for Teaching and Scholarship"
https://libguides.brooklyn.cuny.edu/digitaltoolbox

Nation Writing Project
https://www.nwp.org/

Merrow, John. *The Influence of Teachers: Reflections on Teaching and Leadership*. Jossey-Bass, 2011

"Steve Brill's Report Card on School Reform"
By Sara Mosle, *The New York Times*, August 18, 2011
https://www.nytimes.com/2011/08/21/books/review/class-warfare-
by-steven-brill-book-review.html

"Make Schools More Human"
The pandemic showed us that education was broken. It also showed us how to fix it.

"The fundamental job is to partner with families to raise successful human beings. The pandemic is helping many of us to think about our students in a fuller and more holistic way; we should remember that when the crisis ends."

By Jal Mehta, *The New York Times*, December 23, 2020
https://www.nytimes.com/2020/12/23/opinion/covid-schools-vac-
cine.html

Sir Ken Robinson, author and educator
TED2006, February 2006
"Do schools kill creativity?"
https://www.ted.com/talks/

sir_ken_robinson_do_schools_kill_creativity?language=en
TED2010, February 2010
"Bring on the learning revolution!"
Sir Ken Robinson makes the case for a radical shift from standardized schools to personalized learning—creating conditions where kids' natural talents can flourish.
https://www.ted.com/talks/sir_ken_robinson_bring_on_the_learning_revolution?language=en
The TED Interview, December 2018
"Sir Ken Robinson (still) wants an education revolution"
https://www.ted.com/talks/the_ted_interview_sir_ken_robinson_still_wants_an_education_revolution

"School Flexible Learning Spaces, Student Movement Behavior and Educational Outcomes among Adolescents: A Mixed-Methods Systematic Review"
https://www.researchgate.net/publication/348006491_School_Flexible_Learning_Spaces_Student_Movement_Behavior_and_Educational_Outcomes_among_Adolescents_A_Mixed-Methods_Systematic_Review

"What science tells us about improving middle school"
By Kelly Field, The Hechinger Report, August 16, 2021
https://www.pbs.org/newshour/education/what-science-tells-us-about-improving-middle-school

"The Activists Working to Remake the Food System"
By Ligaya Mishan, *The New York Times*, February 19, 2021
https://www.nytimes.com/2021/02/19/t-magazine/food-security-activists.html

"America must embrace civics and history instruction for the sake of our democracy"
By the Washington Post Editorial Board, March 2, 2021

THE LEGACY OF HARLEMLIVE

THE LEGACY OF HARLEMLIVE

https://www.washingtonpost.com/opinions/america-must-em-
brace-civics-and-history-instruction-for-the-sake-of-our-democ-
racy/2021/03/02/b9814476-7877-11eb-9537-496158cc5fd9_story.html

"Massive investment in social studies and civics education proposed to address eroding trust in democratic institutions"

By Joe Heim, *The Washington Post*, March 1, 2021
https://www.washingtonpost.com/education/civics-social-stud-
ies-education-plan/2021/03/01/e245e34a-747f-11eb-9537-
496158cc5fd9_story.html

Experiential Learning

Boston University, Center for Teaching & Learning

"A comprehensive guide to experiential learning, providing valuable insights and strategies for incorporating hands-on experiences into education"
https://www.bu.edu/ctl/guides/experiential-learning/

Experiential Learning Institute

Learn about the core principles and benefits of experiential learning through this resourceful website, offering in-depth information and valuable resources.
https://experientiallearninginstitute.org/resources/
what-is-experiential-learning/

Northern Illinois University, Center for Innovative Teaching and Learning

An instructional guide on incorporating experiential learning methods into the classroom, enhancing student engagement and understanding.
https://www.niu.edu/citl/resources/guides/instructional-guide/ex-
periential-learning.shtml

294
294

Association for Experiential Education

Discover the principles and practices of experiential education through this authoritative source fostering experiential learning excellence.
https://www.aee.org/what-is-experiential-education

Frontiers in Psychology, Experiential Learning

Read a research article exploring the psychological aspects and impact of experiential learning on students' cognitive development.
https://www.frontiersin.org/articles/10.3389/fpsyg.2021.771272/full

Experiential Learning, International Experiential Learning Community

A concise overview of experiential learning, providing valuable insights and practical information for educators and learners alike.
https://www.experientiallearning.org/info/
what-is-experiential-learning/

Lewis-Clark State College, Inspiration for Teaching and Learning

Explore the concept and benefits of experiential learning through examples and inspirations from Lewis-Clark State College.
https://www.lcsc.edu/teaching-learning/
inspiration-for-teaching-and-learning/experiential-learning

Northeastern University, Center for Experiential Learning

A hub for experiential learning resources and opportunities, fostering immersive and impactful learning experiences for students.
https://experiential-learning.northeastern.edu/

The City as School, Experiential Learning at Its Core

Discover how experiential learning is central to The City as School's educational approach, providing real-world learning opportunities to students.
https://www.cityas.org/

Alternatives to College

"How you got screwed by the education system"

The true purpose of the American education system seems to be to make sure kids are unprepared for the adult world

By Allen Marshall, *Salon*, March 25, 2018

https://www.salon.com/2018/03/25/
how-you-got-screwed-by-the-education-system/

Café Momentum

Café Momentum is a nationally recognized nonprofit restaurant and professional training facility. We create holistic, individualized plans for young people to begin addressing the issues they've had to confront throughout their lives.

(Source: https://cafemomentum.org/about/)

"Why We Desperately Need to Bring Back Vocational Training in Schools"

Nicholas Wyman, *Forbes*, September 1, 2015

https://www.forbes.com/sites/nicholaswyman/2015/09/01/why-we-
desperately-need-to-bring-back-vocational-training-in-schools

"The Best Way to Learn Anything Comes Naturally. You don't need school."

https://jessicalexicus.medium.com/the-best-way-to-learn-anything-
according-to-a-tenured-professor-fb9d93f90d31

"College Not for You? You Can Make The Same Amount of Money In Half The Time Doing This."

Somewhere down the road, trade schools got a bad rep. That perception needs to change.

By Michael Schneider, *Inc.*

https://www.inc.com/michael-schneider/college-not-for-you-you-can-
make-same-amount-of-money-in-half-time-doing-this.html

Race and Education

"Beyond the game. We teach black boys sports are their only hope. What if we let them dream bigger?"
By Martellus Bennett, *The Washington Post*, February 1, 2019
https://www.washingtonpost.com/news/posteverything/
wp/2019/02/01/feature/we-teach-black-boys-sports-are-their-only-
hope-what-if-we-let-them-dream-bigger/

"The Great Divide: Stop Holding Us Back"
By Robert Balfanz, *The New York Times*, June 7, 2014
https://opinionator.blogs.nytimes.com/2014/06/07/
stop-holding-us-back/

"From Struggling High Schooler to College Freshman"
By Jessica Schnall, *The New York Times*, December 30, 2014
https://www.nytimes.com/2014/12/31/nyregion/from-struggling-
high-schooler-to-college-freshman.html

"Can George Clooney and a new LA high school make Hollywood crews more inclusive?"
By Ryan Faughnder
June 21, 2021
https://www.latimes.com/entertainment-arts/business/
story/2021-06-21/caa-george-clooney-team-for-l-a-based-school-to-
improve-inclusion-on-film-sets

Parenting

"'Let them be kids!' Is 'free-range' parenting the key to healthier, happier children?"

By Emine Saner, *The Guardian*, August 16, 2021

https://www.theguardian.com/lifeandstyle/2021/aug/16/let-them-be-kids-is-free-range-parenting-the-key-to-healthier-happier-children

Let Grow

Let Grow believes today's kids are smarter and stronger than our culture gives them credit for.

https://letgrow.org/

https://letgrow.org/our-books/

"How Parents Are Robbing their Children of Adulthood"

By Claire Cain Miller and Jonah E. Bromwich, *The New York Times*, March 16, 2019

https://www.nytimes.com/2019/03/16/style/snowplow-parenting-scandal.html

"The Anti-Helicopter Parent's Plea: Let Kids Play"

By Melanie Thernstrom, *The New York Times*, October 19, 2016

https://www.nytimes.com/2016/10/23/magazine/the-anti-helicopter-parents-plea-let-kids-play.html

"What Happened to American Childhood? Too many kids show worrying signs of fragility from a very young age. Here's what we can do about it."

By Kate Julian, *The Atlantic*, April 17, 2020

https://www.theatlantic.com/magazine/archive/2020/05/childhood-in-an-anxious-age/609079/

"Utah's 'free-range parenting' law said to be first in the nation"

By Meagan Flynn, The Washington Post, March 28, 2018
https://www.washingtonpost.com/news/morning-mix/wp/2018/03/28/utahs-free-range-parenting-law-said-to-be-first-in-the-nation/

Volunteering

Grassroots Volunteering

Grassroots Volunteering is a resource connecting travelers to causes and communities in the places they travel. The site consists of a dual database of organizations all over the world.
http://grassrootsvolunteering.org/

Youth Empowerment

Full Circle Youth Empowerment

We at Full Circle Youth Empowerment Inc. are a team of highly trained professionals who believe in the resiliency of our youth who have therapeutic needs and have experienced many adversities in life. We strongly believe with our specialized services, the commitment of families, and the collaboration with our community providers, our youth will receive the necessary support to overcome challenges, improve their outcomes, and successfully transition into adults. We are fostering hope. We are empowering lives along their journey. We are building a community for youth to flourish. (Bridgeport, CT) (Source: https://www.fcyecenter.org/)

Partners for Youth Empowerment

Partners for Youth Empowerment's (PYE) mission is to unleash the creative potential of young people. For 25 years, guided by this

mission, PYE has been working to shift the field of youth work to respond to the deeper needs of young people for meaning, purpose, creativity, and connection. (Bolinas, CA)
(Source: https://partnersforyouth.org/)

New Urbanism / Walkable Cities / War on Cars

Communities around the world are rethinking the reliance on the automobile, redesigning cities on a human scale that allows programs that encourage human interaction to thrive.

Congress for the New Urbanism
A planning and development approach that focuses on human-scaled urban design, based on the principles of how cities and towns have been built for centuries.
https://www.cnu.org/

Walkable Cities. Project Drawdown.
An approach to city planning, design, and density that maximizes walking and minimizes driving, resulting in decreased emissions.
https://drawdown.org/solutions/walkable-cities

Streetsblog
A resource for information on reducing dependence on cars and improving conditions for walking, biking, and transit.
https://www.streetsblog.org/

"Why is 'Walkability' the New Must Have for Movers?"
By Marisa Sanfilippo, MYMOVE, May 6, 2022
Describes the benefits of living in a walkable neighborhood, including increased social networks, and how to determine the walkability of a new neighborhood.
https://www.mymove.com/city-guides/walkability-new-must-movers/

Jeff Speck

Jeff Speck, author of *Walkable City: How Downtown Can Save America, One Step at a Time*, has been recognized for his work in urban planning and promoting walkable communities.
https://www.jeffspeck.com/

Cars Ruin Cities

An advocacy website promoting the idea of freedom and independence in choosing whether to drive or not, and advocating for cities to be designed better.
https://carsruincities.info/

The War on Cars

A podcast that discusses the ongoing conflict between cars and the city and provides news and commentary on developments in the fight to undo the damage wrought by the automobile
https://thewaroncars.org/

Transportation Alternatives

An organization dedicated to promoting safe, equitable streets in New York City and working with communities in every borough to build a future that meets their needs
https://www.transalt.org/

"Inside the movement to remake America's city streets"

An article detailing the movement to remake city streets in America with a focus on pedestrian safety and the impact of the COVID-19 pandemic on this movement.
By Thebault, Reis, *The Washington Post*, March 15, 2023
https://www.washingtonpost.com/nation/interactive/2023/pedestrian-safety-covid-pandemic/

Artificial Intelligence

Google's AI for Everyone
This is a free course on Coursera that provides a general introduction to AI. While it's not tailored specifically to youth, it's accessible for older teens and could be a starting point for educators.
https://www.coursera.org/learn/ai-for-everyone

MIT Media Lab's Scratch Programming
While Scratch is fundamentally a platform for teaching kids coding, they have been integrating AI and machine learning concepts into their platform, making it a friendly entry point for young learners.
https://scratch.mit.edu/

AI4ALL
This is a nonprofit dedicated to increasing diversity and inclusion in AI. They run education programs for high school students, particularly from underrepresented backgrounds.
https://ai-4-all.org/

Machine Learning for Kids
This platform provides projects and resources to help kids understand machine learning concepts using simple block coding similar to Scratch. https://machinelearningforkids.co.uk/

Youth and AI Labs at Stanford
This Stanford initiative focused on researching and creating learning experiences for young people to explore AI.
https://ai.stanford.edu/

IBM's Teacher Advisor with Watson
While more educator-focused, this platform uses AI to provide teachers with strategies and resources to improve student learning. https://www.ibm.com/ibm/responsibility/initiatives/activitykits/teacheradvisor

The Evolving Landscape of AI Education for Youth

As AI continues to permeate every facet of our lives and shape the future of technology and innovation, it is imperative for educators and youth to remain abreast of developments in this domain. The resources listed above represent just a snapshot of the rapidly expanding landscape of AI education for young learners. We strongly encourage educators, parents, and students to actively seek out and engage with new platforms, courses, and organizations that emerge in the realm of AI. Staying informed and proactive will ensure that our youth are well equipped to harness the transformative potential of artificial intelligence while also maintaining a discerning perspective on its ethical and societal implications.

References in Books, Research Papers, and Websites to HarlemLIVE

"Using Participatory Media and Public Voice to Encourage Civic Engagement"

By Howard Rheingold, Stanford University, Communication Department

2008, Aspen Institute

Another collaboration of teachers and students uses video to give Harlem youth a worldwide forum to highlight issues that matter to them. HarlemLIVE blog, "Harlem's Youth Internet Publication," directly addresses civic issues of interest to Harlem youth, and HarlemLIVE video produces and publishes teen-created videos about civic and cultural issues. HarlemLIVE "began in early 1996, at the beginning of the internet revolution, with just five students, one laptop, a digital camera, and an advisor."

https://www.issuelab.org/resources/881/881.pdf

"Youth as E-Citizens: Engaging the Digital Generation"

By Kathryn Montgomery, PhD, Barbara Gottlieb-Robles, and Gary O. Larson, PhD

2004, Center for Social Media School of Communication, American University

HarlemLive is notable for the community spirit that infuses the writing and for enabling its participants to come to terms with many of the social, political, racial, and cultural issues that affect their lives.
https://dra.american.edu/islandora/object/socialmediapubs:28/datastream/PDF/view

"Online Content for Low-Income and Underserved Americans: A Strategic Audit of Activities and Opportunities"

2000, The Children's Partnership

HarlemLive (http://www.harlemlive.org/) is Harlem's online publication by teens. Approximately 60 students from public high schools located in the Bronx, Brooklyn, and Manhattan develop and maintain this award-winning interactive journal about life issues for teenagers of color. On the Web site, one can read about events and happenings, poetry and memoirs, and view a gallery of photos. The aim of the site is to empower leaders to be caretakers of tomorrow by building a network of information from within the community. Harlem Live has been recognized nationally for its contributions to the online world of youth of color, receiving praise from international as well as national leaders.
https://www.childrenspartnership.org/wp-content/uploads/2019/05/Online-Content-for-Low-Income-and-Underserved-Americans-The-Digital-Divides-New-Frontier_March-2000.pdf

Bridging the Digital Divide: Technology, Community, and Public Policy

By Lisa J. Servon

2008, Blackwell Publishing

Harlem Live was initiated in 1996 by Richard Calton. Calton had started a similar project from within a school but was frustrated by the limitations of being in a school setting. It was difficult to take the kids out of school without insurance being an issue, for example. Calton also recognized the benefits of working closely with very small groups of students, something that was very difficult in the context of the public schools.

Digital Generations: Children, Young People, and the New Media

By David Buckingham and Rebekah Willet

2003, Lawrence Erlbaum Associates

Harlem-Live is an Internet-based youth publication launched in 1996. It has a close relationship with the Playing2Win community technology center in Harlem, which hosts the publication on its Web site and provides office and production space for the publication's editorial team. Columbia University and a number of other local organizations provide additional support.

Technology and Social Inclusion: Rethinking the Digital Divide

By Mark Warschauer

2004, MIT Press

HarlemLive is a high-quality online publication, with general news reports, articles on community issues, arts and culture articles, photo galleries, a creative writing section, and a special women's section. The publication thus provides current, topical information by and for the Harlem community. Equally important, HarlemLive has trained several hundred Harlem young people as journalists, photographers, media administrators, Webmasters, and public speakers. The publication thus serves as a focal point for young people to develop and showcase their technical and communication skills while they address issues of concern to the community and create original content that helps give the community voice.

Listening to Harlem: Gentrification, Community, and Business
By David Maurrasse
2014, Columbia University Press

Education and Technology: An Encyclopedia
By Ann Kovalchick and Kara Dawson
2004, ABC-CLIO

Technicolor: Race, Technology, and Everyday Life
By Alondra Nelson, Thuy Link Nguyen Tu, and Alicia Headlam Hines
2001, NYU Press

The African American Experience
By Sandy Donovan
2010, Lucent Books

Electronic Resources Librarianship and Management of Digital Information
By Mark Jacobs
2013, Routledge

"Community media and the politics of youth."

2003, First Monday Journal 8(11)
Clearly one of the great potentials of the Web—and this enormous time of migration toward digital technologies—is in fostering new community content partnerships. What the Web affords is for everyone to be a producer and not just a passive consumer of the media. Youth in particular are extremely adept at using multimedia, as demonstrated by youth-directed media centers, such as HarlemLive in New York City and Street Level Youth in Chicago.
https://firstmonday.org/ojs/index.php/fm/article/view/844/753

ACKNOWLEDGMENTS

The process of creating this book would not have been possible without the vital contributions of several key individuals. My profound thanks to my initial editor, Isidra Mencos, whose swift and meticulous efforts guided this book through its most challenging stages and whose interviews with many HarlemLIVE alumni and participants significantly enriched its content.

I am immensely grateful to Cynthia Simmons, a long-standing HarlemLIVE mentor, advisor, and angel, for her invaluable insights and thorough review of the manuscript. Additionally, HarlemLIVE alumna Gisely Colón López provided invaluable comments.

My friend Margot has been a steadfast source of encouragement, providing useful suggestions throughout this process. Crafting a book is indeed multilayered, and I am deeply appreciative for her assistance.

Kirin Alolkoy provided vital copyediting and proofreading services.

In conclusion, I extend my deepest gratitude to all those, named and unnamed, who contributed to this project.

Thank you all for your invaluable contributions in bringing this narrative to life. Your efforts have allowed the vibrant voices and compelling stories of HarlemLIVE's participants and alumni to be heard, inspiring others through their resilience and creativity.

Special thanks to Claire's Kitchen Cafe, located on the ground floor of my building. This cafe provided a sanctuary for me when concentration at home proved challenging. The ambiance, coffee, and subtle hum of conversations in the background offered the perfect environment for my writing sessions. This space became an extension of my workspace, and for that, I am deeply grateful.

ABOUT THE AUTHOR

Richard earned a Bachelor of Arts in Journalism, accompanied by a minor in Computer Science, from New York University. Additionally, he holds a Masters in Education as a Reading Specialist from City College of New York.

Spanning over three decades in education, technology, and journalism, Richard dedicated 10 years to teaching in NYC schools, 8 of which were in East Harlem. Afterward, he supported district-wide technology initiatives for 3 years and served as an adjunct faculty member at Teachers College, Columbia University, while also assisting with various projects at the Institute for Learning Technologies.

In 1996, Richard founded HarlemLIVE, Inc., aiming to harness the power of emerging Internet technologies to provide a platform for students to engage in journalism. This book not only chronicles HarlemLIVE's impactful journey but is also a testament to Richard's advocacy for integrating journalism into school curricula and his vision of a civics-driven educational landscape. His hope is to leverage the narratives in this book to further his mission, exemplified by initiatives such as localized newsletters that demonstrate how journalism can foster community while building skills.